Race, Sex, and the Freedom to Marry

LANDMARK LAW CASES & AMERICAN SOCIETY

Peter Charles Hoffer
N. E. H. Hull
Series Editors

For a complete list of titles in the series go to www.kansaspress.ku.edu

PETER WALLENSTEIN

Race, Sex, and the Freedom to Marry

Loving v. Virginia

UNIVERSITY PRESS OF KANSAS

© 2014 by the University Press of Kansas

All rights reserved

Published by the University Press of Kansas (Lawrence, Kansas 66045), which was organized by the Kansas Board of Regents and is operated and funded by Emporia State University, Fort Hays State University, Kansas State University, Pittsburg State University, the University of Kansas, and Wichita State University

Library of Congress Cataloging-in-Publication Data

Wallenstein, Peter, author.

Race, sex, and the freedom to marry : Loving v. Virginia / Peter Wallenstein.

pages cm

Includes index.

ISBN 978-0-7006-1999-3 (hardback) — ISBN 978-0-7006-2000-5 (paper)

ISBN 978-0-7006-2048-7 (ebook)

1. Loving, Richard Perry — Trials, litigation, etc.

2. Loving, Mildred Jeter — Trials, litigation, etc.

3. Interracial marriage — Law and legislation — Virginia I. Title.

KF224.L68.W35 2014

346.7301'63 — dc23

2014019707

British Library Cataloguing-in-Publication Data is available.

Printed in the United States of America

10 9 8 7 6 5 4 3 2 1

The paper used in this publication is recycled and contains 30 percent postconsumer waste. It is acid free and meets the minimum requirements of the American National Standard for Permanence of Paper for Printed Library Materials z39.48-1992.

CONTENTS

The laws at issue in some landmark law cases seemed at the time like Ayers Rock in the Australian outback—dominating a landscape, so solid and immovable that one could hardly conceive of the landscape without them. But the passage of time leaves such landscapes behind; one can barely make out the outcropping in the distance. Such a case arose out of the miscegenation laws of the American South. For many decades before 1967, no southern state would recognize a "mixed marriage" of a "person of color" and a "white" person. Virginia's own law was a nineteenth century contrivance to prevent race mixing enacted at time when legislators believed that the bloodlines of the white race would be corrupted by intermingling with other races. The US Supreme Court accepted this position, and would not hear of it changing, until Richard Loving, a white man, and Mildred Jeter, part African American, part Native American, brought a suit to validate their Washington, DC, marriage in the eyes of Virginia law.

Peter Wallenstein has brought their story to life. That story is not just a Supreme Court case ending bans on mixed marriage, but a richly and deeply conceived story of a place—Caroline County, Virginia—and the people who lived in it from its settlement, through the Civil War, into the Jim Crow era and beyond. Wallenstein's account is not one sided, although his views are clear enough. With his empathetic portraits of the people, their land, and the changing society of rural Virginia, he enables the reader to follow the Virginia story from slavery to freedom, and from mere freedom to equality. For example, Leon Bazile, the Virginia judge who denied their petitions, was as much a part of that landscape as the couple. There are many other, similarly compelling portraits in this stirring tale.

Seamlessly interwoven into these personal stories is the larger narrative of race in American history, the case here serving as a microcosm of changing attitudes toward race. Indeed, 1967, when the Supreme Court decision came down, was a moment in time so full of history that one almost cannot comprehend today how much was at stake in the Lovings' suit. By locating the *Loving* case in the long arc of the story of race,

Wallenstein reminds all of us just how much depended on the arguments of two young lawyers and the open-mindedness of nine old men.

Wallenstein knows the places and the people first-hand. The result is legal history from the heart as well as the head, a book on the case like no other.

Beginning in early 1808, a drama played out in Virginia, as Annie Gray and seven other people held as slaves in Caroline County sued for the "recovery of their freedom." The people being held in slavery included Annie's children and grandchildren: Dick, Peter, Moses, Sam, Phobe, Esther, and Phillis. Much was at stake — some people's freedom, someone else's property. The outcome hinged on events in colonial Virginia from some fifty years before, in the 1750s and 1760s, well before the American Revolution, around the time of the French and Indian War. Thomas Wyatt had purchased a young woman named Molly from the estate of Thomas Conner, and her social and legal identity back then was crucial to her daughter Annie's case many years later. Some white people who had material knowledge were "unable from age and infirmity" to come to Caroline. So they gave their testimony in depositions, taken not just in next-door Spotsylvania County but also some 150 miles to the west, in Lynchburg. The process unfolded slowly, as depositions and deliberations continued into 1809 and then on until late 1810.

As someone held in slavery in early national Virginia, Annie Gray had one legal right — to sue for her freedom. Or as the Virginia Supreme Court of Appeals phrased it: "Persons in the status of slavery have no civil rights, save that of suing for freedom when entitled to it." A 1795 Virginia law spelled out the procedure. On presentation of a petition for recovery of freedom, the court assigned the person an attorney, who must investigate and "make an exact statement to the court of the circumstances of the case, with his opinion thereupon." If persuaded that the case should go forward, the court summoned the "possessor" to answer the complaint.

One key way to win such a freedom suit was to demonstrate descent, in the maternal line, from a free Indian woman, because, under a 1662 law, children took their status, slave or free, from their mothers. Over the years, in order to determine the merit of claims for freedom, a number of cases in the Virginia courts had developed guidelines for judicial understanding of the colony's eighteenth-century history. As late as 1682, the Virginia legislature had provided for the enslavement of Indians. Yet a 1705 act had authorized "a free and open trade for all persons, at all times, and at all places, with all Indians whatsoever." "Dick and Patt, Indians," for example, won a 1793 case that had gone to Virginia's highest court, which declared that, after 1705, "no American Indian" could be "reduced into a state of slavery." Nor could their descendants be enslaved, at least in the maternal line. Subsequent discovery of an earlier law, with the same language, pushed the date from which no additional Indians could be pressed into slavery back to 1691. In *Hudgins v. Wright*, a decision handed down in November 1806, or little more than a year before Annie initiated her effort to obtain freedom, Jackie Wright and her three children successfully used the 1795 law, together with their Indian ancestry, to secure their freedom.

Annie followed the procedures laid out in the Virginia statute, suing Christopher Terrell, the person who presumed to hold her in slavery, for "trespass assault and battery and false imprisonment." When presenting her petition in August 1808 to the Caroline County Court, Thomas Lunsford Lomax, the man who represented her, argued that the eight were "descendants of a certain Jenny Gray dec'd an Indian entitled to freedom + by virtue of that descent are also entitled to their freedom but are illegally detained in slavery." The case was variously titled *Annie et al. v. Terrell, Dick et al. v. Terrell,* and *Terrell v. Terrells Negroes.* To retain his property, Christopher Terrell had to successfully answer the charge and rebut attorney Lomax's declaration that "I am of opinion that the petitioners are entitled to their freedom." He would need a lot of help. The depositions might provide it.

Thomas Wyatt's widow Susannah Wyatt reported from Lynchburg that around 1754, some fifty-four years earlier, her husband had bought "a Negro Girl named Molly," who was "sold as a slave," from the estate of one Martin Conner. Richard Fouracres, who had lived on Thomas Wyatt's place at that time and for a number of years afterward, said the sale took place in Essex County (just east of Caroline County), where Wyatt lived at the time, but that they all soon moved to Spotsylvania County (just west of Caroline), where, Susannah Wyatt and Richard Fouracres agreed, Wyatt sold Molly as a slave to Joel Parrish. According to Susannah Wyatt, her husband had owned Molly for "several years" before selling her to Parrish, who had come calling to inquire, as Richard Fouracres put it, where he might "get a likely girl large enough to spin," and Molly was right there in the room working at spinning.

Mrs. Mary Minor said she had lived within a half mile of the plantation of Joel Parrish for forty-five years and had visited often with the Parrish family, and they with her, and she appears to have resided there, if not at the time of, at least not long after the sale of Molly to Parrish. Waller Lewis was another Spotsylvania County neighbor with knowledge of the people and the facts. Each of these four white Virginians helped piece together the story of Molly and her family for the Caroline County Court.

Jenny—was she an Indian entitled to her freedom? If so, then the train of facts regarding Molly and her children and her daughters' children would follow, as each child would follow the status of the mother. Held as a slave, each mother would have had slave children; if she were free, however, her children would each be born free, and so would her daughters' children.

Testimony from the deponents pointed in other directions, though at the same time complicating the picture of the late colonial society where Tidewater and Piedmont joined at the fall line, where Fredericksburg lies on the Rappahannock River. All recognized that their social world included people of color who might be free, or indentured, or enslaved, and it included people who might be Indian, or African, or European, or any combination.

According to Susannah Wyatt, Molly's mother was, to the best of her knowledge, "of Affrican birth as she always spoke broken English." Waller Lewis said Molly's mother was "an African called Jenny," also living with Wyatt in Spotsylvania County. Richard Fouracres, asked whether he knew Molly's mother, said yes; asked if she was "Virginia born," he replied, "no she was outlandish [foreign-born] and called Ebo Jenny." All three characterized Jenny as by no means Indian, but of African birth, of the Ebo nation, one of the many thousands of involuntary recruits from West Africa who, during the first half of the eighteenth century, arrived as slaves on tobacco plantations in Tidewater Virginia.

Waller Lewis gave far more detail in his assessment of Jenny's geographic background and her ethnic place in Virginia society. He knew, he said,

the said Parrish's woman called Moll who is said to be the mother of the plaintiff [Annie] having seen her at different times, and that her Hair Complexion Features and general appearance in his judgment were altogether African without any other admixture whatever, which he believed would not be the case [had she] been mixed with the Indian as it was said, because he has among his negroes a family that is said to be akin to the Indian and he thinks the mixture still appears very plainly in their hair and Complexion, tho' as he supposes from what he has heard, the Blood must have been mixed at least as often if not oftener than it would have been in the said Moll.

Another mother and daughter named Jenny and Molly also made their appearance in the depositions. Susannah Wyatt reported that during the time her husband owned the slave Molly, "a free Negro named Jenny lived in the family," and that she knew there to be "no kindred between the said Molly and [that] Jenny." Waller Lewis told the court that "a free woman also named Jenny lived in the said Wyatt's family at the same time who had a Daughter called Molly who was bound to the said Wyatt" and "Wyatt sold her time to a man named Gabriel Jones." At the time of the sale of Molly's time to Jones, she still had two more years on her indenture. Richard Fouracres, for his part, said Wyatt had "two free negroes living with him by the names of Jenny and Molly the daughter of said Jenny."

Perhaps the best guess one can make is that this "free woman" or "free negro" Jenny had herself been the daughter of a black man (or an Indian man) and a white woman. A law passed in 1691 — in the same session of the General Assembly that had evidently put an end to Indian enslavement — banned interracial marriage that involved white Virginians. Indians and whites could freely engage with one another in commerce, in other words, but not in marriage. Should a white Virginian marry a nonwhite, he or she was to be banished from the colony within three months of the marriage. Therefore, if the wife was the white partner, her children would presumably be born elsewhere and not be the concern of Virginia law or Virginia society. But what if there were no marriage, but a mixed-race child was born to a white woman anyway? Under this new law, she would have to pay a substantial fine or, if unable to pay, be sold into servitude for five years. Either way, the child would be a servant for far longer, well into adulthood.

Under the 1691 law, this Jenny would have been sold as a servant for thirty years or, if born after 1705, as she likely was, for thirty-one years. Under a law passed in 1723, her daughter, if born before the mother finished her time and obtained her freedom, would also have been sold as a servant for thirty-one years. (In 1765, the House of Burgesses stepped back a bit from the draconian measures of earlier years, but only a bit, as a new law set the term at eighteen years for females and twenty-one for males—but these would not have applied to the "free negro" Jenny or her progeny through 1764.) Let's say Jenny was born in 1707 and Molly in 1726: if so, Jenny's thirty-one years would be up in 1738 and Molly's in 1757. By the time Richard Fouracres and the other witnesses came upon the scene, Jenny was beyond the age of thirty-one and had outlasted her indenture, but her daughter Molly had not yet done so. Any child this Molly had while still bound would also be unfree. The use of the term "free negro" in Molly's case did not connote actual freedom, but only prospective freedom from long-term servitude, as distinguished from perpetual enslavement.

So we return to Annie and her case. Annie may have been trying to attach herself to the other Jenny and Molly, selecting as her mother the other Molly and as her grandmother the other Jenny, or she may have been making what she thought was a genuine case that her grandmother was an Indian who should have been free. But there are clues that suggest other strands of freedom, or stabs at obtaining it, from many years before.

Susannah Wyatt reported that, some time after being sold to Parrish, Molly had asked Wyatt to buy her back, but he had refused. In a variant of that story, told by Waller Lewis, "it began to be reported that Jenny Gray, a sister, as he is informed, of the plaintiff Annie [thus another daughter of Conner estate Molly and granddaughter of Ebo Jenny], intended to try to obtain freedom." Moving to information that seems to have come from Richard Fouracres, Lewis spoke of how, soon after Parrish bought Molly, he came to Wyatt "very much alarmed at a story the girl had told him that she was to be free," and offered him some money so as to be shed of the bargain, and Wyatt "had the mother of the girls immediately called in and directed the said Parrish to examine for himself." According to Lewis, Parrish "was convinced the story the girl had told him was wrong and went away again well satisfied."

Mary Minor gives the most satisfying account of these events. She had, she reported, "never heard from white or black a word about

Freedom until after John Parish son of Joel Parish began to make preparation to remove to Kentucky." At that point, she said, Jenny told her that "some people persuaded her to sue for her freedom, rather than go to Kentucky and leave her Husband; and Jenny at the same time said if John Parish would sell her to Waller Lewis (who owned her Husband) and not carry her to Kentucky she would never sue for her Freedom." So Annie's reportedly African-born grandmother Jenny, who had evidently found a new husband in Spotsylvania County, feared she would lose him because she would be moving to Kentucky, another place at the end of the earth. She was choosing, if she could, to be forever a slave in Spotsylvania, still together with him, rather than a slave in Kentucky, separated from her husband and perhaps other members of her immediate family, including her children and grandchildren.

Mary Minor also said that "to her knowledge the old woman Molly mother to Jenny and Christopher Terrells [other] Negroes lived and died as slaves." Not only that, but no testimony from any of the witnesses supported the contention that Annie and her children and grandchildren were descended from an Indian entitled to her freedom.

Annie wanted to be free. She wanted her children and grandchildren to be free as well, and they no doubt wished to join her in that new status. Caroline County's clerk of court John Pendleton and a number of other people, including the deponents and justices of the peace in other counties, had been called upon to contribute to the deliberations by the members of the court as to whether, when Annie exercised the only right she had as a slave, they should conclude that they were, like her court-appointed attorney Lomax, "of opinion that the petitioners are entitled to their freedom."

They did not. In November 1810, the court ruled against Annie's petition. She and her children and grandchildren were slated to remain in slavery.

But in the process of reaching that conclusion, the members of the court heard testimony that touched on the encounter of Indian, African, and European; of free, enslaved, and indentured Virginians (both for the usual terms of around seven years and for the much longer periods of thirty or thirty-one); and of people of various mixtures among the three great peoples who had lived in the Caroline County area over the preceding two or three generations. They heard testimony, too, that touched on the migration of Virginians, of all racial identities, as tobacco cultivation made its way from low country to upcountry, from Tidewater to Piedmont and then across the mountains and on to a much farther western part of Virginia, the Kentucky country. Both before the American Revolution and after it, even within slavery, much was to be lost, or gained, as Virginians changed residence.

Family was everything, whether to an elderly Jenny trying to stay near her husband or—a half-century later—an even more elderly Annie trying to gain freedom for her children and grandchildren. One hundred and fifty years after Annie filed her petition in 1808, matters of race and family would retain their salience in Caroline County, Virginia.

In 1958, 150 years after Annie's petition, Richard Loving, a white man, and Mildred Jeter, a teenager who would describe herself variably as Indian and as part black and part Indian, wanted to marry, but had the impression they could not do so in Virginia. So they made their way to the nation's capital, Washington, DC, married there, and then returned to their native Caroline County — believing, expecting, hoping that the marriage they had contracted outside the state would be respected, accepted as valid, back in their home state and county. In this belief, this expectation, this hope, they rudely learned they had been incorrect, as she found out the night she and Richard were hauled out of bed and off to jail for their crime of marrying each other.

Mildred Loving died in 2008, one month to the day before her fiftieth wedding anniversary, and two hundred years after Annie's petition. She, like Annie, had just wanted to be free. She found that her racial identity was a tremendous obstacle to freedom, but she sought to find freedom despite the unpromising legal materials available to her. This book explores the long historical background to the 1958 marriage of the couple who wanted to be Mr. and Mrs. Loving — and the story of what followed their marriage.

Much as the law of race had enormous impact in shaping freedom from slavery, it related to other major strands of American history. Across the nineteenth and twentieth centuries the law of race and marriage was often intertwined with the law of race and education, in particular public schools. Nor were race and religion ever far apart. Religious ideas long reinforced the law of race and marriage. Yet in the generation after World War II, religious ideas and organizations did much to bring an end to the old law of race and marriage. People struggled, in their own minds and in the public sphere, over the relative strength of church authority and secular law, especially when those two seemed to diverge or conflict.

What happened along the way sometimes looked inevitable, as if it could have gone no other way, and arguments in courtrooms, whether by lawyers or judges, often deployed rhetoric to that effect — only one possible outcome could arise from a particular trial concerning interracial sex or marriage. But in fact, contingency can just as readily be seen as shaping the course of events. People often acted in ways that changed their own lives and changed, too, key elements in the broader society, setting the stage for future developments in law and society.

The story of the Lovings and the case they took to the US Supreme Court involved a community, an extended family, and in particular five main characters, as well as such key dimensions as race, gender, religion, law, identity, and family.

Richard Loving and Mildred Jeter, and the marriage they made and sought to have recognized, are of course the central characters, different in temperament but committed to each other. Also central to the way their story made its way to the resolution it did were their two young attorneys, Bernard Cohen and Philip Hirschkop, one of whom first took up the case and got it launched, the other of whom came on board later and proved crucial to bringing it to a successful conclusion. And then there's Leon Bazile, the crusty local judge who presided twice over their case and who, while generally perceived subsequently as a buffoon, a cartoon character out of some old Jim Crow movie, must be understood as well.

The community in which Mildred Jeter and Richard Loving grew up is often seen as unique, nowhere much replicated in the state, the region, or the nation. But it may help us to approach the Loving story as though—while having its own special features, an understanding of which is vital to following the story—it also was perhaps far more typical than not, embodying features that could be found in many communities. Hardly only in Central Point did two realities very much diverge, the official version that governed race relations and family formation and the on-the-ground adaptations and accommodations that permitted many things to happen and be more or less accepted, even if the dominant culture frowned on them, and even if official policy outlawed them. The world of Jim Crow segregation could, no doubt about it, prove ruthless in formulating its mandates and applying them to individuals across the landscape. But individuals' beliefs and behavior and experiences cannot be reliably predicted on the basis of such official renderings of the way society was supposed to work.

The story of the Lovings is captivating precisely because it is a love story, set against impossible surroundings, something of the Capulets and the Montagues in William Shakespeare's play *Romeo and Juliet*. Moreover, its historical significance makes it a story worth knowing, and knowing far better than has ever been possible before. More than just their own story, compelling as that might be, their saga stands as a proxy for countless other couples in countless other communities, across the length and breadth of American history in time and space. Most of the thirteen colonies, and the vast majority of the American states, for many years maintained a legal environment on race and family akin to the one the Lovings encountered in the aftermath of their wedding. The eventual resolution of their case brought largely to an end the kinds of travails that Richard and Mildred Loving experienced toward the very end of well over two centuries of such laws.

One key element that must be explored relates to racial identity: how race is understood, how one is racially identified, who gets to decide a person's identity, as well as when, where, and how it matters. In a society in which people have generally been routinely classified as "black" or "white," Mrs. Loving insists, in effect, that race matters be reconsidered. Was she "Indian"? Was she "black"? Was she part one and part the other? The law of race always had to address the question of, if there were to be a boundary that set one racial identity off from another, where it should be. Virginia's laws on the subject were never identical to all the other jurisdictions that maintained such laws, and Virginia's laws themselves kept changing.

For all these reasons, this book takes two tracks in retelling the history of a major Supreme Court case. On the one hand, it follows the intersecting lives of Mildred Jeter, Richard Loving, Leon Bazile, Bernard Cohen, and Philip Hirschkop. On the other, it surveys the intersections of the broader historical, racial, and legal landscapes within which their story unfolded. So this book is a study of five people, with an emphasis on one family and one community. At the same time, it tours all of American history as it reexamines the ways race, law, and family have been understood and how the Lovings' story can help us reimagine those multiple histories. The story of the Lovings is the story of America, and it is the story of how one case arose and how its outcome went far to transform the nation's legal and racial landscape.

Finally, the emphasis on one community, no matter how representative, is constantly in tension with broader issues. Throughout American history, outside forces have made their way into Caroline County. Some were welcome, at least by some residents; others not, at least by many. Interventions took many forms, including the ways the county's territory and people got caught up in the nation's wars, and also including the ways in which official policy entered, whether from the state capital or the nation's. Conflicts, whether they took military form or judicial, and whether ostensibly over race or power or law, constantly recurred, ready to alter the way people went about their lives, or at least the environment in which they lived.

Race, Sex, and the Freedom to Marry captures and reveals these many currents, even as it depicts a transformation in American law and culture across the twentieth century. It explores the rise, fall, and aftermath of America's antimiscegenation regime, a system that sought to govern people's selection of wives and husbands on the basis of their racial identity.

The core of the Loving story itself is recounted in chapters 4 through 7 and the epilogue. The other chapters place one family and their pathbreaking court case in larger contexts of time and space and thus make even clearer their story's extraordinary broader significance.

Race, Sex, and the Freedom to Marry

CHAPTER I

Family and Community in Caroline County, Virginia

The city of Richmond, Virginia, established during the American Revolution as the new capital of the new state, lies at the fall line of the James River. Washington, DC, laid out in the 1790s as the new capital of a new nation, lies on the Potomac. And midway in between, the city of Fredericksburg emerged at the fall line of the Rappahannock River, which also serves as the northern boundary of neighboring Caroline County. Interstate 95, built in the 1950s and 1960s, connects the three cities.

To get from Fredericksburg to Bowling Green, Caroline's county seat and largest town, one goes southeast on State Road 2 for some twenty miles. Driving south through the town on US 301, one passes through a neighborhood of big churches and fine houses, then past the new courthouse and the old jail on the left, the jail where Mildred Loving spent several nights after her arrest in 1958. On the right, a mile or so south of town, is the county's Community Services Center and library, the building that housed the old Union High School that Mildred Jeter attended. Across the highway, as if in counterpoint, a historical marker points out the location, a few miles away, of the long-ago home of Edmund Pendleton (1721–1803), a leader in Virginia during the Revolution and in the law and politics of the new state.

Another mile south, turn left onto State Road 721, and you are a dozen miles from Central Point to the east, where Mildred Jeter and Richard Loving grew up in the 1950s in worlds both separate and overlapping. The roads are paved now, unlike back in the 1940s and 1950s, though mostly still narrow. A half-dozen miles in, at Sparta, Route 721 cuts off to the right, but you continue straight, on 630, for another half-dozen miles. With St. Stephen's Baptist Church on the right, and its cemetery on the left, just ahead is the Central Point intersection, with the derelict old store and post office at Central Point, still carrying the mostly legible name on a sign high overhead, P. E. Boyd Byrd. One option is to turn right, on 625, and head south toward Byrds Millpond and line into King and Queen County. Continue east on 630 instead, and just a few miles ahead is Essex County. Or turn left, north under a pine canopy toward the old post office at Passing, on what is known both as Route 625 and as Passing Road. Continue north beyond Passing and you find Naulatka (pronounced "no-la-ka"), at the edge of Fort A. P. Hill, and then Supply; or turn right, and Route 637 takes you into Essex County and on toward Hustle. Or turn left, instead, and head west toward White Lake. Each of these places appears in the story of the Lovings.

Back south of Bowling Green go straight, instead, continuing south on US 301, and forty miles away is downtown Richmond, where one can visit the state capitol building. Designed by Thomas Jefferson, it houses the General Assembly, which passes the Commonwealth's laws, like the Racial Integrity Act of 1924, under which Mr. and Mrs. Loving were convicted in 1959. Not far away is the building on Broad Street, a monument to the New Deal, that for many years housed both the Virginia State Library, where the state's records are kept, and the Virginia Supreme Court, where the laws are applied to cases like the one the Lovings brought in 1966 on appeal regarding their convictions and exile for their marriage between a "white" man and a "colored" woman.

Marking History in Caroline County

Captain John Smith, the year after landing at Jamestown in 1607, made his way up the Rappahannock River to the area that would much later become Caroline County. White contact with the region therefore dated back nearly the entire four hundred years when Virginia commemorated the events of 1607 in 2007, though not until some years after John Smith's visit did colonial settlers begin to make their homes and plantations in any part of the area. Caroline itself was formed in 1728 out of three of the counties that today surround it: Essex, King and Queen, and King William. In the years before 1728, as well as in subsequent generations, slaves toiled in the tobacco fields, built the roads, and worked on the waterways of Caroline County (especially the Rappahannock River and the Mattaponi), by their labors creating the economy and infrastructure of the area, and creating families and communities as well.

On a visit to the county in the twenty-first century, one encounters reminders of three great wars in US history. A sign in front of the courthouse in Bowling Green recalls the night in April 1781 that Lafayette camped there on his march from Maryland to Richmond. Along Route 2 north of Bowling Green are many signs identifying the Washington-Rochambeau Route, taken by French and American troops while making their way in September 1781 toward what turned out to be the climactic military engagement of the American Revolution, at Yorktown, and designated in 1975 as part of the Revolution's bicentennial celebration.

The Civil War saw a tremendous amount of action in the vast space between Richmond and Petersburg, to the south of Caroline County, and in and around next-door Fredericksburg. Again at the courthouse, one sees the ubiquitous monument to Confederate forces who fought another war of independence, but one with no decisive Yorktown to give the rebels victory. In late April 1865, after Robert E. Lee's surrender at Appomattox, John Wilkes Booth, the Shakespearean actor and assassin of President Abraham Lincoln, died, four miles south of Port Royal, when he refused to surrender to pursuing US forces at the farm of Richard H. Garrett. Markers to those events are located in Port Royal and several miles down Route 301.

Port Royal is a small town nestled near the southern bank of the Rappahannock River, a major waterway that long connected the plantations of the county to the Atlantic basin. The Rappahannock is named after the predominant group of Native Americans who inhabited the region at the time John Smith made his visit, long before conflict erupted between thirteen colonies and the British Empire, or between eleven Confederate states and the new nation that had emerged from the Revolution. Along the entire northern boundary of Caroline County, only the long bridge at Port Royal crosses the Rappahannock.

Route 301 takes drivers southwest from Port Royal toward Bowling Green—each town home to only a few hundred residents—and then on toward Richmond. It cuts south through Fort A. P. Hill, named after a Confederate general from Virginia and established in 1941 in preparation for the fighting of World War II, in much the way and at just the time that the Pentagon went up in Northern Virginia to bring the War

Department under one massive roof. The county lost roughly one-third of its territory when Fort A. P. Hill came along. A great number of families, white and black, whose ancestors had long lived on the land found themselves dispossessed. Descendants of any local Indians still living in the area found themselves dispossessed yet again.

Freedom and Family

In the late colonial and early national periods, especially on the eve of what became the American Revolution, various slaves and servants in Caroline County went to court seeking their freedom. The county magistrate Hugh Noden, before he died, had possession of the Burdette family: Cloe, Dinah, Swaney, Doll, Sarah, and Scilla, all of them very long-term servants as the children of a white mother and a black father. Charles Noden, Hugh Noden's white son and heir, had in mind moving all six to some other place, outside the colony, in the guise of slaves. Other whites intervened, and the Burdettes remained in Caroline, but over the years, as each turned thirty-one, they had to sue Charles Noden individually to obtain the freedom that was their due at that age.

Sarah Mann was herself the mulatto daughter of a black father and a white mother, so she was subject to a thirty-one-year term as servant. While still a servant, she had five children, whom the law also consigned to thirty-one years of servitude: Glasgow, Ceasar, Romulus, Frank, Charlotte, and Hannah Mann. The children's father was a white man, John Sutton, her master. In 1765, approaching her end of service, she claimed that her children should get their freedom when she got hers. Sutton had no interest in seeing her leave or the children get their freedom. She took him to court, and eventually she and her children all shed their status as Sutton's servants.

People held in short-term servitude or eternal slavery, or for that matter in the long-term servitude of a Sarah Mann or a Cloe Burdette, had no power to end the system that controlled them. The best they could do was to work within that system, seeking, by virtue of a law that might provide their own freedom as individuals, a favorable outcome in a court of law. Annie Gray, in her petition arguing on the basis of an Indian ancestry she claimed, pursued one such potential means. The other was the avenue Sarah Mann and her children pursued. Harry Ralls went to court in 1770 against his mistress, the widow of John Stevens, arguing that as the son of a white woman and a black father, he should be free at thirty-one. But the court, reaching back to the circumstances of Harry's birth in 1739, determined that while his father may well have been white, his mother was a black woman named Beck, and if she was a slave, any child she had must be a slave.

Two of the key figures in the political life of revolutionary or early national Virginia lived in Caroline County. The death of his father came even before he was born, but Edmund Pendleton was apprenticed to the clerk of the Caroline County Court, and there he learned much about the law and the ways of the courts, and he grew up to become a member of both Virginia's plantation elite and its political elite. As he developed his holdings, Pendleton found, as did other planters in the 1750s, that slaves seemed always in short supply, especially Virginia-born slaves.

Upon Virginia's declaration of independence in 1776 and the adoption of its new state constitution, Pendleton served as the first speaker of the new House of Delegates. He presided at Virginia's convention in 1788, where he lent his support to the ratification of the proposed US Constitution. Upon the subsequent reorganization of the state's judiciary, he became the first president (chief justice) of the state's new Court of Appeals.

Always conservative in temperament, Pendleton had taken a cautious approach to the question of declaring independence in the 1770s, and in the 1790s he turned against the policies of the new federal government. His commitments to law, liberty, property, and the judiciary combined to forge his understanding of the crucial role an independent judiciary should play. He was pleased and relieved when Thomas Jefferson defeated the Federalist candidate, John Adams of Massachusetts, in the presidential election of 1800, but, looking for formal safeguards against federal power, he soon wrote a pamphlet titled *The Danger Not Over.*

His nephew John Taylor (1753–1824), who from the age of six grew up with Pendleton and his wife, generally replicated his uncle's political leanings, though he opposed ratification of the US Constitution in 1788. A generation younger than Pendleton, but already a lawyer by the time Virginia declared independence, Taylor served as an officer in the Patriot military forces. Beginning with more resources than his uncle had, and earning considerable sums from his law practice, he had the means to develop into a very prominent planter. He spent most of his life on his tobacco plantation, Hazelwood, but he also served in both the US Senate and the Virginia General Assembly.

To distinguish himself from another Virginia politician with the same name, he took the name John Taylor of Caroline. It was he who in 1798 introduced into the Virginia General Assembly the resolution that James Madison wrote against the Alien and Sedition Acts, one of the Virginia and Kentucky Resolutions. A prolific writer, his publications included *An Inquiry into the Principles and Policy of the Government of the United States*, published in 1814. In his way, he emulated his uncle in articulating a worldview that supported slave-based agricultural life and sharp limits on the power of the federal government. His progeny followed him as planters. Upon his death in 1824, he willed his sons Henry, George, and William P. each a substantial plantation, and his grandsons Edmund Taylor and John Taylor each one as well.

Another white family, by the name of Clark, passed through Caroline County. George Rogers Clark was born in 1752 in Albemarle County, near the place Thomas Jefferson was growing up, but William Clark, the ninth of ten siblings, was born in 1770 in Caroline County. There the boys' father had inherited some land, to which he took his family in about 1756, after defeats in the French and Indian War made life farther west appear overly hazardous and security proved for a time to be more important than opportunity. In 1772, the elder Clark brother migrated to the Kentucky country of western Virginia, and there, during the struggle for American independence that soon followed, he played a central role in securing a huge part of the West from British control, so that it remained part of the United States under the terms of the 1783 peace treaty.

William Clark, too, moved to Kentucky in the 1770s. During the years after a new nation gained its independence, many Americans directed their attention to areas even more vast and even farther west, and in 1803 William Clark joined up with Meriwether Lewis on what became known as the Lewis and Clark Expedition, from the Mississippi River to the Pacific Northwest. They traveled, first and last, up and back, along the Missouri River, through what became the state of Missouri and along the eastern boundary of what became Kansas. These areas later emerged as the bone of contention that drove first the Missouri Compromise of 1820 and then, later, the rise of a new Republican Party in the 1850s (fueled by the Kansas-Nebraska Act of 1854 and the *Dred Scott* decision of 1857), the Republican candidate's victory in the 1860 presidential election, and the secession of Virginia and ten other states that formed the Confederate States of America, the capital of which became Richmond, a mere forty miles south of Bowling Green.

Annie Gray had worked with the material available to her to weave the fabric of freedom for herself and her children and grandchildren. Even that proved beyond her power. But she had no way at all to do more than distinguish a few people kept in slavery from the countless thousands of families who did not even have her story of Indian descent to deploy in a petition in 1808 and a court hearing to determine her freedom from slavery. By contrast, in the summer of 1800 a slave from the Richmond area named Gabriel plotted to end slavery for all his fellows held in bondage. His conspiracy, which reached into Hanover and Caroline counties, failed utterly. But it revealed the desperate dream, persistent and widespread, of nonwhites for freedom in early Virginia.

The experiences of members of several nonwhite or mixed-race families during the years between 1803 and 1860 can each illustrate the roles of slavery and race in shaping freedom and families in Caroline County and the surrounding area. John Mercer Langston, for example, was born in Louisa County, on the other side of Hanover County from Caroline. His father, a prosperous planter with a number of slaves, had once owned Lucy Langston, but emancipated her in early 1806, shortly before a new law went into effect that might have required her, if he had freed her afterward, to leave the state in order to maintain her freedom. He and she were at the time the parents of a daughter, Maria, whom he freed at the same time. In the years that followed, they had three more children, all sons, Gideon (in 1809), Charles (1817), and finally John (1829). In an autobiography published in 1894, the youngest son would describe his grandmother, Lucy's mother, as "a full-blooded Indian woman."

In view of Virginia's law against interracial marriage—in place ever since 1691—Lucy Langston and Ralph Quarles could not marry. But they lived out their final years together, and per his instructions, they were buried side by side when they both died in 1834, first he, then she. Ralph Quarles had provided for his three mixed-race sons to move to Ohio, part of the Old Northwest that the efforts of George Rogers Clark had done so much to secure. There, though black freedom was by no means as expansive as white freedom, it was far greater than anything that John Mercer Langston could have experienced in Virginia, whether in the 1830s or at any other time before the late 1860s. He attended school, something outlawed in Virginia, and in fact graduated from Oberlin College in 1849, earned a degree in theology there in 1853, became a lawyer, and subsequently ran for public office and was elected, all this well before universal emancipation came to Virginia in 1865.

A mixed-race (indeed triracial) young man, John Mercer Langston lived the freedom that his interracial parents had hoped for and had done what they could to provide for him. In Ohio, he married a woman with a biography similar to his, the daughter of a white planter and legislator in North Carolina, Stephen Wall, and his slave Jane. Caroline Matilda Wall—who like her siblings carried her father's name—was freed by him, sent to Ohio, and eventually attended Oberlin, where John Mercer Langston met her in 1850. Conditions would later change in Virginia, and he would be returning. He always worked well with whites, but throughout his life he would identify with, and lead in, the struggle of African Americans for freedom—freedom at all, and then a more expansive delineation of it.

Another native of Louisa County, born there in 1815, was Henry "Box" Brown. In an autobiography, Brown would later speak of how, when his owner died and the property was apportioned among four sons, he was separated at age fifteen from his family. This division, he wrote, "from my father and mother, my sister and brother, with whom I had hitherto been allowed to live," was "the most severe trial to my feelings which I had ever endured." As a young man hired out as a slave in Richmond—an Upper South urban slave, that is, with substantial day-to-day autonomy—he met and married a slave named Nancy, and they lived together and had three children. Then suddenly one day in 1849 he discovered that the four had all been sold away to North Carolina, and once again he was bereft.

Again powerless to retrieve and reconstitute his family, Henry Brown plotted this time to gain his freedom from the slavery that had twice cost him his family. Working with a white friend, Samuel A. Smith, and a free black man, Smith's employee James Caesar Anthony Smith, he had himself boxed up and shipped off via Adams Express to Philadelphia, Pennsylvania. His subsequent writings as Henry "Box" Brown, together with his touring with the famous box in which he had made his escape from slavery, spurred the cause of emancipation. As a fugitive from slavery, he served the abolition cause as an extraordinary witness to the horrors of slavery, even at its best. A black Virginian helped shape developments on the racial front, far from his home state.

Anthony Burns resembled Henry Brown in ways important to them in their personal lives and also to us in understanding family life and freedom under slavery. Born in Stafford County, next door to Caroline, in the early 1830s, he learned to read and write but was separated from his family. Sent to work in Richmond in 1853, he soon escaped to Boston, and, in what became a major incident in national politics, black and white Bostonians tried to prevent his being taken back into slavery under the Fugitive Slave Act of 1850. Hundreds of state militia and federal soldiers were involved in the effort to get Burns on the ship that took him back to Virginia and slavery. Even white northerners unsympathetic to the cause of black freedom often perceived what led one to write: "We are the slaves and vassals of the South." Yet a Richmond newspaper saw things very differently: "A few more such victories, and the [white] South is undone."

Caroline County Population	White	Slave	Free Colored	Total
1820	6,497	10,999	486	17,982
1830	6,499	10,741	520	17,760
1840	6,725	10,314	774	17,813
1850	6,891	10,661	904	18,456
1860	6,948	10,672	844	18,464

Whether through birth to free mothers, manumission by owners, or successful legal action, the number of free people of color in Caroline County grew from 203 in 1790 to 486 three decades later. Most non-white Virginians in the county during the half-century before the 1860s were enslaved. A few may have gained their freedom. And a great many found themselves caught up in the interstate slave trade that took so many nonwhite Virginians south and west to places between Virginia and Texas. But most remained as slaves in the area of their birth to slave mothers. In every US census from the first in 1790 through the last pre–Civil War one in 1860, whites comprised less than 40 percent of the county's total population; slaves were always a large majority. Yet the total number of slaves hardly budged, decade after decade—even during the 1790s, but especially from the 1820s through the 1850s—as large numbers of involuntary migrants left the county behind, with newer slave states absorbing Caroline's entire natural increase, the number of slave births that exceeded slave deaths, especially in the 1820s and 1830s. As for the middle group, neither slave nor white, free people of color numbered 844 in 1860—5 percent of the entire population, 7 percent among all nonwhites.

In the late 1930s, a New Deal program led to the gathering of a great many "slave narratives," the results of interviews with people most of whom had been slaves before universal emancipation came in 1865. About a dozen such interviews took place in Caroline County, or in the city of Fredericksburg, or in a contiguous county.

In Caroline County, Caroline Johnson Harris spoke of marriage under slavery, both in general on her plantation and in terms of her own individual experience. The person to whom she gave her interview rendered what she said as follows:

> Didn't have to ask Marsa or nuthin'. Just go to Ant Sue an' tell her you want to git mated. She tell us to think 'bout it hard fo' two days, 'cause marryin' was sacred in de eyes of Jesus. Arter two days Mose an' I went back an' say we done thought 'bout it an' still want to git married. Den she called all de slaves arter tasks to pray fo' de union dat God was gonna make. Pray we stay together an' have lots of chillun an' none of 'em git sol' way from de parents. Den she lay a broomstick 'cross de sill of de house we gonna live in an' jine our hands together. Fo' we step over it she ast us once mo' if we was sho' we wanted to git married. 'Course we say yes. Den she say, "In de eyes of Jesus step into Holy land of mat-de-money." When we step 'cross de broomstick, we was married.

"Pray we stay together an' have lots of chillun an' none of 'em git sol' way from de parents": That, from someone born in 1843, summed up the most realistic hopes of a young enslaved couple in love in the last years before the curtain fell on slavery and the slave trade in Virginia.

———

Secession, War, and Emancipation

In the winter and spring of the season of secession in 1860–1861, white Virginians were very divided over how to respond to the election of Abraham Lincoln in November, the secession of South Carolina in December, the formation of the Confederate States of America with seven states in February, and the events that followed Lincoln's taking office in March. At a constitutional convention in Richmond called to consider these grave developments, delegates from west of the Blue Ridge tended to oppose secession, those east of it to support it. Delegates' votes on secession were by no means a simple matter of their being proslavery or not, as they could differ very much as to whether they saw slavery as more secure inside the United States or in a struggle for Confederate independence.

Twice the issue was directly voted upon. Shortly before the Confederate firing on Fort Sumter, after which Lincoln called for volunteers from every state to put down the rebellion, delegates voted 90–45 (as historian Brent Tarter has recently determined) against secession; after those events, delegates voted 88–55 for secession. Caroline County's delegate, Edmund Taylor Morris, voted "yes" both times—Fort Sumter did not change his mind. Of the delegates from counties contiguous with Caroline, two voted "no" the first time, but all five voted "yes" on the second vote. Caroline County was located in an area that strongly supported secession, before Fort Sumter and especially after it.

John M. Washington (1838–1918), across his long life, tracked the years from the last generation of slaves before the Civil War, through secession, to the end of slavery and far beyond. During the 1850s, he lived in his native Fredericksburg, but he spent most of the 1840s with his mother and siblings some distance west in Orange County, and he hired himself out in Richmond for the year 1861. In an account he wrote after the Civil War, he tells of his separation at the age of twelve from his mother and siblings when they were sent west to Staunton. He tells, too, of his navigation of a legal and urban social system that included slaves, free whites, and free people of color; of how he learned to read; of his courtship and marriage with a young free black woman, Annie E. Gordon; and of how her children would be born free. But their father, as a slave, would be hard-pressed to assure her protection and well-being or theirs, and Annie's mother was so distressed at her daughter's marrying someone enslaved that she cut ties with her.

Washington recounts, too, his escape in 1862 and his service in the Union military in Civil War Virginia, much of it as a guide on horseback. It seems that his father was white, and his mother had a white father too, so he describes himself from his childhood as "a small light haired boy (very often passing easily for a white boy)." In fact, if three of his four grandparents were of completely European ancestry, then if his mother's father had any European or Native American ancestry, under Virginia law John Washington was legally white, as well as a slave. This background can account for how, when he first entered Union lines near Fredericksburg in April 1862, intent on assisting the Union troops, Washington was taken at first for a white man. As he describes the encounter and "the First Night of my Freedom":

> I told them I was most happy to see them all, that I had been looking for them for a long time. Just here one of them asked me "I geuss you ain't a Secessish, then," me said "I know why, colord people aint secessh." "Why you aint a colord man are you," Said he. "Yes Sir I am" I replyed, "and a slave all my life"—All of them seemed to utterly astonished. "do you want to be free" inquired one, "by all means" I answered.

He returned to Fredericksburg, and some of the troops he was with were ordered to Bowling Green, but his orders took him to Culpeper. On September 1, 1862, he made his way to Washington, DC, where before long he was reunited with his wife, his mother, his grandmother, and other members of his extended family. And there he and his wife raised their sons in a world far removed from the slavery he had known into his adulthood.

Outside of Virginia, Indians could be found on both sides during the Civil War. Inside Virginia, they generally tried to stay away from the white man's war, and some among the Chickahominy and Rappahannock nations even fled to the North. Virginia Indians tried not to antagonize their powerful white neighbors, and so did not generally take action in support of the Union, yet they had no love for the Confederate cause. They were generally classified as "people of color," along with free African Americans, and had to carry freedom papers. They had experienced centuries of struggle, including in recent years, trying to hold on to their land, or even their freedom, and it was Virginia landholders and politicians who had taken it away or had tried to. In this context of push and pull, fourteen men from the Pamunkey nation played important roles for the Union. The war came to them, as it swirled around and then came onto their tiny reservation, and they joined in the war, as river pilots for the Union Navy or as land guides for the army or as spies. William Terrill Bradby, who served as a scout, guide, and river pilot, was one of these Pamunkey men who helped the Union. He served for three years, was wounded in action, and later received a pension.

Stonewall Jackson, after he was shot by terrible error by his own troops in May 1863 in Spotsylvania County during the Battle of Chancellorsville, was transported by ambulance twenty-seven miles to Guinea Station, in far western Caroline County. Located on the Richmond, Fredericksburg, and Potomac Railroad, it was safely behind Confederate lines, and he would be able, it was hoped, to take the train south to Richmond, where he could recuperate. Union troops, however, had cut the rail line, so there he stayed, at Fairfield, the plantation home of the Thomas Coleman Chandler family and of a dozen slave families. Jackson declined the offer of a room in the big house, so the Chandler family prepared a downstairs room for him in the plantation office building, which for years had been used by one of the sons, Dr. Joseph A. Chandler, a graduate of Philadelphia Medical College, as both his home (upstairs) and his medical office (downstairs).

Three of Thomas Coleman Chandler's sons—William Samuel, Thomas K., and Henry M.—had gone off to war wearing Confederate gray. By the time Stonewall Jackson arrived, the senior Chandler had seen the loss of many of his dozens of slaves, as they escaped when Union troops came by, and he was in the process of selling off the place. The elder Chandler long outlived the war. Slavery—like Stonewall—did not. The old plantation became the site of Stonewall Jackson's "Shrine."

President Abraham Lincoln had already issued his Emancipation Proclamation, at the beginning of 1863, months before the fighting at nearby Chancellorsville. By the time Union General Winfield S. Hancock came through Bowling Green in May 1864, the future of slavery looked even more grim for slave owners. That November, Lincoln gained reelection, and in January, following up on a campaign promise, Congress proposed the Thirteenth Amendment. Union victory came in April 1865, bringing a formal end to slavery in Virginia, and the Thirteenth Amendment was ratified in December 1865, bringing abolition everywhere.

When emancipation came, slaves left one world behind and entered a new one. Former slave Louise Bowes Rose, born in 1853, recalled in the 1930s a certain baptism into a new life of freedom on the day word came to her Hanover County plantation that slavery had ended: "Daddy was down to de creek. He jumped right in de water up to his neck. He was so happy he jus' kep' on scooping up han'fulls of water an dumpin' it on his haid an' yellin,' 'I'se free, I'se free! I'se free!' "

Freedom and Reconstruction

During the first decade after universal emancipation came to Virginia, black residents shed slavery in part by attending school and in part by organizing their own churches. According to Julia Frazier, who was born into slavery in Spotsylvania County in 1854, "Colored folks went to the white churches; couldn' have colored churches." Still a child when the Civil War ended and emancipation came, she had soon learned her "A.B.C.'s," in 1865 or 1866. Bacchus White, also a slave in Spotsylvania County, on the large estate of Virginia Supreme Court Judge Francis T. Brooke, said: "Dat day and time de colored people didn't have no colored church, so dey alwa's went to the w'ite church, Round Oak, 'an dar wus a plase 'served fur dem."

In the years after 1865, change in Caroline County, as across the South, can be measured and recounted in terms of families, schools, churches, politics, and migration. Black schools and black churches, in the eyes of most black Virginians, were a vast improvement over white control of churches and black exclusion from schools. After the Civil War was over and slavery had ended, the Freedmen's Bureau, as well as the state legislature, took action to give formal recognition to the families of the county's former slaves; long lists tabulated the many marriages formalized and the children legally recognized.

A Freedmen's Bureau register of families, dated February 1866, reveals glimpses of hundreds of family histories. That very month, a prewar free woman, eighteen-year-old Isabel Freeman, had married a former slave, James Taylor. In April 1865, the exact month slavery ended for her new husband Page Catlett, a free woman, Sally Bird, settled in with him, and they had a baby son a few months later; her older sister, Ellen Bird, had married former slave Helot Garnett at about the same time. Together since about 1802 were eighty-four-year-old John Williams and seventy-nine-year-old Hannah Fells, who had lately been slaves on the Williams Carter place. David Fortune, a free man, and his wife, Charlotte Parker (who had belonged most recently to Philip H. Carter), both of them fifty-three, had been together since about 1836, they said, and were the parents of Henry, twenty-two, Isaac, twenty, David, eighteen, Betty, sixteen, and William, twelve, all of them born into slavery and now free at last. Their oldest sons, Henry and Isaac, had each in 1862 married a slave woman on another holding.

John Baptist and Lilly Timlie, both eighty-nine-year-old natives of the county, had been together for some seventy-five years, since about 1791, had been owned most recently by Dr. Joseph A. Chandler, and had in all likelihood found themselves too immobile to follow their fellow slaves into freedom during the war. John Broaddock Butcher, a twenty-nine-year-old man who had belonged to William P. Taylor, son of John Taylor of Caroline, had been married for about seven years to Polly Robinson, a slave on the James Taylor place. In the postwar world, whatever their other concerns, these two couples would not have to worry about belonging to different masters or about their children being born as slaves. Different owners, one spouse or the other moving from one county to another, worrying about whether children would be sold to the Deep South or about children who already had been—these stories can be inferred from the hundreds of family histories, each of which grabs at the imagination as to how people had been able to act and what they had thought and felt.

The Freedmen's Bureau helped local people of color, some of them free since birth, most of them slaves until 1865, establish elementary schools. Louisa County native John Mercer Langston served for a time in Virginia, and elsewhere across much of the South, as school inspector for the Freedmen's Bureau. Then he moved to the nation's capital, some eighty miles to the north of Louisa, Hanover, and Caroline counties, and organized a law school at the new Howard University, which enrolled both men and women, black and white, but was designed primarily for African Americans, who had no alternative school at which to study law anywhere in the South, where most lived. Down the Mattaponi and York rivers from Caroline, Hampton Normal and Agricultural Institute began operations.

The end of slavery in 1865 led two years later, in 1867, to black political rights. And black voters produced results that not only brought men of color into office but also revealed in yet another way the magnitude and breadth of the interstate slave trade out of Virginia in the generations before 1865. In Texas, Richmond native Richard Allen gained his freedom in 1865 and was subsequently elected to a variety of offices, including state legislator. Dozens of other Virginia natives were similarly elected as black legislators from states across the former Confederacy.

In 1866, the Virginia General Assembly—like the legislatures of all the other former Confederate states, except Tennessee—rejected the proposed Fourteenth Amendment, with its equal protection clause and its encouragement of black voting. To achieve ratification of the amendment, viewed by most northerners as absolutely essential as the basis of a new postwar order for the South, in March 1867 the US Congress mandated new elections to a constitutional convention, with black voters helping elect the delegates. Virginia's 1867–1868 convention was required to develop a new state constitution that would enfranchise black men.

Caroline County voters elected no black legislative candidates in the postwar era. Across much of Virginia, however, former slaves and prewar free men of color alike were elected to the state constitutional convention of 1867–1868 and then, through the end of the 1880s, to both houses of the General Assembly. A native of Caroline County, former slave Lewis Lindsay, was elected as a Richmond delegate to the 1867–1868 constitutional convention. Born free, William Breedlove represented his native Essex County in the same convention. Born a slave, Burwell Toler represented Hanover and Henrico counties in the convention. Several nonwhite legislators from counties not far from Caroline—each of them born free in Virginia—were said to have a combination of black, white, and Indian ancestry. Among these men was Jesse Dungey, who represented next-door King William County for a term in the House of Delegates. So he might be called black, something at least partly true; or he might be termed "mulatto" to indicate a white-black mixture; or he might be denominated "black-Indian" to get at his two nonwhite lines of heritage.

As directed by the new state constitution of 1869, the legislature in 1870 created a new system of public schools for Virginia children. The constitution did not specify whether there should be one integrated system or two parallel systems. The legislature mandated segregation, from the beginning of the public schools, in 1870. Saying there would be public schools was one thing, but funding them was another. One reason to segregate them was to make it more likely that white voters and legislators would support them—and that white parents would send their children.

Regardless, the legislature diverted scarce funds to other purposes, and schools actually declined in number in the late 1870s. The Democratic leaders insisted that the state first make payments on its public debt, left over from before the Civil War and far more burdensome in the postwar economy, when, with poverty widespread, public revenue was harder to come by, taxes more of a challenge to pay. Late in the decade, a "deadly struggle" took place in the General Assembly, as Virginia state superintendent of public schools William Henry Ruffner put it, in which "all the enemies of our school system, within and without the Legislature, combined for its destruction" but "were met and beaten at every point; and thus our glorious system of universal, free education was saved, and saved forever." The Caroline County school superintendent reported, after the close of the 1878–1879 school year, "the suspension of a large majority of our schools during the whole of last year" in light of the "unfortunate circumstances."

White Virginians bitterly divided on this great public policy question, and in 1879 a new political force came to power in the legislature. They were called the Readjusters, from their insistence that the state debt be "readjusted" so as to make it possible to address other public policy concerns, chiefly the tax burden and school expenditures. In one of the more startling developments in all of American political history, a biracial coalition, made up mostly of whites from the western part of the state and black voters from the east, gained a majority of the legislature and election to the governorship—and this came after 1877, the year widely taken by scholars to mark the end of Reconstruction. With great effectiveness, they fulfilled their promises on those great issues, and their accomplishment largely outlived their few years in power, before white Democrats overthrew them. For one thing, the new public elementary school system had been established on a far firmer footing.

Another of their accomplishments was to establish what is today Virginia State University, founded in 1882 as Virginia Normal and Collegiate Institute, just outside Petersburg, some fifty miles south of Caroline County. Former slave Peter J. Carter attended Hampton Institute, spent four terms in the House of Delegates in the 1870s, and later served on the board of visitors of Virginia Normal and Collegiate. In the years to come, many of the black teachers in the segregated Caroline County schools obtained their training at Virginia Normal. Others did so at Virginia Union University in Richmond, or at Hampton Institute, or at St. Paul's in Lawrenceville.

In the 1880s, an offer of the presidency of this black public college drew John Mercer Langston back to Virginia. When the Readjusters lost power, the Democrats changed the terms of control at the black school, and Langston left his position but soon ran for Congress from the Petersburg area of the Southside. He served briefly in the session that ended in 1891—a clear indication of how long black political power persisted in Virginia, just as his leaving the college presidency and instead running for elective office, successfully the first time, unsuccessfully the second, indicated the waning of such power.

Caroline County Population	White (%)	White	Nonwhite	Total
1880	44.1	7,606	9,628	17,234
1890	44.1	7,359	9,322	16,681
1900	45.9	7,667	9,042	16,709
1910	47.3	7,846	8,750	16,596
1920	48.8	7,783	8,077	15,954

Caroline County continued to change. Each census count from the 1880s through the 1940s marked a further decline in the number of nonwhite residents. The white population showed little change in absolute numbers, so the white percentage gradually grew. As elsewhere in Virginia, black citizens—by no means waiting on the "great migration" that would later, for example, take many tens of thousands of African Americans from Alabama's Deep South cotton fields north to Chicago—were making their way north to Washington, DC, and to Baltimore, Philadelphia, and New York City. Yet whites remained a minority in Caroline County until the 1970s. Long before then, the county's population—white and nonwhite alike—took a hit when Fort A. P. Hill took a third of the county's area beginning in the run-up to American entry into World War II.

Caroline County Population	White (%)	White	Colored	Total
1940	49.8	6,934	7,011	13,945
1950	48.6	6,058	6,413	12,471
1960	47.4	6,037	6,688	12,725
1970	47.8	6,659	7,266	13,925
1980	55.4	9,917	7,987	17,904

While this was all happening in the realm of social history, in the realm of political history the great experiment of Reconstruction, with its culmination in Virginia in the Readjuster interlude in the early 1880s, was receding to the vanishing point. In fact, the nonwhite migration out of Caroline can be understood as a response to the defeat of the Readjusters, compounded by the apparent finality of the 1902 constitution, designed to eliminate "every negro voter who can be gotten rid of," as the convention leader Carter Glass exclaimed: "Discrimination! Why that is exactly what . . . this Convention was elected for." Thus it had been determined who the leaders of Virginia, for much of the twentieth century, would be. The electorate would be very small, and very white; and in Caroline County, a version of the state of Virginia writ small, whites—actually, a slim proportion of all whites—made the rules and enforced them.

The Lovings and the Jeters

Most families in Caroline County lived a hardscrabble existence. Few, regardless of their racial identity, enjoyed the privileges of the elite. Whites made their way into the world and through life in possession of at least some of the accoutrements of white supremacy. Yet for most, their privileges were clearly finite, even if sometimes critical. In short, most people, regardless of whether they were identified as "white," "Negro," or "Indian," had little in common with the elite Virginians who framed the laws of race that sorted out people from one another. That is surely true of both the Lovings and the Jeters.

On October 23, 1933, Richard Perry Loving was born, as Twillie Loving and the former Lola Allen supplied a younger brother for their first two children, Ethel and Margaret. He was twenty-eight at the time, she twenty-four, and they were living in Central Point, not far outside the boundary of the huge area that, within eight years, would become Fort A. P. Hill. The baby's birth certificate dutifully identified each parent as "white" and said both had been born in Caroline County, he currently engaged in "general labor" and she a housewife. The midwife who attended the birth was Sallie F. Pratt, a resident of Naulatka. Baby Richard's grandparents were farmers Milton and Lizzie Loving and J. W. and Wally Allen.

A few years later, on July 22, 1939, a baby girl, Mildred Delores Jeter, was born to Theoliver "Jake" Jeter and his wife, the former Musiel Byrd, residents of the community of Whites, a few miles northwest of Central Point, at the lower end of White Lake. The new father was fifty-four years old, his wife twenty-eight. She had been born in Central Point, he in Brandywine, a small community nearer to Port Royal than to Central Point, in an area that soon vanished into Fort A. P. Hill. Both were listed as "colored." Mildred was Musiel's fourth child, but her husband had been married before, to Daisy Richardson, so Mildred had several much older half-brothers as well. Theoliver Jeter said he had been a tenant farmer all his adult life. Musiel Jeter indicated she was a "housewife" and had been so for seven years, the length of time they had been married so far.

During World War II, young Richard turned ten years old, and he was soon, if not already, helping around a neighbor's farm, driving a tractor and doing many of the other things that a farm requires. This was the farm of P. E. Boyd Byrd—variously described as "black" and "Indian," and one of the larger farmers in the community—and for many years Richard's dad also worked there.

Some years later, Richard and Mildred met; then became friends, eventually lovers. And then they set out to marry. Obstacles rose before them—the 1950s version in Virginia of a long history of how courts, constitutions, and state laws had shaped couples' lives for some three centuries, whether in Caroline County or a host of other communities, in Virginia and far away.

CHAPTER 2

Couples, Courts, and Constitutions

During colonial times, the dominant people in much of British North America constructed racial categories that defined freedom, conferred citizenship, and determined the right to marry—and, beyond that, specified who a person could, or could not, marry. Until well into the twentieth century, and across much of the nation, Americans worked to create and impose such categories, or resisted them, or lived within them. Not every colony or state legislated against marriages that might be defined as interracial, and nowhere were all interracial marriages banned. Although laws restricting interracial marriage long predated the Civil War, the heyday of antimiscegenation laws came in the hundred years after the very term "miscegenation" was coined in the run-up to President Abraham Lincoln's reelection bid in 1864. Neither the North nor the South was ever all of a piece, yet the two regions—better described as the South and the non-South—tended to move in different trajectories.

Who was white, and who not? Who was free, and who not? Which people were free to marry, and who were they free to marry? The young couple who in the 1950s and 1960s wanted to be Mr. and Mrs. Loving entered American legal and social history very near, as it turned out, the end of a long line of couples who encountered laws like the ones that threatened their marriage and their freedom—their ability to live as a married couple in Virginia and to stay out of jail for trying to do so.

Some couples escaped prosecution under laws that might have targeted them. Some successfully navigated their way through or around legal bans. Considerable numbers, however, in generation after generation and in most of the American states, found themselves in court over their choice of a marital partner. Some paid steep fines or went to prison. Some lost family property that they had expected to own, or to continue to own, on the basis of their longtime marriage to a person who had recently died: they lost both their partner and their property. White supremacy appeared not only in the guise of exclusive sexual access by white men to white women but also in the guise of transfers of property from nonwhite to white but not in the other direction.

Chesapeake Beginnings to America's Antimiscegenation Regime

Among the British North American colonies, Maryland and Virginia acted first to regulate interracial sex and especially marriage. Slavery became a part of the society and legal system in every colony, though not everywhere did laws emerge to keep free people from marrying no matter their racial identities. New York and New Jersey never passed such laws, nor did New Hampshire or Connecticut. Maryland, by contrast, in the 1660s threatened any white woman who married a black man that, as a consequence, she would become a slave and her children after her would be slaves. Generations later, the enslaved descendants—in the female line—of "Irish Nell," for one, would go to court, many of them with success, in the quest to gain their freedom as the descendants of a white woman who, they argued, should never have been enslaved in the first place.

Virginia legislated the rule in 1662 that, regardless of the racial identity of the father, children born to slave women would be slaves, while children born to free women (regardless of their own race) would be free. Over the next thirty years, new questions emerged, and the House of Burgesses addressed each in turn. If, for example, slaves ran away with servants, those servants if caught would have additional years tacked on to their terms of unfreedom; since slaves had no additional time to give, the servants would incur their penalties as well.

The Virginia legislature first took action against various forms of interracial marriage as early as 1691, midway through the colonial era. The 1691 law spoke with disgust of "that abominable mixture and spurious issue" that would no doubt increase unless white women were prevented from having sex with nonwhite men. In the assembly's words, "that abominable mixture and spurious issue" would take place "as well by negroes, mulattoes, and Indians intermarrying with English, or other white women, as by their unlawfull accompanying with one another." By that language was especially meant interracial sex and marriage involving a white woman and biracial children by a white woman. White women who had sex with a black man or an Indian and conceived a child, but nonetheless could not get married, had a special punishment: they were fined, and, if unable to pay, they were sold as servants for a period of years. And the child? Sold as a servant until the age of thirty-one, which, though not perpetual enslavement, was a very long term of unfreedom. This term was reduced in 1705 to a mere thirty years, but then it was extended in 1723 to the next generation when any woman in that status herself had a child.

One central question, of course, is why so many white men in Virginia worked so hard to keep a legal barrier between themselves and so many of their neighbors, and why they maintained the effort for centuries. Wherever the idea originated, and historians have done a great deal of work to figure this out, many whites from colonial times saw themselves as embattled in a struggle to maintain civilization against people of different religions and races. The law of 1691 emerged in part from this concern. As slavery developed, economic motivations—protecting and enhancing the value of an investment in a certain form of property, maintaining control over a labor force—drove such laws as the 1662 one that defined the child of a slave mother as a slave even if the father was white. These two notions came together, reinforced each other.

The seventeenth-century laws of race and marriage in Maryland and Virginia were designed to generate and reinforce a system of designated candidates—huge categories of them—to hold positions of social subordination and economic dependency. Framers of these laws aimed for white supremacy, certainly, but, more particularly, a system of privileged white adult male supremacy, open to accommodate new members who met the prevailing criteria, but structured to restrict entry by racial others. A large and servile labor force was wanted. So was sexual access to all women, and exclusive access to white women. The men who made the rules did not make rules to restrict their power, but rather to enhance it. Rules about race and about labor made by the House of Burgesses, itself democratically elected by landowning white men, were intended for governing other people.

New England in the 1810s

Not all New England colonies and states had laws against interracial marriage, but Massachusetts (beginning in 1705), Rhode Island (starting in 1798), and Maine (after it separated from Massachusetts) did for many years. Massachusetts repealed its law in 1843, and Maine and Rhode Island did so in the 1880s, long before the time of the Lovings. In the years before repeal, though, couples encountered those laws in ways that prefigured many of the issues that made their way into the second half of the twentieth century. The Lovings experienced legal obstacles and snares both similar to and different from the ones those faraway, long-ago couples had.

No white folks in Massachusetts said that Ishmael Coffee had committed a crime, though the law banned marriages between whites and "negroes" or "mulattoes." But they did argue whether, as a "mulatto" who had taken as "his supposed wife a white woman," his marriage was "void." And they also argued over whether the couple's daughter, Roba, was herself "white" or "mulatto." The couple resided in Massachusetts in the 1760s but got married in Rhode Island, which had no law as yet to keep them from marrying, and then returned "immediately" to Massachusetts. Over the next half-century, three legal questions arose: (1) Was their Rhode Island marriage valid in Massachusetts? (2) Was Roba a "white" person who could therefore legally marry a white man? (3) Was the Massachusetts law of race and marriage, in fact, in accordance with constitutional law at the time?

This last question arose in the litigation, but it is not entirely clear what meaning the challenge had. Perhaps it aligned with the state's 1780 constitution, which declared: "All men are born free and equal." That language proved, in the early 1780s, to be the basis on which people held in slavery in Massachusetts brought freedom suits, suits for their freedom, suits that they won; slavery in the state crumbled, and the first US census, in 1790, counted no slaves there at all. Alternatively, did the challenge to an out-of-state marriage, one that originated in a place where the marriage was perfectly legal, seem to present a problem under the new US Constitution, which required each state to recognize contracts validly undertaken in another state?

The three big questions—the validity of the couple's marriage, the racial status of their daughter, and the constitutionality of any impediments in Massachusetts to legal recognition of their marriage—arose in two court cases because each of the three people fell into deep poverty, their state's law of public support depended on a person's place of "settlement," and no town fathers wished to take on financial burdens that could be rightly passed on to another town. Rather, they went to court to get their responsibilities clearly determined.

Roba's place of settlement was Medway until 1789, when she married Christopher Vickons, whose settlement was in Natick. Was she white? Was their marriage valid? These matters arose after Vickons died, and she and their child, both "indigent," needed public support. Medway would support them unless (1) the law against her marriage was constitutional *and* (2) she was a mulatto. Given those two conditions, her marriage would be invalid, and her place of settlement would have never shifted to Natick. However, change either of those conditions (that is, if she were actually white or the law unconstitutional), and then her place of settlement would have shifted to Natick through her marriage.

The Massachusetts Supreme Court, in view of how it ruled on the question of Roba's racial identity, found it unnecessary to rule on the question of the law's constitutionality. Of course she was white, said the court in its 1810 decision. A "mulatto" was the child of a "black" person and a "white" person, half and half, whereas she was the child of a mulatto man and a white woman, thus three-quarters white. Natick was responsible and must therefore reimburse the town of Medway for the expenses of supporting Roba and her child.

Some years later, Roba's parents found their half-century-old marriage itself in court. Aged and ailing, they needed public assistance, but the town they were living in, Medway, insisted that another town, Needham, was their place of "legal settlement" and should be supporting them. Needham would accept responsibility only if the couple had a legal marriage, something the trial court ruled that they in fact had. On appeal, in 1819 the Supreme Court of Massachusetts upheld the trial court. A marriage, it ruled, if valid "according to the rules of the country where it is entered into, shall be valid in any other country." The Massachusetts law, even though itself constitutional, did not affect a marriage imported from a state that had no law restricting it. An interracial marriage was "only void, if contracted within this state, in violation of its laws."

––––––––

Dred Scott and the "Deepest Degradation"

The Massachusetts law against interracial marriage did not void the marriage that Ishmael Coffee entered into in Rhode Island. But it did play a significant role in litigation that erupted two generations later and hundreds of miles away.

Freedom suits by people challenging their enslavement arose again and again in America between the 1760s and the 1840s. Among them were those in Massachusetts in the 1780s, Annie's petition in early national Virginia, and the most famous of all, Dred Scott's journey through the American court system, from the state courts of Missouri to the US Supreme Court, between the late 1840s and the late 1850s. When the US Supreme Court ruled against him in 1857, one key consideration was whether Dred Scott could be a US citizen, thus whether he could rightly bring his case into a federal court.

To bolster his conclusion, Chief Justice Roger B. Taney drew upon the history of colonial and state laws against interracial marriage. Most of the original thirteen states — eight of them as of 1776 — had such laws. Taney felt no need to dwell upon, or even notice, the four that never did — New Jersey, New York, New Hampshire, and Connecticut, with Rhode Island initiating such a law in 1798. Nor did he bother to notice that Pennsylvania repealed its law in 1780, or for that matter that Massachusetts repealed its in 1843. But he did stress that Massachusetts reenacted its in 1786 — right after, he might have noted, slavery came to an end there — and in fact added to the previous penalties for violations by whites.

Taney observed that it would be "tedious" to run through all such laws, and he chose to notice the laws of just two colonies or states, one in the North and one in the South, Maryland and Massachusetts, but he let them stand as though the two represented universal white public opinion as exemplified in public policy of long duration. So the presence, and the persistence, of these laws undergirded Taney's assertion that the founders could not have meant to include black Americans within their language of rights, within "the people" in whose name they spoke. These laws against marriage between "the white race" and the servile race, he wrote,

> were still in force when the Revolution began, and are a faithful index to the state of feeling towards the class of persons of whom they speak, and of the position they occupied throughout the thirteen colonies, in the eyes and thoughts of the men who framed the Declaration of Independence and established the State Constitutions and Governments. They show that a perpetual and impassable barrier was intended to be erected between the white race and the one which they had reduced to slavery, and governed as subjects with absolute and despotic power, and which they then looked upon as so far below them in the scale of created beings, that intermarriages between white persons and negroes or mulattoes were regarded as unnatural and immoral, and punished as crimes.... And no distinction in this respect was made between the free negro or mulatto and the slave, but this stigma, of the deepest degradation, was fixed upon the whole race.

Reconstruction

Four years after Justice Taney penned those words, Abraham Lincoln took office as president of the no-longer United States. War soon broke out as the Confederate States of America pressed its bid for independence, and to win the war President Lincoln eventually moved as commander-in-chief toward emancipation.

Two journalists had wicked fun toward the end of 1863. President Abraham Lincoln had issued the Emancipation Proclamation at the start of the year, and in the coming year he seemed likely to run for election to a second term in the White House. Doing what they could to undercut Lincoln's prospects of success in the coming campaign, David Goodman Croly and George Wakeman, two Democrats playing as though Republicans, put together a creative but entirely bogus pamphlet that pretended to celebrate the coming racial equality that the Republican Party's policies might bring to America: *Miscegenation: The*

Theory of the Blending of the Races, Applied to the American White Man and Negro. In that brave new world, old taboos would vanish, and the biggest change of all would have black men marrying white women.

Lincoln won against his Democratic opponent in November 1864, and the Union did as well against the Confederate States of America the following April. In the two or three years that followed Lincoln's victory in the election and the Union Army's victory in the war, tremendous change came to American law and politics and the Constitution. The questions that Croly and Wakeman had raised turned out to be very real, and the term "miscegenation" that they contrived turned out to be widely used as a substitute for the traditional term, "amalgamation." Might black men marry white women, and white men marry black women? Might it be legal? Might state laws and state constitutions, even in the South, permit it? Might the US Constitution prohibit states from preventing it? Not before the end of the 1870s, or even later, would answers everywhere come into focus.

Much was in doubt for a number of years, and much contested. The Thirteenth Amendment, ratified in December 1865, put an end to slavery across the land, though in most places, including Virginia, it had been declared abolished many months earlier. During the first year after the war, southern state legislatures enacted laws to accommodate—and contain—the changes that an end to slavery released. Some of those laws, most notably Mississippi's, appeared to leave a key feature of slavery intact by stipulating that black residents could not legally come into possession of their own farm land, so most of them would have to continue to work for whites. In response, Congress passed the Civil Rights Act of 1866 to declare African Americans citizens, with rights that included the purchase of land and the making of other contracts.

To safeguard the Civil Rights Act against subsequent repeal or judicial invalidation, Republicans proposed the Fourteenth Amendment, which incorporated the key provisions of the Civil Rights Act and also addressed what had emerged as an absolutely critical matter, the fact that former slaves would no longer count as "three fifths of all other persons" but, instead, as full persons themselves, even as it was their former owners who voted with that increased representation in the US House of Representatives and the electoral college. Yet all but Tennessee among the former Confederate states rejected the proposed amendment. So in order to obtain ratification, the Republican majority in Congress forced the matter in the other ten states by removing the current governments, providing for their replacement, and granting political rights to black men. Black men as well as white men voted in elections to choose delegates to new state constitutional conventions, conventions that had to provide black voting rights under the new governments to be established. Then the new legislatures elected under those new constitutions had to ratify the Fourteenth Amendment, and only then would Congress agree to seat US senators or members of the US House of Representatives sent from that state. In short, black southerners, as well as white southerners, would make the rules that applied to all citizens. There had never been anything like it in American life, and certainly not in the South, where the vast majority of black Americans lived. *Dred Scott* from a decade before had been decidedly overturned, though how thoroughly and how permanently remained to be seen.

As of 1867, every state in the South had a law, whether recent or ancient, against black-white marriage, but very soon after that the Solid South was no more. During Reconstruction—after the election of delegates to those new constitutional conventions, followed by new legislatures chosen under those new constitutions—seven states of the former Confederacy removed their laws against interracial marriage. The legislatures exercised their discretion to do so in Florida, Arkansas, Mississippi, South Carolina, and Louisiana. State courts, applying their respective understandings of the mandates of the new legal and constitutional order, declared against such laws in Texas and Alabama as well as in Mississippi and Louisiana.

The Alabama Supreme Court ruled in *Burns v. State* (1872) that the Civil Rights Act of 1866 "confers . . . upon the negro in express terms . . . the right to make and enforce contracts, amongst which is that of marriage with any citizen capable of entering into that relation." Similarly, the Louisiana Supreme Court ruled in 1874 that "the Civil Rights bill . . . invested [Cornelia, a 'colored' woman] with the capacity to enter in the contract of marriage with E. C. Hart, a white man, and to legitimate her children by him born before said marriage, just as if she had been a white woman." According to the Texas Supreme Court in 1872, "the law prohibiting such a marriage [as that between A. H. Foster, a white man, and Leah Foster, his former slave] had been abrogated by the

14th Amendment to the Constitution of the United States." Declared the Mississippi Supreme Court in 1873, "with the adoption of" the 1868 state constitution, "former impediments to marriage between whites and blacks ceased."

Other state supreme courts, however, in both the North and the South, ruled otherwise. Two of these were Georgia and Indiana. In *Scott v. State* (1869), the Georgia Supreme Court upheld a lower court conviction for interracial "cohabitation" despite a marriage ceremony. Conceding an end to slavery and a beginning of black civil rights and even black political rights, the court nonetheless insisted that the "conquering people" of the North had not yet "required of us the practice of miscegenation, nor have they claimed for the colored race, social equality with the white race." Neither the Civil Rights Act of 1866 nor the Fourteenth Amendment had any bearing on Georgia's capacity to outlaw interracial marriages, insisted the court, and ban them it had.

What about interracial marriage in the Reconstruction North? Thomas Gibson had some African ancestry, Jennie Williams had none. They married in April 1870, and ten days later an indictment came down. The trial judge—convinced that the Civil Rights Act and the Fourteenth Amendment governed the matter, overriding the state law against black-white marriage—quashed the indictment. The state appealed! The prosecution wanted not only to punish the infraction but to have the state's highest court uphold the statute for use in other cases.

As the Indiana Supreme Court mused in *State v. Gibson* (1871), "If the federal government can determine who may marry in a state, there is no limit to its power." But, the court ruled, there were limits, and Gibson had to go on trial for his supposed marriage and face the possibility of a prison sentence of between one and ten years as well as a big fine. The Gibsons moved on and escaped prosecution. But the court's ringing endorsement of a state's authority to regulate marriage—a state where the traditional law against black-white marriage was not an outgrowth of slavery there—did much to bolster southern judges in their inclination to find a way to exempt miscegenation laws from the reach of the Fourteenth Amendment.

In Virginia: Andrew Kinney and Edmund Kinney

Virginia's prewar law against interracial marriage had changed since the first edition of it in 1691, but the essentials remained intact, though the original sentence of banishment for the white party had long since been replaced by a fine. In the absence of a valid marriage, both parties who "lewdly and lasciviously . . . cohabit together" were subject in the 1870s to a fine of between $50 and $500.

This was the situation when Mahala Miller and Andrew Kinney decided to get married. They traveled in November 1874 from Augusta County to Washington, DC, had a wedding, and returned to their home in the Shenandoah Valley. They had been together since soon after the Civil War, for they had had three sons beginning as early as 1867. Though their marriage may have been an attempt to escape prosecution for living together out of wedlock, it instead brought the wrath of local authorities down upon them. Charged with "lewdly associating and cohabiting" with Miller, Kinney protested that they were married, and at trial his attorney asked the judge to instruct the jury that the marriage was "valid and a bar to this prosecution." Instead, the judge instructed the jury that the marriage was "but a vain and futile attempt to evade the laws of Virginia." The jury convicted him, and he paid a $500 fine, but he appealed the outcome to the Virginia Supreme Court.

In *Kinney v. Commonwealth* (1878), a unanimous appeals court upheld the verdict. Rejecting the Massachusetts precedent from 1819, the court declared there to be "no doubt" as to the authority of a state "to declare who may marry, how they may marry, and what shall be the legal consequences of their marrying." If the couple wished to live as husband and wife, they must change their place of "matrimonial residence" to a place "where the laws recognize the validity of such marriages." As for Virginia's law, it was a crucial part of "our cherished southern civilization, under which two distinct races are to work out and accomplish the destiny to which the Almighty has assigned them on this continent." Such "connections and alliances so unnatural that God and nature seem to forbid them, should be prohibited by positive law, and subject to no evasion."

The next federal population census, in 1880, nonetheless showed the couple still together, still living in Augusta County, and, by that time, the parents of five sons. But if local authorities let them alone after the initial hefty fine, Virginia legislators saw their marriage and the publicity that followed their trial—as they appealed to the state supreme court in their challenge of the state's authority to enforce the current law—as a call to action, to add to the force of Virginia's "positive law" and make it more expressly "subject to no evasion."

A new law, enacted in March 1878, changed the punishment for interracial marriage from a fine to a two-to-five-year term in prison. A penalty identical to that for marrying within Virginia awaited any black-white couple seeking to evade the Virginia law by going out of state to get married in hopes of returning to Virginia as a married couple. What we might term the "Andrew Kinney bill" was soon applied to another man named Kinney, together with his wife, for their DC marriage.

Edmund Kinney, described as a black man, and Mary S. Hall, a white woman, made their way from Hanover County in October 1878 north to Washington, DC, where they had a wedding ceremony, and then back to Hanover County. Both were soon charged with violating the new law, and both were sentenced to five years of hard labor in the state penitentiary.

They appealed their plight to federal Judge Robert W. Hughes, but he could find no constitutional basis for intervention. The Fourteenth Amendment's privileges and immunities clause, he asserted in *Ex Parte Kinney* (1879), did not prevent a state from violating the privileges of its own citizens, and the equal protection clause in no way limited a state's discretion "to regulate the domestic relations of its own citizens." Regardless, both parties, white and black, had been charged with the same crime and given the same sentence, so where was the violation of equal protection? And the matter of comity, in which one state recognized contracts entered into elsewhere? Might the couple lawfully import their marriage despite the state's new law? On this the judge was also adamant. The couple could not bring into Virginia—"in violation of her laws," contrary to Virginia's "public policy"—"the marriage privileges of a citizen of the District of Columbia" any more than they might the privileges of a polygamous citizen of Utah.

State Laws and Interracial Marriage, 1870s–1920s

Would courts align their rulings on interracial marriage with the approach in Georgia, Indiana, and Virginia or with the approach taken for a time in Texas, Alabama, Mississippi, and Louisiana? Aaron Green, a black man, and Julia Atkinson, a white woman, married in Alabama in 1876 and soon found themselves in court for their marriage. Relying on the 1872 decision in *Burns*, which had thrown out Alabama's miscegenation laws, they appealed their convictions to the Alabama Supreme Court, the same court that had issued the *Burns* decision, but with an entirely new slate of judges. What they heard there offered no comfort, no exoneration. Cheerfully relying in part on the Indiana ruling in *State v. Gibson*, the Alabama appeals court in *Green v. State* (1878) expressly overruled *Burns*. The ruling in another case that same term, *Hoover v. State* (1878), utterly repudiated *Burns*: "The former erroneous ruling of this court furnishes no excuse which we can recognize." Like the *Gibson* case in Indiana, each of these opinions went on at length, and with gusto, in working out the rationale for the state's committed adherence to the antimiscegenation regime. Also like *Gibson*, each would be called upon in the years ahead to bolster rulings elsewhere.

One by one, the seven former Confederate states that had abandoned their laws against interracial marriage returned to the fold. In Texas, where not only a state court but a federal court had ruled against the miscegenation laws, the antebellum norm soon snapped back into position. In 1877, federal district Judge Thomas Howard DuVal, declaring the Texas miscegenation statute "obsolete and inoperative" under the Civil Rights Act of 1866 and the Fourteenth Amendment, freed Lou Brown, a white woman who had married a black man. Even he changed his mind within two years, in *Ex Parte Francois*, after the Texas Supreme Court, in *Frasher v. State* (1877), had overruled *Bonds v. Foster* and also another such case, *Honey v. Clark* (1873).

No federal court would rule as Judge DuVal had, if ever so briefly, until *Loving v. Virginia*—and, as with other rulings against miscegenation laws, it would be forgotten by historians and judges, at first shunned as illegitimate, then neglected because it had been buried in the past. State judges in antimiscegenation states would construct a history that denied an alternative past that once was. Lies would be repeated as facts until they became indisputable facts.

South Carolina was back on board via legislation in 1879, Florida by 1881. Texas had its statute restored first by the 1877 court ruling in *Frasher v. State*, then by legislation in 1879. Mississippi not only restored its statute in 1880, or at least enacted a new one, it also—for emphasis, and so no future state court could rule against it—placed it in the new state constitution of 1890. So did Florida in 1885, South Carolina in 1895, and Alabama in 1901. Some states that had never suspended their laws also constitutionalized the restriction—Tennessee in 1870, North Carolina in 1875. Beyond the symbolic importance given the policy by placing it in a state's constitution, the gesture also prevented the legislature from ending the ban on black-white marriage and, of even greater significance in view of developments there or elsewhere during Reconstruction, ended any likelihood that a state judge might rule against the ban.

By the mid-1890s, public policy in the South was uniform in its opposition to black-white marriage. The final two states to rejoin the others and reconstitute the Solid South were Louisiana and Arkansas. The Louisiana legislature, after several failed efforts, managed to pass a new law against interracial marriage in 1894, two years before the Supreme Court ruled on the state's 1890 transportation segregation statute in *Plessy v. Ferguson*. The Arkansas Supreme Court, in *Dodson v. State* (1895), denied that the Arkansas law had ever gone missing. It had always been in full force, the appeals court declared as it upheld the indictment and conviction of a black man, Thomas Dodson, and a white woman, which came after the Dodsons had been married for nearly two decades.

Yet during those same years, five states in New England and the Midwest moved in the other direction, repealing their laws: Illinois (1874), Rhode Island (1881), Maine and Michigan (both in 1883), and Ohio (1887). Gone was the early post–Civil War patchwork pattern in which the states east of the Mississippi River showed no strong regional differentiation, aside from the Border South's uniform stance against black-white marriage. North of the Mason-Dixon Line and the Ohio River, by the 1890s Indiana was the sole holdout, maintaining the statute that its supreme court had upheld in *State v. Gibson*. South of that boundary, no exception could be found at any time between 1895 and 1967.

In yet another pattern, a whole raft of new states in the West enacted laws against various forms of interracial marriage. As was always the case, every one of the new laws attacked black-white marriage. Most also addressed the presence of Chinese men and, later, men from Japan. Many of these laws also refused to recognize marriages between Caucasians and American Indians.

As of 1874, the year of the Illinois repeal, only four western states had miscegenation laws: Nebraska, Nevada, Oregon, and California. As new states entered the Union, most supported laws against some forms of interracial marriage. By 1913, the year after the last of the contiguous forty-eight states was admitted, the only exceptions to universal participation in the antimiscegenation regime, among all the states west of the Mississippi, were Kansas, New Mexico, and Washington. So by that time, most of the outliers—the states that did *not* have laws against interracial marriage—were in New England or the Midwest.

In December 1912, Congressman Seaborn Roddenbery of Georgia tried to impose on every state at least as much of the law of race and marriage as was found in his home state. He proposed an amendment to the US Constitution: "Intermarriage between negroes or persons of color and Caucasians or any other character of persons within the United States or any territory under that jurisdiction is forever prohibited, and the term negroes or persons of color, as here employed, shall be held to mean any and all persons of African descent or having any trace of African blood."

The proposed amendment did not carry. It did not make it out of Congress, so the question did not arise as to whether three-fourths of the states would adopt it. The fact was that thirty out of forty-eight states maintained miscegenation laws (if not in 1912, then by the end of 1913, the year Wyoming signed on) and eighteen had no such statutes. Even if all thirty with miscegenation laws agreed to a federal amendment, at least six of the remaining eighteen would have had to join in as well. The likelihood was not good, perhaps, but Congressman Roddenbery did what he could.

Failing to get his amendment, the congressman could nonetheless sleep soundly knowing that Georgia's law was safe for the foreseeable future from interference—by the Georgia legislature, the Congress, or the federal courts. When he died the next year, he had become sufficiently notorious that Jeffrey Thomas Wilson, an aging former slave in

Norfolk, Virginia, noted in his diary, with no evidence of regret: "Congressman Roddenberry of Ga is dead." Meanwhile, the social and legal world of *Plessy v. Ferguson* rolled on. Roddenbery's home state of Georgia itself deployed its autonomy in setting the color line by considerably expanding in 1927 the number of racial groups assigned to the nonwhite side of the line.

When Roddenbery's proposal failed, as things turned out, the nation was just about to plateau in its commitment to the antimiscegenation regime. After 1913, no new states joined up, though none stepped back anytime soon either. The number of states with laws restricting interracial marriage held at thirty all the way from 1913 to 1948. Virginia remained steadfast among them.

Interracial Marriage at the US Supreme Court

From time to time between the 1880s and the 1930s, the Supreme Court ruled on matters related somehow to interracial marriage, though never addressing the issue directly. In *Pace v. Alabama* (1883), the Court heard the case of Tony Pace and Mary Jane Cox, one of them black—that is, with at least one-eighth black ancestry, or one black great-grandparent —and the other white. By the time they got together, the Alabama Supreme Court had reversed the Reconstruction-era ruling in *Burns v. State* (1872) that the state law against interracial marriage violated the state constitution, the Civil Rights Act of 1866, and the Fourteenth Amendment. Therefore the Alabama law against black-white marriage was up and running again.

So they were not married, nor could they be. Nonetheless they lived together, or so the state charged, and they were found guilty and sentenced to two years in prison. Had they both been white, or both black, they would have had the option of marrying, and if, instead, they remained unmarried, their maximum penalty for a first offense would have been a misdemeanor charge that carried a minimum fine of $100 and a possible term of six months in jail. As an interracial couple, whether married or not, they were subject to a felony conviction that carried a prison term of at least two years and as many as seven. They appealed their plight to the Alabama Supreme Court, which upheld the outcome at their trial. They went on to the US Supreme Court, which gave them another hearing.

The couple's lawyer, John R. Tompkins, never contested the Alabama law against interracial marriage; rather, he agreed with it as "good law." But he did object to the disparate sentences that an interracial couple suffered for their cohabitation. On the other side, Alabama Attorney General Henry Clay Tompkins conceded nothing. Of course the state could ban "intermarriage of persons of the two races." And of course it could then also ban "illicit intercourse between them, the end to be accomplished by each prohibition being the same—the prevention of the amalgamation of the two different races." States retained full authority, he insisted, to legislate on matters of marriage, and "the policy of the law has always been to punish acts of criminal intimacy between those who are forbidden to marry with greater severity than where no such prohibition exists."

The Alabama attorney general offered to the justices of the nation's highest court a specious history lesson on bans against interracial marriage—bans that, though they were not obviously being contested, were nonetheless the foundation for the next step to justifying a greater penalty for cohabitation if interracial. That question had been before a number of state courts as well as lower federal courts, he declared, "and in every instance the validity of such laws has been upheld." That exceptions from a decade earlier could be found in Texas, Mississippi, and Louisiana, as well as in his own home state of Alabama, one would never have known from his assertion. *Burns v. State* might as well have never happened.

Unanimous in its ruling, the nation's highest court adopted the state of Alabama's reasoning from stem to stern. Even Justice John Marshall Harlan signed on, the justice who would famously dissent in a more famous segregation case, *Plessy v. Ferguson*, thirteen years later. Writing for the Court in *Pace v. Alabama*, Justice Stephen J. Field bought the rationale that the Fourteenth Amendment had no play, that equal protection was in no way compromised by the disparate sentences. The sentences were equal for Pace and Cox: each was found guilty of the same charge, and each was in the penitentiary for two years. They had not been convicted of the same charge that, for a white couple, would have carried lesser penalties. Rather, they had been convicted of an entirely different crime, and the law they broke "prescribes a punishment for an offense that can only be committed where the two sexes are of different races."

An 1888 decision by the Supreme Court, in *Maynard v. Hill,* had nothing to do with race but everything to do with marriage. In no uncertain terms, the Court's ruling in *Maynard* left matters of marriage up to states to sort out.

In 1896 the Supreme Court determined in *Plessy v. Ferguson* that the Fourteenth Amendment said nothing that might prevent a state legislature from requiring racial segregation on passenger trains. Speaking for an 8–1 majority, Justice Henry Billings Brown pointed toward the widespread segregation of public schools. Even the District of Columbia had such schools, he said, schools whose segregation was authorized by the same Congress that proposed the Fourteenth Amendment. Marriage, too, was segregated in many states, and here he parroted the falsehood earlier told to the Court in *Pace v. Alabama,* and surely known to be false by one justice. Edward Douglass White—a native of Louisiana elected as a zealous Redeemer to the state senate in 1874, the year the state supreme court there ruled the miscegenation statute unconstitutional, and a member of that court beginning in 1878—was appointed to the Supreme Court in 1894, the year Louisiana restored its miscegenation statute. Nonetheless the US Supreme Court asserted that no court had ever invalidated an antimiscegenation law: "Laws forbidding the intermarriage of the two races may be said in a technical sense to interfere with the freedom of contract, and yet have been universally recognized as within the police power of the State."

In a case two decades later, the Court heard lawyers speak again about laws against interracial marriage. A number of cities, including Baltimore and Louisville, adopted ordinances in the 1910s designed to segregate black residential areas from white ones. Issues of racial justice came up, as did the property rights of white homeowners who wished to sell or rent to whoever would buy or lease. Supporters of these ordinances equated the various kinds of segregation laws, which, they observed, "have existed for many years separating black from white in schools, in railroad cars[,] and in the matter of marrying." The other side, seeking to invalidate the racial restrictions in housing, did not contest segregation in transportation, education, or marriage, but wished to distinguish the issue at hand, which concerned property rights. The

Court threw out the ordinances, but nothing had happened that might suggest that laws against interracial marriage were at all constitutionally suspect. In *Buchanan v. Warley*, a housing case, as in *Pace v. Alabama*, ostensibly a cohabitation case, both sides agreed: the Fourteenth Amendment had no power against laws that banned interracial marriage.

Cases before the courts across the long history of the antimiscegenation regime revealed varied political and constitutional connections among miscegenation laws, on the one hand, and voting, housing, education, and transportation, on the other. In Virginia, Richmond's all-white city council—no black candidate had been elected since the 1890s—passed an ordinance in 1911 restricting subsequent land transactions along racial lines. It sought to prevent any people, white or black, from taking up residence on a block where a majority of the homes were occupied by people of the other race. Over time, as a result, with only people of color able to buy in predominantly nonwhite sections of the city and only whites able to obtain property in predominantly white sections, the various sections of the city would grow ever more perfectly segregated along racial lines. That was the intent.

Buchanan v. Warley appeared to invalidate all such ordinances, but some cities continued to enact them. Whatever the Supreme Court had ruled about race and zoning ordinances, it had left what looked to Richmond city authorities like a promising loophole. So the city council tried again, and according to a new ordinance enacted in 1929, people who could marry someone with the racial identity that predominated in a given part of the city were eligible to buy or rent property there, but otherwise not. J. B. Deans, a black resident of Richmond, went ahead and bought a house in a white neighborhood and then went to federal court to obtain an injunction against the city's applying the ordinance to stop him.

This charade proved too flagrant, too transparent, for federal district Judge D. Lawrence Groner. While in no way interrogating the constitutionality of laws against interracial marriage, or for that matter the segregated schools the city's children attended, he ruled that the city had no authority to use marriage euphemisms to subvert what the Supreme Court had ruled about property transactions. The city took the case to the Fourth Circuit Court of Appeals, but that court upheld Judge Groner: "Attempt is made to distinguish the case at bar" from *Buchanan v. Warley* as well as a similar subsequent case from Louisiana, *Harmon v. Tyler*, "on the ground that the zoning ordinance here under consideration bases its interdiction on the legal prohibition of intermarriage and not on race or color; but, as the identical prohibition of intermarriage is itself based on race, the question here, in final analysis, is identical with that which the Supreme Court has twice decided in the cases cited." As if that weren't clear enough, the city took the case to the US Supreme Court, whose opinion in May 1930 in *City of Richmond v. Deans* read in its entirety "Decree affirmed" before citing *Buchanan v. Warley* and the Louisiana case.

Miscegenation matters themselves, when they reached the federal courts during the World War II era, left no imprint. A property dispute from California hinged on whether a widow, Marie Antoinette Monks, was "white" and could therefore have legally married Allan Monks in the 1930s in Arizona. She lost his estate at trial, and multiple efforts to get the US Supreme Court to hear her case fell on deaf ears, the last time in 1946.

Another property case, one in a string of such cases from Oklahoma, went to the Tenth Circuit Court of Appeals in 1944. To the dismay and frustration of lawyer A. L. Emery, he just could not get the attention and assistance of Thurgood Marshall and the NAACP nor a favorable reading of federal law from federal judges. In the end, William Stevens could not inherit Oklahoma property under his 1936 Kansas marriage to Stella Sands, for a lower court had found him to be "of African ancestry" and her to be "white," though also Indian. His marriage was no more valid than was that of Mrs. Monks, and no more the legal basis for retaining, or obtaining, family property. In one case, the Arizona law of race and marriage governed the outcome in a California state court. In the other, the Oklahoma law of race and marriage governed the outcome in federal court.

The Fourteenth Amendment, as late as World War II, had no more power against state laws restricting interracial marriage than it had managed back in the 1870s when state courts from Indiana to Alabama to Virginia insisted that marriage was a state responsibility, that federal authority could not reach it. The alternative past, with its opposing construction of the Fourteenth Amendment, had vanished from historical memory and from constitutional law.

The Law of Race and Schools and the Law of Race and Marriage

One of the mysteries of the law of race, rarely addressed or even recognized, let alone untangled, has to do with where states drew the color line. State laws differed on where they drew it. Majorities of state legislators changed their minds and redrew the boundaries. And the states differed as to whether they employed the same line, at a given time and place, in all venues or rather placed the boundary at different places depending on whether the question at issue had to do with marriage, or schools, or, for that matter, transportation, as had been the case in *Plessy*.

Statutes supply one major category of source material. In addition, various cases that made their way through the courts—not only to trial but also to an appeals court, which thus allows them to be readily found by scholars and used as historical evidence—demonstrated the various ways whiteness could be ascertained and how the rules of race operated. One means was by "degree of blood," which itself might be determined either by lineage—a genealogical exercise, going back a good two or three generations—or by appearance, including skin coloring and hair texture. The other key means examined how people performed race, including who they associated with and where they—the current generation or a previous one—went, in a thoroughly segregated society, to school or church.

Some states applied the same rule everywhere. Oklahoma, for example, applied the same rule in marriage, education, and transportation. So did Texas. Alabama did as well, though changes there in state law moved some people previously "white" across the boundary to "colored," as the one-eighth fraction that had previously applied in Alabama made its way, by 1927, to the one-drop rule: "the descendant of any negro," "without . . . limit of time or number of generations removed." In *State ex rel. Farmer v. Board of School Commissioners of Mobile County* (1933), after one family contested their children's reclassification from "white" to "colored," the Alabama Supreme Court spoke of the restricted right to attend a "school for white children as the law defines white children."

Virginia kept upgrading the white proportion a person had to have in order to qualify as white, but leaders aspired not only to obtain a higher standard of racial purity but to apply it everywhere. Walter Plecker, a leading proponent of white "racial purity" in Virginia in the 1920s, voiced the importance of delineating—ever more definitively—the line between "white" and "colored" and of applying that standard to schools and trains as well as marriage. Speaking of mixed-race Virginians who might try (even in a manner consistent with Virginia law) to pass for white, he urged that a "firm stand" be taken "against their intermarriage with white people," or their continuing "to attend white schools and to ride in white coaches."

Such consistency in a state's laws did not, however, hold everywhere. Arkansas used the formula "any negro blood whatever" in prohibiting "cohabitation." But in transportation, where conductors presumably would have to make on-the-spot judgments about where passengers should be seated, the term was "visible and distinct admixture of African blood."

The most frequent distinction drawn came between education and marriage. In Missouri, the school-segregation statute spoke of all "children of African descent," but the miscegenation statute banned marriages between a "white person" and anyone "having one-eighth part or more of negro blood." In Mississippi, the state supreme court spelled out this kind of distinction in the case *Moreau et al. School Trustees v. Grandich* (1917). Antonio Grandich and his wife went to court when their four children, who had always gone to the local "white" school, were told not to return, on the grounds that they were "members of the colored race." The parents had been married in Mississippi as white people, and now their children, suddenly reclassified as black, "refused to attend the colored school." Their suit claimed them to be "all white with a slight strain of Indian or red blood," and asserted that their exclusion from the white school had "resulted in irreparable damages, humiliation, and disgrace, being classed as members of the colored race."

In turning back the pleas of the formerly white Grandich family, the Mississippi Supreme Court explained the rules of race in that state. The law of marriage clearly applied the one-eighth rule to black racial identity: anything less than one-eighth black, according to the 1890 state constitution, and a person was legally white. Yet in overturning a lower-court ruling about who qualified to attend white schools, the Mississippi appeals court explained why the one-eighth rule had no place in education, why "children having less than one-eighth negro blood" are "not necessarily . . . members of the white race." In education, the court declared, "The word 'white' . . . means member of the white or Caucasian race, and the word 'colored' means, not only negroes, but persons who are of the mixed blood." So, much like Gong Lum and his ethnic Chinese family, who had left behind an unfavorable Mississippi court ruling about racial identity and public schools in the 1920s and moved to Arkansas, the Grandich family moved to New Orleans.

Such a higher standard in education than in marriage was widespread and long-standing. In Ohio, according to the state supreme court ruling *Williams v. School District* (1834), anyone more than half white was to be deemed "white" and could attend the white schools. But a decision a quarter-century later, *Van Camp v. Board of Education* (1859), set a higher standard: anyone with "a visible taint of African blood" might be excluded from schools for white children. In Kentucky a half-century later than that, once it had been claimed that Troy Mullins and his sister Loucreta were perhaps one-sixteenth black, they were barred from attending the local "white" school. Despite assertions that the two children were "as fair as members of the white race," the trial court ruled against them, and the appeals court agreed, in *Mullins v. Belcher* (1911): "The question does not depend upon personal appearance" but rather on whether a person had any "traceable" "negro blood."

With all the attention rightly paid by historians to the universal ban in southern states on black-white marriage (aside from some discontinuity during Reconstruction and wherever the color line was drawn), variations in the treatment of segregation in schools during the Jim Crow era suggest an even greater salience there.

Two Catholics, One "White," the Other "Black"

In October 1947, Los Angeles residents Andrea Perez and Sylvester Davis set off to get a marriage license but were turned back because of California's long-standing miscegenation law. They had met in the early 1940s, before he went off to war, when both were working at a Lockheed Aviation assembly plant, and both attended St. Patrick's Catholic Church. She was Mexican American and therefore—in that time and place—classified as "white," while he was African American and therefore not white. They went to court—to the local court and then to the California Supreme Court. There, the couple's lawyer, Daniel G. Marshall, himself a fellow member of their church as well as a member of the American Civil Liberties Union, urged the right to marry as a First Amendment matter of religious freedom and the sacraments of the Catholic Church, and he castigated what he called the "myth and superstition" of race as an utterly inappropriate basis for denying any couple the right to marry.

The state, for its part, marched out the US Supreme Court decision in *Pace v. Alabama* (1883), deflecting the Fourteenth Amendment; *Maynard v. Hill* (1888), placing authority over marriage clearly in the hands of the states; *Reynolds v. United States* (1879), a case involving Mormons and plural marriage that just as clearly distinguished between belief and behavior in matters of religious freedom; as well as a long string of state cases upholding laws of race and marriage, including Alabama's 1878 ruling in *Green v. State*, as well as the recent federal court ruling from Oklahoma in *Stevens v. United States*.

Marshall countered with *Burns*, bringing to the court's attention the 1872 Alabama Supreme Court ruling that upheld the authority of the Fourteenth Amendment against a state statute—"lest it be thought," he observed, that the Alabama court had never ruled the other way, or that no previous ruling had done what he was urging the California court to do. In addition, he brought to bear another string of cases, one regarding family, privacy, and the right to marry, starting with *Meyer v. Nebraska* (1923). When the state, having lost the case, petitioned for a rehearing, Marshall had another Supreme Court ruling to call on. In that case, *Shelley v. Kraemer* (1948), the white parties to a restrictive covenant, having agreed never to convey their property to a black family, called on the state judiciary to force a neighbor to follow through on his commitment, and in ruling against judicial enforcement of the covenant the Court spoke against "state action" in the service of such racial discrimination in housing. Marshall now could say: "Just as no court may enforce a restrictive covenant[,] the respondent here [the county clerk] is forbidden, since he is an agent of the state, to refuse a license for reasons of race or color no matter what the statutes on which he relies say."

In this mighty struggle over race and religion, and state law versus the US Constitution, a narrow 4–3 majority of the California Supreme Court ruled in favor of the couple and against the constitutionality of the California statute. Justice Roger Traynor came around in part because of Marshall's First Amendment argument, and three other justices were convinced by Marshall's arguments on race. So, while the First Amendment and the Fourteenth were both critical to this breakthrough ruling, a new interpretation of the Fourteenth Amendment, or at least new to the twentieth century, was the key to the outcome. Putting cases upholding segregation like *Plessy v. Ferguson* aside as irrelevant to the case at hand, Justice Traynor sharply distinguished segregation in other arenas, whether in education or transportation, from segregation in marriage: "A holding that such segregation does not impair the right of an individual to ride on trains or to enjoy a legal education is clearly inapplicable to the right of an individual to marry. Since the essence of the right to marry is freedom to join in marriage with the person of one's choice, a segregation statute for marriage necessarily impairs the right to marry."

With *Perez v. Sharp*, a big state broke away from the antimiscegenation regime. The nation's second most populous state at mid-century had joined New York, Illinois, Pennsylvania, and Ohio as states with more residents than the most populous state that continued to maintain laws against interracial marriage, Texas. Most states—twenty-nine out of the forty-eight—continued their antimiscegenation laws, but California was a big tree to fall.

Ham Say Naim's Quixotic Quest

In the mid-1950s, a Virginia case about interracial marriage went both to the Virginia Supreme Court and the US Supreme Court. Like other cases involving a white person and an "Oriental" or "Mongolian," this one was not about a felony charge but about something else. Either way, it showed the antimiscegenation regime at work, and it gave Virginia's highest state court an opportunity to posture about its unlimited authority over the law of race and marriage.

In June 1952, Ham Say Naim, a sailor from China whose home port was then Norfolk, and a white woman, Ruby Elaine Lamberth, went across the state line to Elizabeth City, North Carolina, where they got married. Both states banned marriages between whites and blacks; unlike Virginia, however, North Carolina permitted marriages between Caucasians and Asians. For some months, the Naims made their home in Norfolk, but in September 1953 Ruby Naim filed a petition in court seeking annulment, either on grounds of adultery or on the basis of Virginia's ban on interracial marriages.

The local judge, Floyd E. Kellam, saw a couple who had gone to North Carolina in order to evade the Virginia law, as much a crime as having had the ceremony in Virginia. He also saw a white woman who wanted out of her marriage to a man of color, though he no doubt disapproved of her choice of a marriage partner in the first place. Of course the marriage was void, and he granted the annulment Mrs. Naim sought, so she no longer was Mrs. Naim and never had been. Mr. Naim, for his part, wanted to stay married, since on the basis of his marriage to Ruby he had applied for an immigrant visa, and unless he remained married he could not hope to become a permanent resident.

Naim's immigration attorney, David Carliner, was intent on doing well by his client. Carliner had become a specialist in immigration law, and in that capacity he had taken on Naim's case. But he had long been allergic to racial discrimination, and in the late 1930s, as a law student at the University of Virginia, he had learned of Virginia's Racial Integrity Act. Finding that he had to challenge Virginia's miscegenation law to help his client on the immigration matter, he saw it as not only a necessity but also a great opportunity. As he put it many years later, "I just jumped at the opportunity to challenge" the Virginia law. He went to work to develop what he thought should be a winning argument in such a matter of blatant racial discrimination. If he lost at the Virginia Supreme Court, perhaps he could prevail at the US Supreme Court. As he remembered the case many years later, it never occurred to him that he ought to argue, on the basis of the US Constitution's full faith and credit clause, that a marriage valid in the state where it was contracted should be recognized elsewhere, since he was convinced the equal protection clause should carry the day.

Looking back on his reception at the Virginia Supreme Court, Carliner observed: "I don't think I've ever been treated with more hostility by judges." One of them, Lemuel Franklin Smith, had voted for the

Racial Integrity Act as a member of the House of Delegates in 1924. Justice Archibald Chapman Buchanan, speaking in June 1955 for a unanimous court, reached for the Tenth Amendment to shield the Virginia statute from the Fourteenth. "Regulation of the marriage relation," he declared, is "distinctly one of the rights guaranteed to the States and safeguarded by that bastion of States' rights, somewhat battered perhaps but still a sturdy fortress in our fundamental law, the tenth section of the Bill of Rights." As for *Brown v. Board of Education*—especially *Brown I* from May 1954 but also just recently *Brown II* in May 1955—and the US Supreme Court's reliance on the equal protection clause, the court saw all the more reason to refuse the finding Naim hoped to get: "No such claim for the intermarriage of the races could be supported; by no sort of valid reasoning could it be found to be a foundation of good citizenship or a right which must be made available to all on equal terms." No language could be found in the US Constitution, he asserted, that would "prohibit the State from enacting legislation to preserve the racial integrity of its citizens, or which denies the power of the State to regulate the marriage relation so that it shall not have a mongrel breed of citizens." Justice Buchanan and his brethren fretted that "the obliteration of racial pride" and "the corruption of blood" would "weaken or destroy," not strengthen, good citizenship.

Naim appealed to the US Supreme Court for a better outcome. Not enough justices of the nation's highest court cared to take on his case in the aftermath of *Brown v. Board*, as mounting evidence emerged that most whites living in the states of the former Confederacy—certainly including those in Virginia—were in no mood to make concessions on school segregation or, indeed, any other facet of segregation. That November, the nation's highest court left Naim to his own devices, and it left the Virginia statutes in excellent working order as they continued to do what they could to safeguard white supremacy and white racial purity.

Virginia's highest court used strong language in upholding that state's laws against interracial marriage and turning back a constitutional challenge to them. Moreover, the US Supreme Court declined an opportunity to hear the case, so the state had the last word. The same high court ruling in *Brown v. Board of Education* that led the Virginia court to sound so feisty neutered the nation's highest court, where at least some justices feared causing even more difficulty on the school front by addressing the matter of race and marriage. The right case might come along, and at the right time, but regardless of whether this was a good case, the time was not good at all.

The turmoil associated with *Brown v. Board of Education* hardly occasioned the only impediment to the Court's taking the *Naim* case, let alone to supplying the outcome that Carliner looked for. No branch of the federal government had yet undertaken any role in scrutinizing a state's laws on race and the freedom to marry. Certainly no consensus had begun to emerge that the antimiscegenation regime should be taken down everywhere. The Court's rulings in *Brown* came at a time when every state outside the South had largely, or even entirely, abandoned legally mandated school segregation. And the situation regarding laws against interracial marriage? In the aftermath of the 1948 *Perez* ruling in California, which raised the number of states *without* laws against interracial marriage to nineteen, Oregon had repealed its law in 1951, Montana its in 1953, and North Dakota followed in 1955. That left nine states with laws against black-white marriage in *addition* to the seventeen states that still segregated both schools and marriage.

Many years later, Carliner had occasion in an interview to muse about the case. Of course he was going to challenge the Virginia law, and of course, he maintained as he always had, the US Supreme Court should not have ducked the case. Then again, he conceded, the time may well not have been right to obtain the ruling he sought, so perhaps the quest was quixotic: "As an attorney representing a particular point of view, I think that my responsibility was to push for what I thought in the interest of the goal was right. The Justice of the Supreme Court has a larger frame of reference to decide what is right." Or as he also put it: "I was too early in trying to challenge the miscegenation statute"; "I was a fool rushing in, but then I'm no angel."

The year before *Naim* came before the Supreme Court, a straight-up miscegenation case, *Jackson v. Alabama*, also went to the Court, and the time was hardly good for addressing it either. This was in 1954, between the May 1954 and May 1955 decisions in *Brown v. Board of Education*. Three justices—Hugo Black, William O. Douglas, and Chief Justice Earl Warren—voted to hear it. Their brethren, however, mindful of the fierce opposition in much of the South to the prospect of school desegregation, believed it prudent to just let Linnie Jackson, a black woman, finish out her prison sentence in Alabama for violating the state's law against her relationship with A. C. Burcham, a white man.

The Law of Race and Marriage in the 1950s

Beginning in 1948 a number of states abandoned their allegiance to the antimiscegenation regime, but none did so in the South. Once the key dynamics were in place, as whites sought a system that guaranteed social subordinates and economic dependents, simple demography kicked in to heighten all other considerations. In Caroline County — always majority nonwhite, usually by a wide margin — political control seemed essential. And then there was that cluster of sexual phobias and privileges, each with a powerful concern to be addressed. Virginia's miscegenation laws held sway from the 1690s on, their power persisting past the middle of the twentieth century, even as Richard Loving and Mildred Jeter were courting in Caroline County.

CHAPTER 3

Identity and Community in the Midst of Multiple Faiths and Races

St. Stephen's Church in Central Point—in far eastern Caroline County, near the boundaries of Essex County to the east and King and Queen County to the south—originated in 1872, seven years after the end of slavery. Writing a half-century later, in 1924, local historian Marshall Wingfield said its building (not the original one) was "the largest and most costly house of worship in Caroline, white or colored." He set its value at about $20,000 and the size of the congregation at nearly three hundred. As for their racial identities, he wrote: "There are few members of this congregation who have as much as one-half negro blood. The people of the church and community are, as a whole, very nearly white and, out of their community, could not be recognized or distinguished as colored people. It is said that the predominating blood in them is that of the Indian and white races." Wingfield noted that M. W. Byrd—the child of a nonwhite family whose freedom dated well before the Civil War—had by that time been serving the church as clerk for more than forty years, since within about a decade of its founding. Writing many years later, anthropologist Helen Rountree noted: "In the absence of a tribal church before 1964, some Caroline County Rappahannocks attended St. Stephen's Baptist Church, which had a multiracial congregation (whites, blacks, and Indians)."

St. Stephen's Church, the church Mildred Jeter grew up in as a child and, as Mildred Loving, attended for the rest of her life, alerts us to the triracial makeup of the Central Point community. Or it casts doubt on the suitability of the conventional rhetoric of "black" and "white," or even of "Caucasian," "African American," and "Indian" or "Native American," as discrete categories with clear boundaries that are well suited to being applied to each person in a community of individuals.

Historian Arica Coleman did some interviewing in the early

twenty-first century in the Central Point area on the matter of racial identity. One of her informants, unwilling to be identified in public, given the deep feelings in that locale on the matter, offered one assessment:

> The "we only white and Indian" thing was what the old folks said, and some people still like to believe that, but it's not true. There was a lot of mingling down here between the Blacks, the whites, and the Indians. Not just in Central Point, but all over Caroline County. As far as the Rappahannocks go, they are mostly light skin, but they got Black relatives right here in this area. I know some of them. Honestly, people are so mixed down here you can't say what you are or what you are not.

Such racial indeterminacy held throughout Virginia, throughout the South, throughout America. Homer Plessy, the Louisiana man who in the 1890s brought the court case *Plessy v. Ferguson*, was so fair of feature that one could hardly know looking at him that he had any black ancestry at all. Yet the train conductor who arrested him was supposed to be able, with ample certainty, to assign him to the white car or the "colored" car.

The 1900 census pegged Homer Plessy as "mulatto," not "black," and all seem to have agreed that his features and coloration were such that the conductor would likely not have ordered him to the black car had he not identified himself in racial terms. But the law directed that railway cars be segregated, empowered railway employees to determine racial identity, and required employees and passengers to comply with the segregation statute. Notably, the Supreme Court recognized the arbitrariness of the racial classification without which the specific case before it could never have arisen. This aspect of the case the Court was unprepared to address:

> It is true that the question of the proportion of colored blood necessary to constitute a colored person, as distinguished from a white person, is one upon which there is a difference of opinion in the different States. . . . But these are questions to be determined under the laws of each State and are not properly put in issue in this case. Under the allegations of his petition it may undoubtedly become a

question of importance whether, under the laws of Louisiana, the petitioner belongs to the white or colored race.

So the very opinion in which the court enshrined what became known as the "separate but equal" doctrine also recognized that the state law might or might not be appropriately applied in the way it had been to Mr. Plessy, since perhaps he was white, not "colored." That matter apparently intrigued Justice Henry Billings Brown, who wrote the 7–1 opinion, and the other justices for whom he spoke, but he left it to others to work out the details. As long as segregation persisted in American life, and wherever it did, we can almost hear the Court saying the individual states — their legislatures, their courts — would decide who was white, and who was not, whether it mattered, and how. The major dividing line, as in Louisiana, was between black and white, but what that meant, and how it should apply to the facts at hand, often came up in court cases. So did the fact that Americans were often divided in ways that included Native American ancestry as well as Caucasian and African.

———

Oklahoma Benefits and an Arkansas Marriage

In a manner that contrasted with Virginia's, thus revealing how the *Plessy* observation about state law and racial identity could play out, Oklahoma settled the matter in its own way, from the time of statehood in 1907. Under the Oklahoma state constitution of 1907, everyone was either "white" or "not" — or, rather, "of African descent" or "not of African descent," thus either black or not black — and anyone was "white" who had no African ancestry. Caucasians were committed to distinguishing themselves from black residents, and Indians often sought to do the same.

Therefore, in a state in which large numbers of Indians lived, they were as legally white as their Caucasian neighbors, unless an African American had played some role in the family tree. This legal boundary between individuals classified as "white" and all people "of African descent" definitely applied to education, and it definitely applied to marriage too. Many times in the American past, and certainly in Oklahoma, cases in which the law of race and marriage made its way into the courts had to do with the transfer of property rather than with an indictment for commitment of a felony.

In April 1914, Emily Lewis, a Choctaw Indian, accompanied William Yates, an African American, from Oklahoma to Fort Smith, Arkansas, where state law prohibited whites from marrying blacks but did not mention Indians. So, while Lewis and Yates could not marry in their home state, they could in a neighboring state, and the newlyweds soon returned to Oklahoma, where they lived together at her place in Haskell County until her death the following year. She left no children and no will, but she left her land, her husband, and her parents, who soon sold the land out from under her widowed husband. He challenged their right to seize land he should have possessed as a consequence of his marriage, but in the end the Oklahoma judiciary declared, in *Eggers v. Olson*, that the state's laws "intended to prohibit marriage of the descendants of the African race with any other race in this state." William Yates could derive no benefit in Oklahoma from his marriage to Emily Lewis in Arkansas, and ownership of the land could not transfer out of the hands of "white" people in Oklahoma:

> In the case at bar the marriage was impossible under the statute. Going out of the state to escape the statute, and going through the form of marriage in a state where the inhibition did not exist, and soon thereafter returning to this state, and all in an effort to accomplish indirectly what cannot be done directly, would be a fraud upon the laws of this state by a citizen of this state, and such a marriage can not be recognized by the courts.

Oklahoma law contrasted with Virginia's as to where to locate Indians, as "white" or people of "color." It resembled Virginia's, however, in banning interracial marriage, or rather some kinds of interracial marriage. It also resembled Virginia's in refusing to recognize the validity of a marriage undertaken in a jurisdiction that permitted it when the couple's home state barred it.

One Drop of Indian Blood

Oklahoma entered statehood having already established a racial boundary between people who were "white" and those who were "not," and from day one it placed on the "not" white side of the great racial divide only people, though every person, who had any discernible African ancestry. Most states never did adopt the one-drop rule in their law of marriage, even when they maintained laws against interracial marriage, and those that did so mostly did a few years later. Virginia did so in the 1920s. Glimpses of some court cases along the way will illuminate the timing and significance of the changes enacted by the Virginia legislature and interpreted by the Virginia courts, in just the way that *Plessy v. Ferguson* clearly empowered Virginia authorities to do.

Living in 1877 in Virginia, south across the James River from Richmond, were, as newspapers had occasion to report, Robena McPherson and George Stuart. Though a married couple—they had been married in Washington, DC—they found themselves arrested for the crime of "living in illicit intercourse." Despite their insistence that they were legally married, even because of it, they were convicted and fined. The trial court determined that, while he was white, she was not, and thus their marriage had no validity, was actually a crime, and so could supply them no shield against prosecution. They contested the ruling, and the case went to the Virginia Supreme Court, where their names were rendered Rowena McPherson and George Stewart.

According to a unanimous appeals court decision, the facts suggested that Rowena McPherson was not, after all, "a negro," but a white person under Virginia law. The law of racial identity in Virginia, across the entire nineteenth century, before and after the Civil War and universal emancipation, categorized a person as "white" if of less than one-fourth African descent. According to testimony, Rowena McPherson's father was white, and her maternal grandfather was also white; thus she was at least three-quarters white. To be sure, that fraction would leave her nonwhite in the eyes of the law at that time and place. To be legally "white"—and thus free to marry George Stewart, and he her—she had to be less than one-quarter black.

The case hinged on the racial ancestry of Rowena McPherson's maternal grandmother. Testimony from the family declared that the maternal grandmother's mother—McPherson's great-grandmother—was a "brown skin woman," "half Indian." Thus the court concluded, "less than one-fourth" of Rowena McPherson's "blood" was "negro blood." And "if it be but one drop less, she is not a negro."

Rowena's mother was evidently nonwhite under Virginia law. And this mixed-race background may be why the couple went to the nation's capital for their wedding, rather than getting married in Virginia. But as for Rowena, she was "not a negro." Despite the original arrests and the outcome at trial, the couple had, as the state supreme court viewed the matter, not married across the racial boundary provided under Virginia law, so the marriage was valid. Saved by an unusual form of the "one drop" rule of racial identity, the pair was not guilty. A white man retained his patriarchal prerogative in selecting a wife, and he had no need to pay a hefty fine for the choice he, and his bride, had made.

———

Virginia's Road to the One-Drop Rule of Black Racial Identity

Union victory in the Civil War brought at least three emancipations. First came a universal end to racial enslavement. When the abolition of slavery came to seem clearly inadequate by itself to set the terms of freedom, Congress passed the Civil Rights Act of 1866, the core of which, subsequently incorporated into the Fourteenth Amendment, declared African Americans to be citizens and then spoke of equal civil rights for all citizens. And in 1867, black men in the former Confederacy obtained the right to vote when Congress took further action to ensure ratification of the Fourteenth Amendment. The postwar legal and constitutional changes applied to people of color regardless of whether they had been free before the war or had only recently been emancipated.

Perhaps—this was less certain—those changes freed white people, too, in their choice of a marriage partner. For a time, the question was answered "yes" in Alabama, Mississippi, Louisiana, and Texas, but "no" in Indiana, Georgia, and Virginia. Uncertainty about the answer to this question persisted well into the 1870s in some states, and in fact Louisiana did not restore its statute against interracial marriage until 1894, while the case from that state involving racial identity, railway seating, and a man named Homer Plessy was making its way through the American court system.

Yet there never was a time in Virginia, from 1691 on, that white people could, with legal impunity, marry people of "color." Even there, though, the rules had changed over the years. For one thing, Rowena McPherson's Indian forebears saved her in the 1870s from being consigned to a category of Virginia women among whom a white man like George Stewart could not lawfully take a wife.

And the laws kept changing. The one-quarter rule of black racial identity lasted from 1785 — just after the Revolution — until early in the twentieth century, but then it changed, and a white racial identity became a more exclusive property in Virginia than ever before. In 1910, the legislature jumped two generations. Abandoning the traditional one-fourth marker, a new law leapt across one-eighth (the colonial measure) and adopted one-sixteenth. No longer would having one black grandparent suffice to be classified as nonwhite; beginning in 1910, having one black *great-great*-grandparent would do.

Had the McPherson-Stewart couple been arrested a couple of years later, after a new law was passed in 1878, and had they been found guilty of marrying in violation of the new law, they would each have been sentenced to the state penitentiary for at least two years and as many as five. Had their marriage taken place after 1910, when the boundary between white and nonwhite was moved from one-fourth black to one-sixteenth, her genealogy would have quite clearly defined her as nonwhite and therefore unavailable for him to marry.

Right after the 1910 rule went into effect, a white woman discovered its significance for her. Lucy Moon's first husband, I. B. Grasty, had died and left her in dire straits with two young children. She married again, but her new husband, John Moon, though legally white when she married him, lost his membership in the "white" category under the new rule. And now her marriage was interracial, and she was raising her two young white daughters in an interracial household. Authorities took the children away, for who could countenance their continuing to live in what was now an unsuitable home environment? In the end, she managed to retrieve custody of her kids, but the Virginia Supreme Court had to massage the facts to conclude, as it did in *Moon v. Children's*

Home Society of Virginia, that Mr. Moon was simply not "a colored person within the meaning of our statute." The case had an afterlife. Some Virginia lawyers bitterly assailed the ruling. A white mom got to keep her white kids, and they her. Both daughters later lived as "colored" women.

And in 1924, a new state law pushed the genealogy hunt even further back. Walter Plecker was adamant about clearly identifying people who had, as he wrote repeatedly, "one drop of negro blood," so that they "cannot go to white schools and can never marry a white person in Virginia." The Racial Integrity Act of 1924, which introduced the "one-drop" rule of black racial identity in Virginia, was designed to meet that need. So great were the costs, ever rising, of being identified on the "colored" side of the racial divide—that is to say, the black side—that the chief of the Pamunkey tribe declared in 1928, "I will tie a stone around my neck and jump in the James River rather than be classed as a Negro."

What was termed the first conviction for interracial marriage under the Racial Integrity Act took place in Amherst County in May 1928. A white woman, Mary Hall, had married Mott Hamilton Wood, identified as a man one-sixteenth black who had lived all his life as a white man. When each was sentenced to the minimum two years in the penitentiary, the black *Norfolk Journal and Guide* commented acerbically that the couple might have been better off had they just lived together and raised a family without getting married. After any number of white people urged Governor Harry Byrd to pardon the bride at least, he responded that she should have known her husband to be legally black, and "the necessity of racial integrity is so important," he said, she must serve her term.

Plecker must have been pleased at that conviction, as well as the governor's steadfastness, but then came the case of the former police chief of Phoebus, Emil Umlauf, who came back from New York with a woman of color, the former Lizzie Whitehead, as his bride. Arrested and tried in 1929, they got off when the jury could not agree that he deserved two years in the penitentiary so let the couple go. The trial judge, C. Vernon Spratley (who would serve on the Virginia Supreme Court from 1936 until 1967, through the entire time the Lovings were in the state courts), angrily directed the couple to leave town immediately. Hard pressed to see how the Racial Integrity Act could satisfy its purpose if juries would not convict, Plecker next urged the legislature to reduce the minimum penalty to a single year, which the General Assembly did in 1932.

By that time, Plecker was focusing his energy more on race in the public schools than on matters of race and marriage. Time and again, he managed to get taken out of the white schools children he suspected of having black ancestry. But in Essex County, next door to Central Point and Caroline County, he seemed to meet his match. Kids with what were widely acknowledged to be small amounts of nonwhite ancestry were freely attending schools clearly designated as white. And the children seemed to play without the slightest sense that racial identity distinguished any of them from any others. When fingered, one family folded, but a second resisted and took the matter to court. There, circuit court Judge Joseph W. Chinn — who himself would soon be raised to the state supreme court — ruled that the Racial Integrity Act failed to define black identity, except by inference. It only defined a "white" person; moreover, it made no mention of schools, only marriage. So the 1910 definition, setting the boundary at one-sixteenth black, continued to stand with regard to racial identity and the public schools, and the children of Lizzie Tate and Tom Robinson, as Judge Chinn worked out the evidence, were less than one-sixteenth black, so the law could not bar them access to that "white" school in Essex County. Whereas a white racial identity usually required at least as much "white" ancestry in education as in marriage, in this rare instance, in Essex County in the late 1920s, the identity requirements to attend a white school proved less stringent.

A story in the *Richmond Times-Dispatch* pointed out the significance of Judge Chinn's ruling. "Any child having less than one-sixteenth Negro blood, not only can attend a white school," said the writer, "but must attend it, and is by law prevented from attending a colored school." The same, he went on, would seem to apply to Virginia's public institutions of higher education. University of Virginia professor of history Richard Heath Dabney expressed concern that his institution, the state's preeminent college, might be invaded. (It is far from clear that Professor Dabney had similar concerns about the occasional ethnic Chinese student who studied at the University of Virginia from the 1920s on, or about Art Matsu, half-Japanese and the best football player ever to represent the College of William and Mary, or Cato Lee and other Chinese students at Virginia Polytechnic Institute, or their counterparts at the Virginia Military Institute.)

So the General Assembly completed its work by passing the Racial Integrity Act of 1930. Here, even more than in 1924, is where the one-drop rule of black racial identity took firm hold in Virginia law. The stories from Essex County drove the engine of further legislative reform. One category of people, actually two categories, remained who though not fully white—that is, they had some known nonwhite ancestry—were not black. The "Pocahontas exception," enacted over Plecker's opposition in 1924, exempted people—many of them elite Virginians, including high state officials—who had minuscule Indian ancestry dating from the seventeenth century. The new law exempted the few people who, if at least one-quarter Indian and less than one-sixteenth black, lived on either the Pamunkey or Mattaponi reservations. Jim Crow had gone to school from the very first day of classes in 1870. But now the refinement of the one-drop rule had gone to school as well. On that policy "white" Virginians could agree, as they would continue to agree, nearly to a person, until well after the US Supreme Court decided *Brown v. Board of Education.*

A "Colored" Family in Caroline County

John Mercer Langston illustrates how nonwhite Virginians could be free from slavery, but he had to leave the state to find greater freedom. Both before and after the Civil War, many free people of color in Virginia remained in their native state rather than leave for some more promising place. Revealing an alternative image of "colored" freedom in Virginia is a family in Caroline County. Mildred Jeter's mother and grandmother both had the last name Byrd, and—albeit with missing values along the genealogical journey—a free family in the Central Point area can be tracked back to before the Civil War. A free man of color, Mordecai Byrd, according to the 1850 census, was twenty-five years old, his wife Mary was twenty-four, and they had a one-year-old son, Ellett. Living in the same house were three members of the Fortune family, also people of color. Were they Native American? African American? We cannot tell from the census how they identified themselves, or how others, including the census taker, might have classified them. All we really know is that they were indicated as other than white.

A decade later—on the eve, as things turned out, of secession, civil war, and universal emancipation—this free family of color had grown. The census often shows people aging a couple of years more or less than the intervening decade would suggest, and in 1860 Mordecai Bird, listed as thirty-seven years old, and his wife Mary, thirty-five, had three daughters and three sons, the youngest of them also named Mordecai, age two. Mordecai Sr. was a laborer who owned $40 worth of personal property; he and his wife were both listed as illiterate. Also living in the Central Point area, according to the 1860 census, were other free non-white families, with similar ages and structures, such as those of Joseph and Olympia Fortune and of Isaiah and Elizabeth M. Fortune.

Mordecai the younger, reportedly born on Easter Monday 1859, before the Civil War, lived until August 1954, shortly after *Brown v. Board of Education*. As a young man, he may have left the area and for a time run a store in Richmond or in Washington, DC, before returning in the 1880s to live out his life in Central Point. He bought the former home of his late mentor, the lawyer Thomas H. Brooks, in 1892. He ran a store there, and from 1893 to 1936 he was also the postmaster, at more or less the same extended time that he served St. Stephen's Baptist Church across the road as its clerk. When he stepped aside from postmastering in 1936, well into his seventies by then, he apparently did the same with the store. A younger member of the extended Byrd family, his grandnephew P. E. Boyd Byrd, became postmaster then, and his name remains to this day on the store building, though it has long since closed. P. E. Boyd Byrd married the teacher in the elementary school across the road, Miss Jessie Lee.

Mordecai ("M. W.") Byrd and his wife, Bettie (from "Green Mont," at Beazley, on the edge of nearby Essex County), had a number of children around the turn of the century. Among them was Robert Purcell Byrd, born about 1904, who studied for a time at Virginia Union University and, from the late 1920s until World War II altered the course of his life, taught in the local school at Central Point, held at St. Stephen's Church.

Living as a servant in M. W. Byrd's household in 1900 was the twenty-six-year-old Linwood Jeter, who in 1913 likely became the father of Musiel Byrd, Mildred Jeter Loving's mother. Musiel's mom was Susie Byrd.

Leon Bazile and the Problem of Mixed Marriage

Correspondence between Richmond, Virginia, and Anniston, Alabama, was frequent throughout the second half of 1917. Congress had declared war on Germany, and at any time the young man in Virginia might be called for the draft. This was Leon Bazile, who had earned a law degree in 1910 from the University of Richmond, then practiced law, and in 1916 went to work in the office of the state attorney general. There he remained while leaders in the United States tried to navigate their way through the Great War without becoming militarily involved—and yet then, in April 1917, they declared war against Germany and began, in the months that followed, to ship countless thousands of young men off to fight in Western Europe.

Meanwhile, Bazile mounted a campaign for the heart of a young woman in Alabama, whose visit that summer of 1917 to Virginia had been, to his mind, entirely too short. But they found themselves separated, not merely by hundreds of miles, but also by profound religious differences. And he took on the task, as an experienced lawyer, of writing a legal brief that would win his case and her heart. She was Baptist, he Catholic, and they wrestled for many months with what this meant for the prospect of their marrying.

They exchanged books on their respective beliefs, and they spoke constantly of the "problem." He signed his letters "with all my love," she signed hers "your true friend"; for, as she wrote in late June: "Please don't go to so much trouble about solving the problem, Leon, I can never be more than a friend to you." At the same time, she hoped the books she had sent him had arrived and would prove helpful, "if you are determined to write your 'brief.'"

He spoke often of his conviction that her objection was rooted in a prejudice that he had to overcome. On July 1 he wrote her: "Possibly if you were descended from as many Roman Catholics as I am from Baptist ministers we would have had no difficulty in finding a middle ground, but as it is at present you are prejudiced towards my faith, and while I by no means belittle your faith I have so much confidence in the truth of the teachings of my faith. Only by convincing me of the error of the doctrines of my church and the truth of the doctrines of your church can my viewpoint be changed."

The very next day he wrote again:

> My Dear Virginia:
> ... I have only set forth my side of the issue as strongly as I knew how, and in so doing have followed the line pursued in my legal briefs—the only form of literature I am capable of producing.
>
> I was away from Richmond Saturday and did not get your letter until this morning. I was glad to hear from you but fearfully disappointed that you should inform me again that we could only be friends. I love you, and don't propose to give up merely because you say we can only be friends. If I abandoned my cases when my opponent tried to discourage me I would never win. In a matter of so much greater importance to me than anything else life has to offer[,] you are very much mistaken if you think I'm going to give up so long as there is the remotest chance of my winning you.
>
> ... Please continue to write to me, and I am sure that eventually we will solve the problem that now so greatly troubles us. With all my love, I am
> sincerely,
> Leon

On July 8, he wrote: "I'm still working on the Problem and feel assured that we will be able to solve it eventually. When I have acquired more knowledge I will send you another installment of the 'Brief.' Please write to me." Within another two weeks, though, he reported that he had been drafted—"they got me on the first call." Promptly she replied:

> My dear Leon,
> Your letter has just come and I have had a big cry because you have to go to war. If you work for the state, you can be exempt. Leon, I just can't give you up. I didn't know it would mean so much to me.

Would it be wrong for me to hope you are not strong enough? So many men here have been turned down who have never been sick.

Indeed, developments on the war front heightened his recognition of his own feelings. On July 30 he told her:

now that I have to prepare to renounce all things that have been heretofore worth while, I realize as I never did before[,] when what I now face was not a certainty but only a possibility, how much it means to have to lose you. All things else have become insignificant.

And she retorted fondly, on August 2:

Leon, dear,
Of course I am going to see you again. You are very much mistaken if you think you are giving me up with your law practice and everything else.

At the same time, she asked him for a photograph of himself, so "that I may see you daily." He promptly promised to send one but wanted one of her as well, "just large enough to be carried in my pocket."

The war had made her even more precious in his eyes, and it had alerted her as to how much she cared, too. Nonetheless, in early November, the couple reached a crisis. Western Union brought him a telegram: "CAN NEVER AGREE UNLESS YOU LEAVE YOUR CHURCH AM SORRY VIRGINIA."

Try as Bazile might to craft an appropriate "brief," November slipped away, and then December came and went, and still no resolution. In the early weeks of 1918, however, they somehow finally found a way to resolve "The Problem." His papers are missing whatever correspondence may have passed between them during that critical time. But on January 25 — on the eve of his wedding to Virginia Bowcock — Leon Bazile wrote out, on stationery of the office of the attorney general of the state of Virginia, the final terms of their marital contract as regarded all religious matters:

My dear Virginia:

I agree that I will never coerce you or in the slightest manner interfere with your practicing your religion in any way that you see fit.

I will not require you to be present at the baptism of the children.

I will go with you to your church except on second Sundays and
on special occasions.

I agree with you that the clause relating to the education of the
children as Catholics does not mean that they must be educated
in Catholic schools, but only means that they must be taught their
catechism.

While the children when old enough will have to go to the Catholic Church when I go[,] they can on other occasions go to your
church with you.

His brief had not convinced her to convert, but she had come to realize how much she loved him, and he had overcome her key objections.
Despite her doubts of June and July, and her ultimatum in the November
telegram, she had largely accepted his terms. He would not be leaving his
church, nor she hers. Their children would be raised as Catholics, but he
and they would go with her to her church far more often than not. They
had solved "The Problem," and their mixed marriage could go forward.
Yet she, and he, having crossed one community boundary but not another, would not be attending St. Stephen's Baptist Church.

Soon he was writing her from France, where he spent much of the
year following their wedding. Once again, they had to pursue their relationship through letters. Once again he found himself writing love letters, but this time they had resolved their "problem," and he was writing
his wife, not someone who insisted she could "never be more than a
friend." Their mixed—interfaith—marriage lasted nearly fifty years,
until his death.

———

Leon Bazile, Private and Professional

Hanover County shares a border with Caroline, along Caroline's south-
western boundary. Aside from his tour of duty during World War I,
Leon Maurice Bazile (1890–1967) lived his entire life in Hanover County,

Virginia, where he had been born. His great-grandfather and grand-father had emigrated from France, living for a time in New Jersey (where Bazile's father was born) before moving to Virginia in the 1850s, where the family practiced farming in general and wine growing in particular, as they had in France. The pioneer Baziles of Virginia spoke and wrote mostly French, and they attended St. Ann's Catholic Church in Ashland.

Leon Bazile remained for fourteen years in the office of the state at-torney general, except for his service in France during World War I. He became assistant attorney general in 1921, held that position until 1930 (during which time he dealt with such cases as involved black voting rights, residential housing segregation, and interracial marriage), and then returned to the practice of law in the private sector. Elected three times by the voters of Hanover and King William counties to represent them in the Virginia House of Delegates, he served during the 1936, 1938, and 1940 sessions. Then, in 1941, he became judge of the Fifteenth Judi-cial Circuit, a district that included Hanover, Caroline, and other coun-ties nearby as well as the city of Fredericksburg.

Questions related to the Racial Integrity Act came to the office of the attorney general. After a couple was refused a marriage license in Rock-bridge County some months after the act went into effect, they chal-lenged their racial classification as one white, Robert Painter, and one "colored," Atha Sorrells. Walter Plecker, who attended the November 1924 hearing, was outraged when the local judge, Henry S. Holt, ruled the evidence from Plecker's fistful of birth certificates insufficient that Atha Sorrells was anything other than white, or at least had any black ancestry. Judge Holt wrote out a lengthy opinion, in which he worried about the lack of due process under the law as well as the placement of the burden of proof on the applicant for a marriage license.

Plecker wanted the decision appealed, but guidance from the attor-ney general's office dissuaded him—better to let this one loss go, for the act might be declared unconstitutional. This advice came in a letter from assistant attorney general Leon M. Bazile, on November 26, 1924, addressed to "My Dear Mr. Powell": "If you and Dr. Plecker wish the case to go to the Court of Appeals, this office will take it there, but the thought has occurred to me that inasmuch as the law seems to be work-ing all right outside of Judge Holt's circuit, we would run the risk of losing a great deal on the chance of reversing him in one case."

Across his long life, Leon Bazile followed an avocation as local historian, with an emphasis on his portion of western Hanover County. He was active in the celebration in 1936 of the two hundredth anniversary of Patrick Henry's birth in Hanover County and active also in the subsequent restoration of the Hanover Courthouse. The old building remained in use until 1978, long after the judge's death in 1967, after which it came to be used mostly for tours and weddings. Tales are told about how, as a Catholic, Judge Bazile detested signing final divorce decrees, so they would pile up in his office. When he went on vacation, the substitute judge would make his way through the pile.

His ethnicity and religion aside, Bazile was a representative figure throughout the half-century era so closely associated with Harry F. Byrd Sr. Leon Bazile had substantial experience in all three branches of the Virginia state government. An accomplished professional, he was also an urbane member of Virginia's cultural and political elite. At the same time, he embodied the persistence of the dominant political culture of Tidewater Virginia two centuries earlier. Patrick Henry's portrait continues to hang high on the front wall of the old Hanover County courthouse; Judge Bazile's portrait hangs lower down on the right wall.

Race and Schooling

Andrew "A. P." Young, the son of a slave father, was born in 1886. He obtained his elementary education in the 1890s in the community of File, a couple of miles from Sparta, in a one-room school called the "red schoolhouse," to which he would walk. William A. Vaughan, a white boy born in 1895, attended such a school for white children in the little community of Mica, a few miles north of Bowling Green, in a part of Caroline that would later become Fort A. P. Hill.

Across the long age of segregation and disfranchisement, schooling supplied one measure of what black citizens of Caroline County could do in a world in which they had little say in running the larger community. The state legislature enacted a law in 1906 calling for a high school in every county. If only one high school was set up, however, it would be strictly for white children, so black kids and their parents were left to fend for themselves. A "white" high school, Lee-Maury High School, was set up, in a new building constructed with public funds in 1913. A "colored" near-equivalent followed, building on nonwhites' efforts in the 1890s to establish some kind of secondary schooling for children in Caroline who could not attend the white schools.

When the county agreed to supply assistance across the racial divide beginning in 1914, a private school that the Sunday School Union had established, the Bowling Green Industrial Academy, was partly folded into the public school system as the Caroline County Training School. Money from the Sunday School Union and from the Rosenwald Fund made a new building possible in 1921. And in 1929 the school had gained accreditation and, commemorating the community group that had inaugurated and then continued to support the herculean effort, was renamed Union High School.

Meanwhile, segregated, small local elementary schools continued to operate in the many communities scattered throughout the county, as they did throughout Virginia. The Rosenwald Fund helped greatly in the early 1920s not only with the emerging high school but also with eight local elementary schools. One of these, the one-room school at Ruther Glen, cost $1,556—$500 from the Rosenwald Fund and the rest from the colored community. The school board covered teachers' salaries.

School Superintendent William A. Vaughan's biography helps illustrate life and schooling in Caroline County, as well as the intervention of great outside events. After three years of study at Richmond College, he sailed to France on the *Mercury* to fight in World War I, notably in the Argonnes offensive. After a year away, he returned, uninjured, to Virginia and his life as a student. He finished at Richmond College in 1920, taught at Hargrove Military Academy in Chatham for a year, and then became superintendent of public schools in his native Caroline County in 1921. He held that position until he retired in 1963. He took a year away, though, in 1929–1930, to earn a master's degree in education from the University of Virginia; his thesis was titled "A Survey of Certain Aspects of the Public School System of Caroline County, Virginia." During World War II, Vaughan had responsibilities on the home front, rationing fuel oil to county residents and serving as county chairman in charge of war bond sales.

A teacher at Union High School, a "colored" teacher of course, also illustrates life in the Jim Crow era as well as how the residents of

Caroline County contributed to World War II. The US military remained segregated as the nation entered the war in December 1941. Reginald A. Beverly, a native of Ruther Glen in Caroline County, had graduated from Union High School in 1933 and from Virginia State College for Negroes in 1938, then taught at the Louisa Training School for two years, and returned to Union High in 1940 as a science and math teacher. Already World War II loomed, and a few weeks before Pearl Harbor his draft notice came. On December 5, as he recalled many years later, he went to school, took roll, and then rode a bus from Bowling Green to Richmond to report for duty. As he explained, the army needed surveyors but did not have time to first teach soldiers math, and here he was a math teacher, so he was sent to surveyor school. He spent the war in the far Pacific Northwest as regimental surveyor for the 95th Engineer Regiment. "We built 300 miles of the Alcan Highway," he reported, "from Dawson Creek, British Columbia, through the Yukon Territory to Alaska." After the war finally ended, Beverly returned to his post at Union High. He soon married, and his wife, Bessie, taught next door at Union Elementary School.

Another family can depict the longer story of black Caroline County in the century after emancipation. A resident of Bowling Green, Rev. A. P. Young was eighty-nine years old when he spoke with *Caroline Progress* reporter Jacque Mason in June 1975. He was more or less retired by then, but he had been a Baptist minister and a high school teacher for a great many years.

Andrew "A. P." Young was born on June 27, 1886, in Caroline County, the son of Wilson L. Young. He explained the origins of Jerusalem Baptist Church at Sparta: "My father was a slave. The members of Jerusalem Baptist Church [had been] members of Salem Baptist Church," he said, but "when they were set free, the pastor, Andrew Broaddus, told them that they could go out and have a church of their own or sit in the balcony of Salem Baptist Church and take no active part in the church. My father and the others decided to separate from the church. On June 6, 1886, they organized Jerusalem Baptist Church," thus three weeks before the birth of his baby Andrew. For thirty years, Wilson Young served as church superintendent. His son served as pastor of Jerusalem Baptist from 1930 to 1975, and also at Shiloh Baptist Church in Bowling Green for forty-nine years. A. P. Young may well have adopted the practice, as black men often did, of going by his initials so that white folks couldn't readily call him by his first name, as was the custom according to which people of color were expected to use the honorific "Mr." and "Mrs.," but whites did not accord the same respect to nonwhites.

Young graduated in 1906 from the Bowling Green Industrial Academy (an early edition of what became Union High School). After passing the state teacher's examination, he taught in another one-room schoolhouse, Jerusalem Elementary, for a year. He earned a bachelor of divinity degree in 1911 from the Virginia Theological Seminary and College in Lynchburg, and he soon began preaching at Baptist churches in the area surrounding Caroline County, as well as teaching high school. While a minister at one of those churches, he met his wife, Gertrude Nash Norman, a graduate of Hampton Institute. He taught at Union High School from 1926 until he retired from teaching in 1951, at the age of sixty-five, shortly before Mildred would have begun attending there. He long continued his other career, preaching.

Irene Quash Fields, who grew up in Dawn (in a southern nook of Caroline) and graduated from Union High in 1947, described the difference having school bus transportation made. There was none for nonwhite students in the county before 1937, though her father, contractor William Quash, lobbied all through the 1930s to get the school board to agree to provide transportation for them. Meanwhile, her oldest sister, Gladys, went to New York and lived with their aunt in order to go to high school. Without bus transportation to Union, her older brothers Fred and William could not get to the high school, and by the time transportation came along, they were working and did not wish to stop, so they never attended. Their sister who came along at just the right time enrolled at Union in 1937 and graduated in 1941. As for that bus from Dawn, the school board agreed to cover the cost of a bus body, but told the parents they would have to get it from North Carolina. One of them, farmer Wortham Fields, bought a chassis, and he and his oldest son, Malcolm, "sat on milk crates" for seats as they drove it to Raleigh to collect the bus body.

Meanwhile, as long as elementary students were going to their local one- or two-room school, they had to make their own way, even if it meant walking a few miles each way. Students from across the county and across the 1930s and 1940s have reported such stories. Getting a bus ride to the high school did not necessarily reduce the walking distance. Florence Coleman Bryant, Union High School class of 1940, recalled: "Getting to the school bus [that would take them to the high school] was no easier for the children from my neighborhood than walking the two and half miles to St. John Elementary School had been." Their "well-worn path" took them "through a dense forest, past a gristmill and a millpond, across a footbridge, onto a hard surface highway, and, finally, to the bus stop." Bert Twiggs Nichols, class of 1948, walked three miles to get to the bus stop for Union: "The bus for White kids," she recalled, "passed our homes to pick them up at their gates," and the white kids who were thus pampered "yelled out the windows 'niggers' and spit on us" as they rode past the black kids walking.

Racial Integrity

The 1924 Racial Integrity Act put an end to the official presence in Virginia of anyone identified as an "Indian." Or at least it did for all but the people living on one or the other of Virginia's two small reservations for the Pamunkey and the Mattaponi. Even twins were divided as to their identity if one, an "Indian," lived on the reservation and the other, "colored," lived elsewhere. Plecker insisted that all "Indians" had some African ancestry, and therefore must be identified as colored. In some respects this changed nothing. Officials in Caroline County insisted that no change in nomenclature would be necessary, as they had always classified Indians as colored.

Walter Plecker may have directed otherwise, but a number of Caroline County residents continued to self-identify as Indians. This they did, to limited effect, in various ways. Plecker, representing the authority of the state of Virginia, tried to be sure that the US census of 1930, to be taken six years after passage of the 1924 Racial Integrity Act (and the same year as the successor act of 1930), would count no Indians; people who identified themselves as Indians, by contrast, sought to retain that identity. Local census takers were caught in the middle. On the 1930 census sheet for Caroline County that includes the family of M. W. Byrd and his wife Betty, census taker John C. Harris wrote—in the two spaces normally reserved for the state in which each person's parents were born, so overwritten, above "Virginia" — "mixed blood — Rappahannock Tribe." The adult children of M. W. and Betty Byrd still living at home included R. Purcell Byrd, listed as a twenty-four-year-old teacher in the public schools.

For dozens of other residents of Caroline County, the same information appears in those spaces. The added information did two things at once, identifying people as "Rappahannock" and declaring them "mixed blood." The census taker giveth, and the census taker taketh away. On the one hand, the people so identified could be understood as Rappahannock and therefore Indian; on the other, they would be understood as "colored," which is to say, not white and therefore "Negro."

During World War I, we are told, a number of men from the Caroline area who identified as Indians enlisted in white units, not black units, though certainly other men — among them Theoliver Jeter, later the father of Mildred — went into "colored" units. When World War II came along, those who had been "Indians" (they or their elders) and therefore "white" a generation earlier expected to be and do the same. Again, the Racial Integrity Act marked a transition from one era to another, and again Plecker jockeyed with federal officials, as did Virginians who identified as Indians and wished that identity to be respected. Some young men, when drafted into the war, refused to enter unless they were permitted to join white units. Such, this time, was not permitted. Much was at stake for the men. Acceding to a "Negro" designation would threaten their life chances thereafter, and more immediately doing so would curtail their options in the nation's segregated military, probably — to judge from World War I — consigning them to a combat support role.

Several men from Caroline County were prosecuted for refusing to be inducted — inducted, that is, into black units. Three went on trial in January 1943. Robert Purcell Byrd, Oliver Wendell Fortune, and Edward Arnall Nelson, each of them contending that he was Rappahannock, were found guilty of dodging the draft because they refused to be inducted except on their own racial terms. Sentenced each to a two-year term in federal prison, they declared their intent to appeal their convictions and sentences, but federal district Judge Robert N. Pollard denied them their request to stay free on bail and instead returned them to confinement.

Opposition to this treatment arose, but Plecker stood firm. Thousands of "mulattoes," he warned, were "striving to pass over into the white race by the Indian route." In the end, however, Robert Purcell Byrd and the others did not serve their full terms in prison. According to Rev. Fall's history of Caroline, Byrd "and several other Indian boys were sent to Boston to do defense work, where he lived since," except for a few years in the 1950s, "when he returned to Central Point to care for his aged mother & father." Anthropologist Helen Rountree tells how, when they determined to call themselves "conscientious objectors," their sentences were commuted, and they spent the rest of the war working in hospitals with other conscientious objectors.

Rev. Fall might be telling the story himself, or he might be relying on a 1968 letter from Robert Purcell Byrd; but one way or the other, in his book on Caroline County, Robert's father, Mordecai W. Byrd, child of the earlier Mordecai Byrd, is termed "a Rappahannock Indian."

"So Mixed Down Here You Can't Say What You Are"

The unnamed local resident who said that "people are so mixed down here you can't say what you are or what you are not" was surely on to something about racial indeterminacy, at least in his or her corner of the world. But the state enforced its determination to "say what you are or what you are not." Within the white side of the great racial barrier, Leon Bazile struggled to overcome the clearly defined difference between a Baptist and a Catholic. Soon thereafter he and Walter Plecker went to work in helping erect or maintain a clear boundary between people classified as "white" and people of "color." In the world that Bazile and Plecker would establish, people who were deemed "white" scurried to maintain — in fact tighten — the definition and consolidate their place within it. People defined as on the other side of the boundary struggled within it, or to move across the line in that binary. Or, in word or deed, they denied there was a proper binary in the first place or that they should be confined within it.

Plecker's assertion about "striving to pass over into the white race" gives the lie, of course, to any pretense that "separate but equal" offered even a semblance of "equal." The tremendous disparity in life chances that came with being defined as black rather than white gave tremendous incentive to close the gap by any means available, which might entail changing residence, changing racial identity, or doing the first to achieve the second. It also offers one explanation of why people might try to hold on to an Indian identity, so as not to be immersed, as they might see it, in a group from which there could be no escape, and in which there was very little hope of advancement, because whites would not permit it—quite aside from resisting the conceit that someone else might presume to tell them who they were, or who they were not, or to tell them and the world that one part of their family background should obliterate another side.

Thus the divergent paths of conscription and citizenship taken during World War I and World War II by Leon M. Bazile, Theoliver Jeter, and Robert Purcell Byrd. And thus the very different schooling and marriage worlds of A. P. Young and William A. Vaughan. Could a young couple in love bridge these two worlds, bring together two vastly different legal identities into a legally recognized marriage?

CHAPTER 4

An American Love Story

Richard Loving and Mildred Jeter

As the presence of Fort A. P. Hill demonstrated, Caroline County never was a separate world, cut off from developments throughout Virginia, the South, the nation, or the globe. The law of race and schooling, like the law of marriage, originated in the state legislature and governed behavior in Caroline County. When young Richard began school in 1939, he attended a segregated white school, as demanded under the original school statute of 1870 and the state constitution of 1902. The elementary school for white children out his way, a large modern building at Sparta, had five or six teachers each year covering the seven grades, from Lottie L. Broaddus for first grade on up to M. Elizabeth Pitts for seventh. Each of them had a bachelor's degree from either Mary Washington College or William and Mary. The bus Richard rode to school took him west on Sparta Road from the Central Point area.

When the war ended, and Mildred turned six, she too went off to the local school, but in her case it was to one of the many small "colored" schools. If she had lived a few miles farther south than she did, she might have traipsed off each morning with her sister and brothers to St. Stephen's Church, the brick structure where Central Point Elementary School met, sometimes with one teacher, sometimes two. As it was, she attended the Sycamore School, north from Central Point up Passing Road toward Supply, but heading west a bit on Beverly Run Road just north of Passing toward the community of Whites. Aside from his service during World War I, Jake Jeter never did live far from his birthplace at Brandywine, and though Mildred's mom was from Central Point he raised his family several miles away.

The Sycamore School, one of the nine Rosenwald schools in Caroline, had been built just after World War I so was a quarter century old by the time Mildred enrolled. Covering the original costs of construction were the local black community, with $1,675, and the Rosenwald Fund, with $500. Built of wood according to one of the standard Rosenwald designs, it had two classrooms, but no indoor plumbing, electric lights, or central heating. On occasion it had two teachers, consistent with the design, but most of the time one teacher held classes for all seven grades. Mildred's teachers were, for the first two years, Nellie M. Jones, who had studied at St. Paul's and resided in Supply, and then, for the next few years, Kathryn Green Amy, who had a bachelor's degree from St. Paul's and lived in Whites.

An Incipient Civil Rights Movement during Mildred's Childhood

As Mildred made her way through elementary school during the presidency of Harry S. Truman, he made civil rights a central item on his agenda for the nation. He issued an executive order that the US military end its policy of racial segregation, and he appointed the President's Committee on Civil Rights. More than that, he had his Justice Department participate in the argument of Supreme Court cases against segregated higher education, and he appointed the President's Commission on Higher Education, whose report urged an end to segregation in colleges and universities.

In 1948, the US Supreme Court ruled in a case on higher education from Oklahoma, *Sipuel v. Board of Regents of the University of Oklahoma*, that the old stateways on race would be given greater scrutiny than had been required before, and "separate but equal" must include far more of the "equal" than it often had. Also in 1948, a split decision by the California Supreme Court, *Perez v. Sharp*, declared the state's miscegenation law unconstitutional. In marriage and schooling alike, the segregated past was coming under effective challenge, at least to some degree and in some places.

In the fall of 1950, in a particularly rural part of rural Prince Edward County, fifteen-year-old Barbara Johns suddenly realized what she must do. Her elders in the black community had been unable to make progress in obtaining a better high school, and Barbara came up with a plan that might get results. In April 1951 her vision and her plans to implement it came to fruition. In what we might call the first mass nonviolent direct action of the modern Civil Rights Movement, all of the more than four hundred students at the Robert R. Moton High School in Farmville walked out. They wanted a shiny new high school that matched the one their white neighbors and cousins attended. But the NAACP had shifted course in the previous year and would no longer support a court case that simply sought to seize more of the "equal" in "separate but equal." Rather, the group would consider taking this case only if the black community in Prince Edward signed on for a direct constitutional attack against segregation itself. Agreement reached, the case went into the federal court system the next month. Resolution came three years later, when it was decided as part of the package of cases known as *Brown v. Board of Education.*

So when Mildred Jeter finished elementary school in the early 1950s, segregated schooling, like segregated marriage, remained consistent with the law of the land. But in May 1954, just before she turned fifteen, the Supreme Court declared it unconstitutional for states to mandate segregated schools. A unanimous high Court ruled that the old formula from *Plessy v. Ferguson*, at least so far as it related to public education, was no longer in operation. Schools must desegregate. A follow-up decision a year later, also called *Brown v. Board of Education* but distinguished as *Brown II*, laid down guidelines for achieving school desegregation, with the lower federal courts overseeing the process, state by state, county by county, even school by school.

In December 1955, the Montgomery Bus Boycott erupted in Deep South Alabama after a black woman, Rosa Parks, declined to obey the bus driver and give up her seat to a white man, as southern chivalry and Alabama law dictated. A year later, after a year of walking and carpooling by black residents instead of riding segregated buses, a Supreme Court ruling, *Browder v. Gayle*, directed that the buses operate on a nonsegregated basis. Montgomery authorities actually complied, and the boycott came to an end.

In Virginia, meanwhile, some white taxpayers in Hanover County went to court, arguing that the one million dollar bond issue approved there in 1953 to construct new schools had been absolutely understood to contemplate segregated schools. But now that the Supreme Court had ruled against such schools, either the bonds might be used to construct "non-segregated schools" or the bond issue should, as they urged, be nullified as in violation of the intent of the voters who approved it. Circuit court Judge Leon Bazile ruled in early June 1955 in their favor, improving at the same time on the opportunity to castigate the nation's highest court for making bad law. The only schools white taxpayers could have been voting to support back before *Brown v. Board of Education* were, he noted, under Virginia law, categorically segregated. His ruling was widely seen as having broad application, far beyond a single county. According to one dissenting opinion expressed by a white mother in Hanover County, "it seems like a shame that a little question like who's to sit next to who has to stop the school program it took us ten years to get going."

The state of Virginia responded in 1956 to the threat of desegregated schools by enacting "Massive Resistance," a multipronged policy that required the governor to close any school that a federal court ordered desegregated or that—as at least one community in Northern Virginia, Arlington County, appeared likely to do—went ahead on its own to desegregate. Working from one cardinal rule, that no white child need ever attend school with a black child, the legislature barred any local option that might desegregate any K–12 school. Under such rules, one or more white schools in various places in Virginia—the city of Norfolk, the city of Charlottesville, and Warren County—were indeed closed when court orders finally came in fall 1958. In Caroline County, the board of supervisors had already—in 1956, the year after *Brown II*—voted in favor of withholding all county funds from the schools rather than permitting them to be desegregated, so the county had signed on, in its own direct way, to what the legislature was mandating in general.

In July 1958, word came from school Superintendent William A. Vaughan that two new schools were planned for Caroline County, slated to open for fall the next year, both racially separate. Regardless of the Supreme Court's rulings in *Brown v. Board of Education* some years before, the county would perpetuate a segregated school system. Also in July, in a wedding on the white side of the great racial divide, Vaughan's daughter Ann married New Jersey resident Henry A. Riggenbach. No legal challenge there.

A Time to Marry

Meanwhile, in the Central Point area in far eastern Caroline County, the two young daughters of Theoliver and Musiel Jeter began courting. In April 1953, fifteen-year-old Garnett Jeter married a twenty-three-year-old laborer from nearby Rexburg, in Essex County, named Raymond Hill. Sometime in the spring of 1956, Mildred discovered she was pregnant, and on January 27, 1957, she had a son, Sidney. The midwife was Richard Loving's mother, Lola Jane Loving, who delivered most of the children in the area, since, as a neighbor later put it, the local doctor was "always late."

As early as 1950, Richard Loving, at about the age of seventeen, began stopping by the home of friends of his, where he made the acquaintance of their eleven-year-old sister, Mildred Jeter, a year or so younger than her big sister Garnett. Mostly he came to see his friends, the two girls' older brothers, with whom he shared both an interest in music and an interest in cars, but she eventually became an attraction as well. Over time across the 1950s, they developed a friendship, and eventually they began courting. He went by "Rich"; she, growing long and slim, had come to be known as "Stringbean," which he shortened to "Bean."

Young women often found themselves pregnant in the 1950s, and often they quickly followed the cue as indicating it was time they got married: in a "Dear Abby" column from that era, after a writer expressed great concern about a child who had arrived a mere seven months after the parents' wedding, Abby replied not to worry, the child was on time, the wedding might have been late. Mildred, however, continued to live at home unmarried with her parents, and that's where Sidney lived, too. He took his mother's name, so he was Sidney Jeter. Years later, when at age sixteen he applied for a Social Security number, he listed Richard Loving as his "stepfather."

Having been dating Richard for some time, Mildred discovered in early 1958 that she was pregnant again. We cannot know now just what kinds of thoughts went through Mildred's mind, or Richard's, but we can imagine Richard thinking perhaps they should get married. One might as readily imagine Mildred saying, "Honey, if we're going to be having babies, should we maybe get married?"

Mildred made observations over the years that offer further clues to their thinking and the world they lived in. In whatever way they each saw the other in terms of race, they were aware that some people in the community did not, or might not, take kindly to their courting across racial lines, quite aside from what might be made of their marrying. She once observed that Richard thought nobody would bother them if they got married, as if he thought they might be bothered if they did not. She did not know there was any law against their getting married, she would say, but Richard seemed to think there was, that they could not get married in Virginia. So Richard proposed that they go north some eighty miles to the nation's capital and try to have a wedding there. And that is what they did.

It seems that they made a first trip north on May 24, a Saturday, to apply for a marriage license. On Monday, June 2, they went back. Mildred's brother Otho (also Richard's friend), as well as her father, made the trip as well, to give them company and to serve as witnesses to the wedding. Judging from when her second child was born, in October that year, she was at least four months pregnant by the time she visited the nation's capital for her day trips in quest of a marriage license and a wedding certificate. Theoliver Jeter had lived a long time—he was in his seventies by this time—and one can suspect that he had never thought a child of his would be marrying a white person. He may well have been apprehensive, for himself, for his daughter, for the entire family. But he had known Richard from young man to adult, and he could see that each of the two young people had chosen the other for a very serious relationship. He would do what he could to help them make their way.

As Mildred later explained, not knowing a pastor in the District, they selected a name from the phone book. The name they picked was Rev. John L. Henry. Reverend Henry conducted the ceremony at his place at 748 Princeton Place, NW, and the foursome piled back into the car and drove back to Caroline. Richard and Mildred returned to Caroline County a married couple, Mr. and Mrs. Loving. They lived together with Mildred's parents, their bedroom on the main floor, her parents' bedroom upstairs. There they lived as husband and wife, without incident or apparent apprehension, through the rest of June and into July. Whether from pride and joy, or to signal their marriage and ward off any doubters, they hung their marriage license on the wall of their room. By July, Mildred was nearing six months pregnant with her second child.

———

Arrest and Trial

Late one night, around 2 o'clock or so in the morning, they awoke to the glare of flashlights in their faces and the sounds of strange men in their room. It turned out to be the county sheriff, Garnett Brooks, as well as his deputy and the county jailer, Massie Samuel and H. Q. Taylor. Sheriff Brooks demanded to know who they were, sleeping together as they were in that room. Mildred stammered: "I'm his wife." Richard pointed toward a document hanging on the wall: "We're married. That's our marriage license." The sheriff scoffed: "That's no good here," or something to that effect.

Mildred was not quite nineteen years told, at least five months pregnant, and the mother of a young child. She was terrified, jolted awake, uncertain. "I couldn't believe they were taking us to jail," as she remembered that night many years later, in the 1990s. Looking for help, looking to her mom, "I went upstairs, sat on the bed, talked with my mother," she reported. "Make them go away," she pleaded. There are times when moms cannot help, cannot fix things.

They were hauled off to the county jail, in Bowling Green, an antique structure, next to the courthouse, that had been constructed in 1902. Built of brick, it had four rooms downstairs, where Richard was put, and four more up, where Mildred was kept. From a summer 1964 report of an inspection of the jail, six years after her ordeal, we can get a sense of the skanky physical environment that Mildred, in particular, encountered. The building was described as "inadequate," and the plumbing in "the room on the second floor used for the segregation of females or juveniles" as not only "obsolete" but also "entirely out of order." The jail had no kitchen on the premises; meals were provided, twice a day, from a nearby restaurant. The menu was fixed: breakfast consisted of "sliced bologna, fried egg, bread, and kool-ade"; supper brought "pickled pigs feet, stewed corn, green lima beans, bread, and kool-ade."

Richard was released the next day on bail, she not for several days more. Richard and other members of the family were given the clear understanding that if they tried to get her out, he would be put back in. One can imagine the emotional turmoil that Mildred felt—thrown into jail, where she was kept day after day, night after night; separated not only from her parents and her husband but also from her firstborn, who was not yet eighteen months old; and some six months pregnant too. Even worse, "it about scared me to death," she'd recall, when the jailer spoke of letting a white male prisoner into her cell for the night. One can also imagine what Richard was going through—also seized by authorities in the middle of the night; jailed himself, though for only one night; and not only forcibly separated from his wife but helpless to protect her or ease her plight.

Phyl Newbeck observes in her book on the Lovings that Sheriff Brooks usually went about his business alone, but in this case, a nonviolent crime, he took along the entire police force the county could muster. Sheriff Brooks's successor—Ottie Moore, who defeated Brooks in his bid for reelection—later commented that anyone in that position would have had to follow through, in more or less the manner that Sheriff Brooks did. The law was waiting, as standby authority should a perceived need arise to call on it, and the various members of the law enforcement community would predictably carry out the assigned roles should a complaint be made. Who made a complaint the Lovings never knew, they said, though friends thought Richard must have antagonized someone; one of their lawyers, Phil Hirschkop, later mused that perhaps a victory by Rich's racing team had riled a rival, maybe the sheriff if he had a team.

Whatever the doubts Richard may have had about whether they could marry in Virginia, or whatever apprehensions he may have had should they carry on and not marry, he failed to understand that the same law that prevented their marrying in Caroline County also made it a felony to go to DC, marry, and then return as husband and wife. He failed, too, to comprehend that, though white and nonwhite might mix on an informal basis, in fact often did, and usually with no legal consequences, the mere fact of their marrying made it more likely, not less, that they would be visited by the sheriff in the way they were. He had had the audacity to formalize their relationship.

So, while the couple had been dating each other for a considerable time, their DC marriage came only a few weeks before their arrests for the felony of interracial cohabitation. They had gone formal, had gotten married, and were living together, in the home of the bride's parents.

On October 13, according to the local paper, the Caroline County grand jury indicted the couple, Richard Loving, "alleged to be white," and Mildred Jeter, "alleged to be colored," for the crime of going out of state, marrying, and returning, "contrary to the state law against mixed marriage. Loving and the Jeter woman will be tried on January 6. Judge Bazile will be the presiding judge." Donald Loving had been born on October 8, five days before the indictments came down.

At the end of December, the county sheriff, Garnett Brooks, as well as his deputy sheriff, Massie Samuel, and the county jailer, H. Q. Taylor, each received a summons to appear at 10 o'clock on the morning of January 6 as a witness in the trial of defendants "Jeter and Loving." Circuit court Judge Leon Bazile would indeed be presiding, at the courthouse in Bowling Green. Representing the couple was Frank B. Beazley, a veteran Bowling Green lawyer in his sixties who, back when Mildred was a young child, had served four terms in the Virginia House of Delegates.

One wonders how the couple, perhaps especially Mildred, prepared for their trial date. Mildred and her mom must have talked about how, if she and Richard were sent off to the penitentiary, whether for a year or for five years or something in between, toddler Sidney and baby Donald would be growing up with their grandmother for some considerable time. Who among the couple's four parents attended to give their moral support? We can imagine Judge Bazile peering out at the scene that day in his courtroom, with Mildred's dad perhaps looking after Sidney while her mom held Donald. And just maybe he mused on his own mixed marriage and long happy family life, once he and his bride broke through the barriers that their different religious faiths had posed. Perhaps the patrician Leon Bazile even saw in the plebeian Richard Loving something of a kindred spirit, not bound by other people's rules of love and marriage, not deterred by big challenges in such matters. The judge had to have considered his limited apparent discretion in the penalty to be imposed, since the statute was clear about the one-year minimum in the Virginia penitentiary as well as the five-year maximum.

One recent account of the Loving story has it that Judge Bazile "imposed the maximum penalty." He did no such thing. Why, we might ask, not? According to the barebones account of the proceedings, the couple pleaded "not guilty," and both sides agreed to proceed without a jury. The evidence in, as well as the arguments for each side, the couple changed their pleas to "guilty." Judge Bazile pronounced sentence, "one year each in jail." But he promptly suspended the sentence, "for a period of twenty-five years," provided Mildred and Richard both "leave Caroline County and the state of Virginia at once and do not return together or at the same time" during that twenty-five years.

"The prisoners" paid court costs and left the building, the county, and the state. The judge had found a way to navigate a law that required him to convict, but then, having given the lightest possible sentence, suspended even that, though in a manner that still deprived the family of a lot of their freedom. In order to live free as "Mr. and Mrs. Loving," they would have to do it elsewhere.

Banished

The couple went back to DC, this time to live and work, not just for a day trip. There they could live as "Mr. and Mrs. Loving." Mildred had a cousin living in DC, Alex Byrd, together with his wife, Laura. They lived at 1151 Neal Street Northeast, in a black part of town, and that is where the Lovings—Richard, Mildred, Sidney, and Donald—took up residence. Richard, perhaps with some tips from Alex and Laura, went out to find work. Mildred mostly stayed home and looked after the two children.

The couple knew they could not live in Virginia, for as many years ahead as they could envision. They were far less clear on the judge's meaning, however, that they could not return for visits together. From time to time, each of them came back to Caroline; in fact both did.

On March 28, the day before Easter Sunday, they were back in Caroline County, where they found themselves arrested for violating the terms of their parole. Richard later observed, "We'd been down there a few times," and Mildred amplified: "In January they had the trial, . . . but the way I understood it," the family could come back to visit, "So that Easter we came back, and they got us again." Released on $200 bond, this time they were ordered to be back in Caroline County together, at the courthouse, at 10 o'clock in the morning on April 13. They explained what had happened, though not what happened after their arrest, and did not address why they hadn't been sent to jail for the year in accordance with their original sentence.

Some months after the Lovings pled guilty in Caroline County, the office of the Virginia attorney general assured the clerk of the Rockingham County Circuit Court that of course no marriage license should be issued to a Caucasian man and a Vietnamese woman, for such was "specifically prohibited" by the Racial Integrity Act. Yet just a couple of years later, while Richard and Mildred were living in exile in the nation's capital, a marriage took place back in their home county that called into question once again the charges that had been brought against them, even as it probably revealed again the role of Fort A. P. Hill and the nation's military in shaping social relations and helping determine marriage partners. In June 1962, Billy B. Huff, a twenty-five-year-old native of South Carolina and currently a student living in Doswell (across the line in Hanover County), married a schoolteacher named Lorraine Sanae Hayashida, a native of Maui, one of the islands of Hawaii. They obtained their marriage license in Caroline County. One supposes that he had gone out of high school into the military, had been stationed for a time in Hawaii, perhaps at Pearl Harbor, and had subsequently been stationed at Fort A. P. Hill. Now he had settled in the nearby community, the pair had stayed in touch, and they were marrying. Officiating at their wedding in the village of Penola (a few miles southwest of Bowling Green) was W. Roy Carner, a Baptist minister living in Ashland who had been presiding over marriage ceremonies since 1920.

What makes the couple particularly notable, of course, is her ethnicity. Her parents were clearly ethnic Japanese: her father's name George Shigeto Hayashida and her mother's maiden name Edith Nakamura. He identified himself on their application for a marriage license as "white"; and she was permitted to enter a dash — a piece of punctuation that offered up a lot less information than the identical dash that indicated the number of times each had been previously married. Did they get a pass because he had recently been in the military? Because he was from out of state, and she too? Because the rules had softened? Because neither was a local "colored" person, or neither was African American? Whatever was going on, the Racial Integrity Act should have barred their wedding in Virginia, so their evidently untrammeled success in getting married locally revealed the capricious enforcement of Virginia's laws of interracial marriage.

Sometime during the spring of that first year in exile, Mildred realized that she was pregnant again. Despite the warnings to stay out of Virginia, she went back to Caroline County for the birth, which took place the day after Christmas 1959. Her third child, like the first two, would be born there. As before, the midwife would be Richard's mother. But then the family resumed their lives in DC, far from home. Mildred had three young children to care for, and Sidney and Donald had a baby sister, Peggy.

But they continued to make their way back to the Caroline County area. As their daughter Peggy would put it many years later, "They gonna come back together. They gonna take their chances." Usually they stayed in a nearby county. Robert Pratt, "Tony" then, and a toddler, many years away from becoming a history professor, would play with Sidney, mostly, who was just a little older. This was in Battery, about seven miles east of Central Point, in Essex County. Pratt's grandfather and great uncle ran a boarding house, where Mildred's sister Garnett Hill and her husband and two young sons, Jerrell and Warren, were living at the time. Pratt remembers Mildred driving up, parking, going inside with the children, and then—a decent interval later—Richard, coming in from the other direction and following suit. Mr. Loving rarely came out until he was about to drive away to DC again.

———

Massive Resistance and Judge Bazile, 1959–1963

Meanwhile, on Lee-Jackson Day, January 19, 1959, just days after the Lovings' trial and banishment, two courts overturned a core component of Massive Resistance as a constitutionally permissible way for Virginia to respond to any court order that a school be desegregated. In *Harrison v. Day*, the Virginia Supreme Court pointed out, in a 5–2 decision, that the state constitution continued to require the maintenance of an effective system of public schools throughout the state. The two dissenters took a position similar to that taken by Judge Bazile in an earlier case; they held that the state constitution did no such thing—that it required both the maintenance of a system of public schools *and* that they be entirely segregated, and if the segregation mandate no longer held, then neither did its companion, that if one fell so did the other. On the same day, in *James v. Almond*, a federal district court ruled that Massive Resistance violated the equal protection clause of the Fourteenth Amendment. In those jurisdictions where the governor had ordered schools closed, the doors soon reopened.

Complying with the letter of the court rulings, the General Assembly ended any direct effort to maintain absolute statewide segregation; but, suddenly rediscovering the merits of local option, it expressly authorized local jurisdictions to do what the state no longer could. At the state level, Massive Resistance was done; at the local level, not so much. In Prince Edward County, authorities had determined shortly after *Brown II* to get out of the public schooling business as of the day a court order came down to desegregate there. In May 1959, the court order finally came, and Prince Edward did not hesitate to follow through on the plans it had put in place four years before. When late summer came, the public schools of Prince Edward County were chained shut. The school buses no longer ran, no longer took "colored" kids to "colored" public schools and "white" kids to "white" public schools. The Prince Edward Academy was quickly taking shape to accommodate most whites. In Caroline County, the board of supervisors had taken the same stance as had Prince Edward, but no court order came in the early years, and white residents of the county had time to find other ways to accommodate or evade the new educational order.

In marriage, too, resistance to interracial couples of the sort that Mr. and Mrs. Loving had chosen to be, with one party white and the other not, remained total—or at least Billy Huff and his bride aside. Such marriages were still banned by state law for all Virginia residents, whether the marriage took place inside the state or elsewhere. No court had ruled such laws unconstitutional in Virginia. Schools might slowly desegregate, at least in some places. The law of marriage, it appeared, would stay in place. And the correspondence of Judge Bazile reveals the ways in which the two questions—schools and marriages—remained closely connected in the minds of many white Americans, especially white southerners.

A "True Texan," writing often from Louisiana, filled the mailboxes of prominent white southerners who included federal district Judge C. Sterling Hutcheson, who was dealing with litigation regarding school desegregation in Prince Edward County, and Virginia circuit court Judge Leon M. Bazile. Included in those notes were phrases like "nefarious plans to subjugate the entire white South." A reference to Rev. Dr. Martin Luther King Jr. in January 1959, shortly after the Lovings' convictions, spoke of King's "desire to see every jail in Alabama filled with decent white citizens, both men and women." We are, "True Texan" fretted, "headed for complete Mongrelization."

Other folks weighed in as well, each assuming the judge to be receptive, each urging him to stay true to the faith. From Nevada came a solicitation in March 1959 for support for FOCUS, a group promoting an amendment to the US Constitution that would uphold white Americans' "freedom of choice" to associate with themselves and not with others. (The irony appears in "white American" Richard's being prevented from his own "freedom of choice" as to who to associate with in marriage.) Also in 1959, but from Falls Church, in northern Virginia, came a message datelined "Territory of Virginia," with white southerners characterized as "in bondage."

There is no need to conclude that Bazile signed on in full to the worldview of every such writer. But there is no basis for denying his general sympathy with such, either. Bazile's reading often included volumes on the Civil War and the Confederacy. His papers include his musings on segregation in schools in the aftermath of *Brown v. Board of Education.* For example, he wrote Governor J. Lindsay Almond Jr. in 1959 regarding proposed amendments to the state constitution related to school desegregation. Certainly if the schools were in fact going to be desegregated, he wrote, the state's requirement of school attendance would have to go. In January 1960 he requested a copy of a speech given by Congressman Dale Alfred of Arkansas on "The Constitutional Crisis: Its Threat to Liberty and the Remedy."

The congressman, a medical doctor, had served on the board of education in Little Rock between 1955 and 1958, exactly when authorities in Arkansas famously defied a desegregation order at Little Rock Central High School. Long an exemplar in the medical profession and in civic life, he took a leadership role in the American Medical Association and served as president of the Arkansas State Opera Company. Also a leader in his church life, he was receptive toward the desegregation of the Episcopal Diocese of Arkansas. But evidently *Brown v. Board of Education* did him in. He won election to the Little Rock School Board in 1955, "quickly established a reputation as an intransigent segregationist" (as his biographer has put it), and, on that springboard, won a write-in election in 1958 to defeat the incumbent congressman from his district as insufficiently opposed to desegregation.

When various white residents of Judge Bazile's Hanover County were organizing an academy in anticipation of the desegregation of the public schools, they issued a mimeographed declaration, "Facts you should know about" Hanover Academy. By March 7, 1959, just weeks after state and federal courts threw out Massive Resistance, plans were already afoot, and in a rush so as to open the new school in September. Without mentioning race or the nation's highest court, the statement spoke to "christian principles" and "free enterprise."

A year later, in March 1960, S. A. Luck Jr., president of the academy's board, wrote Judge and Mrs. Bazile to thank them for their gift of a set of the *Times History of the First World War* for the school's library. The judge was simultaneously offering a gesture of support for the new school and its mission and commemorating his own service in World War I—service of which he was most proud—fighting in the native land of his grandfather and great-grandfather, the first two generations of Baziles in America.

Virginia Supreme Court Justice Willis Dance Miller died in late 1960. Judge Bazile and his friends mounted a campaign to secure his appointment to the court as Miller's successor. Richmond attorney Robert R. Gwathmey III, a member of the board of Hanover Academy, blind-copied the judge on a letter to Governor J. Lindsay Almond: "Now more than ever we need a good conservative constitutional jurist on the court"—someone cut from the same cloth as Justice Miller. Despite endorsements by local bar associations and other people seeking to be heard, Bazile was passed by, in favor of Harry Lee Carrico, also a circuit court judge, but a far younger man, from Fairfax County.

Bazile served as vice president, then president, of the University of Richmond Law School Association. He followed David John Mays '24, the Pulitzer Prize–winning author of a two-volume biography of Virginia's patrician Revolutionary-era leader Edmund Pendleton published in 1952 and, during the period of Massive Resistance, the chair of the Virginia Commission on Constitutional Government, a major tool in the campaign to maintain segregated schools. Mays took credit for the appointment of Justice Willis Dance Miller in 1947 to the Virginia Supreme Court. As a member of the board of trustees of the University of Richmond, in 1965 Mays was the only member of the executive committee to resist, even that late, the beginnings of desegregation of the undergraduate school there. Bazile followed Mays in many ways. Each was prepared to work within the rules, in fact was committed to doing so — rules, that is, that they and people very much like them made for everyone living in Virginia.

The judge's ties reached back many years with the state's great leader, US Senator Harry F. Byrd Sr., who as chair of the Senate Finance Committee wrote the judge (on the need for cutting back federal spending) three months after the Lovings' 1959 trial: "I often think, Leon, of our close association when I was governor." Again, in reply to the judge's 1959 Christmas message: "I will always remember with pleasure the days spent with you in the General Assembly." And he thanked the judge in early 1964 for a "gracious note" regarding Byrd's candidacy for reelection to the Senate that year.

Developments in education and transportation alike continued to shape Caroline County. Early in the Lovings' first year of exile, word came that work on Interstate 95 would likely begin in Caroline County later in the year. At Union High School, according to the local paper, the new principal, Reginald A. Beverly, no longer just another excellent and experienced teacher there, met with the faculty. As for Caroline County school Superintendent William A. Vaughan, after more than four decades of service he retired in 1963. The system as a whole was assuredly far stronger than it had been when he took it over, and black schools as well as white ones had developed a great deal — schools under "separate but equal" were in fact more nearly equal in Caroline than in many Virginia communities, as Union High School had long demonstrated. But they remained categorically separate, "white" and "colored."

Culture, Law, and Interfaith Marriages across America

Big changes in American culture, in the realm of religion, were under way in the early 1960s. The United States in the quarter-century after World War II was a nation that Will Herberg, in his book *Protestant—Catholic—Jew*, published in 1955, characterized as one in which people, white people, might marry outside their ethnic lines but rarely outside their faith. Irish Catholics might marry Italian Catholics. As for white Methodists, they might reach out and marry white Baptists. People socialized within their circles and married within their cultural worlds, with relatively few straying outside—let alone far outside—those cultural worlds. A great many people had some stake in what we could call religious integrity as well as what had for years been termed racial integrity.

Leon Bazile's marriage between a Virginia Catholic and an Alabama Baptist had long lain outside the norms; but it began to appear a bit less anomalous. As church leaders of every faith could see, in the United States and elsewhere, something was going on in the 1960s that eroded the model Herberg had highlighted. Some Americans within any one religious group married outside that group, leading to expressions of great concern, whether by Protestant leaders or by Catholics, Jews, or Greek Orthodox. All saw what they thought to be a rise in interfaith marriages, and almost all saw such marriages as unsettling, even if they did not necessarily agree as to the frequency or the danger.

The American Jewish Congress sponsored a conference in 1963 on religious intermarriage. Reform Rabbi Joseph Klein of Temple Emanuel in Worcester, Massachusetts, accused rabbis who performed marriages between Jews and gentiles of being "a dangerous element in the struggle for Jewish survival" because they were "contributing to the ultimate destruction of Jewish life." Dr. Leo Jung, an Orthodox rabbi in New York City, agreed. Such marriages, he said, were "morally wrong," often ending "in divorce court" or in "a state of belligerence," and also "unfair to the millions of Jews who have fought for survival."

Archbishop Iakovos, as head of the Greek Orthodox Archdiocese of North and South America, addressed the church's seventeenth biennial congress, held in Denver in 1964. There he included interfaith marriage among the matters that merited the church's concern. During the previous year, the church had performed 7,165 weddings, among which 13 percent were with Roman Catholics and 15 percent were with Protestants. If more than one-quarter of all weddings involving Greek Orthodox brides or grooms were interfaith marriages, he worried, how far into the future would the group be able "to maintain and perpetuate its identity as a Greek Orthodox Church"?

Roman Catholic leaders expressed their own concerns about "mixed marriages," which they tended to define as unions of a Catholic with a non-Catholic Christian. At the Ecumenical Council that met in Rome in November 1964, American leaders were divided over what changes, if any, should be made in the Catholic Church's "laws" governing "interconfessional marriages." Rather than continue to require that, in a mixed marriage, both partners promise to raise their children as Catholics, one proposal with wide support would have required only that the Catholic partner pledge that effort "to the best of his [or her] ability."

Perhaps the first wedding ceremony in the nation at which both a Catholic priest and a Protestant clergyman officiated took place on July 13, 1964. A Protestant from Connecticut, Susan Ekberg, married a Catholic from Missouri, Patrick C. Barker. The ceremony took place in the groom's church, the Church of Ste. Genevieve du Bois, near St. Louis. The bride's parents requested the unusual ceremony, which was then arranged by the Episcopal Diocese of Missouri's Bishop George L. Cadigan and Joseph Cardinal Ritter, the Roman Catholic Archbishop of St. Louis. At the ceremony, the Catholic clergyman, the Rev. T. Leonard Jackson, read the vows from the Episcopal Book of Common Prayer. He and the Protestant clergyman, the Rev. Claudius Miller, both offered prayers and gave their blessing. Father Jackson explained that the couple themselves, in the Catholic view, were the ministers of the sacrament, and the essential component of the ceremony was their exchange of promises.

Responses among Protestant commentators were sharply divided. In an editorial titled "Ecumenical Walking," the *Living Church*, a weekly Episcopalian magazine, celebrated the joint ceremony as "an ecumenical breakthrough." In rebuttal, Protestant Episcopal Bishop John S. Higgins of Rhode Island characterized the event, instead, as an "ecumenical disaster" and suggested as a more apt title "Ecumenical Jaywalking."

Noting that the bride had agreed before the marriage that their children would be raised as Catholics, he castigated the editorial's "indefensible and misguided sentimentality," which, he said, "can only encourage other Anglican brides and grooms to do the same thing. Anglicans in such a situation need help and not betrayal from their leaders."

The *Christian Century* supported the rebuttal and widened its application. Episcopalians, it noted, had been warned against signing prenuptial agreements of the sort that Susan Ekberg had reportedly accepted. "What results from such agreements signed by non-Catholics," declared the magazine,

> is not ecumenicity but capitulation. The non-Catholic party to such an agreement not only — as Bishop Higgins sees it — betrays his or her church but also — as most Protestants see it — betrays any children that may come of the union. It is particularly regrettable that some Episcopalians approve such a one-sided compromise at a time when Catholic bishops are reconsidering their church's demand that non-Catholics in a "mixed marriage" sign away their children's religious birthright.

Tensions persisted over these "mixed marriages." So did the attendant difficulties. And so, too, did some individuals' insistence that obstacles to interfaith marriages be overcome. Even big city mayors sometimes had to appeal to higher authority. In 1966, Hope Vulgaris married Carmen J. Armenti, the mayor of Trenton, New Jersey. It was the first marriage for each of them, but by the end of the day each had gone through two wedding ceremonies, and the same two hundred people attended both services. One ceremony took place at St. James Catholic Church, the groom's church. The second took place at the bride's church, St. George's Greek Orthodox Church. Earlier, the mayor had requested permission for the marriage from Catholic Bishop George W. Ahr, who had refused, so Armenti had flown to Rome, where he had obtained a dispensation from Pope Paul VI. The Rev. Peter Pinci conducted the Catholic service, where he read a letter from Rome granting permission for the wedding.

The Rise of Religious Opposition to Miscegenation Laws

Various religious figures, together with groups of church people (regardless of whether they expressed great doubts about interfaith marriages), voiced a growing opposition to laws and attitudes alike that would ban interracial marriages.

According to the National Catholic Conference for Interracial Justice (NCCIJ), as the group declared at its 1963 annual meeting, interracial marriage in no way violated the rules of the Roman Catholic Church. As long as individuals did not violate the "impediments" regarding incest, bigamy, and "diversity of faith," they should have "the right to decide to marry and the right to decide whom to marry," with neither their family nor the state intruding to thwart their choices in these matters. From this perspective, the marriage of Andrea Perez and Sylvester Davis in California in 1948 was no mixed marriage at all, for although the state viewed them as one white and one not, the church saw two practicing Catholics.

The NCCIJ denounced the expressions of "cruelty" often directed toward people who married interracially: "The Catholic conscience condemns ... the underlying racist philosophy" that so often leads to hostile attitudes and behavior, for "the Catholic dogma, revealed by God, of the unity of the [human] family cries out against this pagan ideology." Not content with statements of faith and prescriptions for toleration, the NCCIJ called for action, as it urged conference members all across the nation to work for the repeal of state miscegenation laws. Moreover, such Catholic groups as the Knights of Columbus should, said the NCCIJ, end any remaining practices of segregating their local organizations. Both conditions were incompatible with the national group's understanding of its religious beliefs and social mandates.

Some Protestant groups took a similar approach to state miscegenation laws. The 1965 General Assembly of the United Presbyterian Church, a mostly white denomination, adopted a statement condemning the "blasphemy ... of racism" and denying any "theological grounds for condemning or prohibiting marriage between consenting adults merely because of their racial origin." Recognizing that interracial marriages could "bring all kinds of tensions within the family," the group did not wish to be misunderstood as actively encouraging such marriages, but individuals must be legally free to make their own decisions. Like the NCCIJ, the United Presbyterian Church called on its members to work for the "repeal or nullification" of miscegenation laws. In their communities and their churches, in electoral and judicial politics, Christians should enlist in a battle to end a system of unjust laws. The next year, the 1966 International Convention of Christian Churches (Disciples of Christ) similarly adopted a resolution urging members to "overcome" state miscegenation laws. The resolution encountered resistance, but the opposition was explained largely as stemming from some people's thinking it "premature," not simply wrong.

Through the 1950s and into the 1960s, the nation's miscegenation laws continued to make public news, because they continued to shape private lives. Yet, after long being cited as the authority for banning marriages across racial lines, God was, it seemed, turning against all laws that banned such marriages. Church leaders and church followers adopted the statements they did because they knew miscegenation laws to be alive and well in many states—and because a changing climate of public opinion saw them as evil rather than good, codes that should be opposed rather than tolerated or promoted.

Mildred Loving Appeals to a New Authority

Meanwhile, life for the Lovings continued mostly in the nation's capital throughout 1960, and 1961, and 1962. Sometime in the spring of 1963, Mildred had had enough. Reportedly her cousin Alex or his wife, sympathetic but tired of Mildred's chronic complaining, was the one who put it into her mind to write a letter to the attorney general of the United States asking for help.

CHAPTER 5

Back in Court, 1963–1966

During the first few years of the Lovings' twenty-five-year banishment, the Civil Rights Movement picked up steam, and in venue after venue the US Supreme Court marked substantial changes in the stance of the federal government and the legal status of segregation. In February 1960, hundreds of students at Virginia Union University marched from their campus to the downtown shopping center to conduct sit-ins, and thirty-four of them were arrested on February 22 at eating places in Thalhimers Department Store. In May 1963, in *Randolph v. Virginia*, the Supreme Court threw out the convictions of the thirty-four on the grounds that, under "equal protection" in the Fourteenth Amendment and "state action" as in *Shelley v. Kraemer*, a trespass law cannot be used to maintain racial segregation.

In the meantime, one of the student protesters, Ford T. Johnson Jr., had been found in contempt of court for failure to comply immediately with a Richmond traffic judge's directive that he sit in the "colored" section of the courtroom—and the Supreme Court also overturned *his* conviction that spring, in *Johnson v. Virginia*. Others among the thirty-four joined the Freedom Riders in 1961, riding against segregation on interstate buses and at bus terminals. Raymond B. Randolph Jr., for one, found himself arrested in Jackson, Mississippi, and sent to Parchman Penitentiary. Each protest action, whether in Virginia or elsewhere, spurred additional actions. In adjudicating the various local cases, the Supreme Court eventually often found itself addressing constitutional law in novel ways under the Fourteenth Amendment.

Also in spring 1963, after more than four years in exile, Mildred Loving had had enough, and she saw an opportunity. For one thing, as she later explained, "I wanted to come home. My family was here, and my husband's family was here." Moreover, she said, "I hate to live in the city." More immediately, in personal terms, a car had hit Donald one day as he played in the street. Sidney came home to tell her about the accident, and she did not know until she reached her younger son whether he was dead or alive. A news account from January 1965 suggests "financial difficulties" as an impetus for their effort to return home from exile—difficulties in finding sustained work come to mind, as well as the costs of covering automobile travel for their frequent visits, even in just one vehicle, let alone in two cars to return home separately. Another explanation for her initiating her new effort has it that the couple had just made another of their visits to Caroline County and had been caught by authorities yet again; and this explanation is consistent with how she soon framed her letter looking for help. All of these considerations pointed her in the same direction. They needed to be back home. They needed help to get there.

In the news, regardless, she saw items about all manner of actions being taken by African Americans against segregationist laws and practices, and also about a new civil rights bill President John F. Kennedy was sending to Congress, although the Civil Rights Act of 1964, when it became law the next year, left marriage as the one remaining pillar in the legal structure of Jim Crow. Had she waited a few months longer, she'd have seen reports of the great March on Washington for Jobs and Freedom, masterminded by A. Philip Randolph—leader of the original great March on Washington Movement in 1941—and by Bayard Rustin and scheduled for that August; but she may have already heard about it in the planning stages. Finally, she had definitely heard about Robert F. Kennedy, the nation's attorney general and the president's brother, who was developing a keen sensitivity to civil rights issues. Kennedy was the chief of the Department of Justice, there in Washington, DC, just a few miles from Neal Street.

So, in her careful penmanship, Mildred Loving wrote Bobby Kennedy, looking for assistance, asking might he be able to help her, inquiring if the new law might be of help to them. Maybe he could fix things. As she recalled many years later, "I told Mr. Kennedy of our situation" and asked "if there was any way he could help us." Mildred wanted his help at the very least in visiting more freely in Caroline County. At best, though she pressed for the more modest outcome, Kennedy would help her and her family move away from Washington, DC, and back home—back to Virginia, back to Caroline County, back to Central Point—for good.

When a letter came to her Neal Street home on letterhead of the Department of Justice, one can imagine her delight and anticipation as she opened the envelope, and then her concern and uncertainty as she digested its brief contents. Kennedy could not help directly, but perhaps something could be done. She should inquire of the American Civil Liberties Union (ACLU).

The ACLU, which had been itching for years to rid the nation of miscegenation laws like Virginia's, had two kinds of presence in the DC area. For one thing, the national organization, headquartered in New York City, had a local office in DC, directed by Lawrence Speiser. For another, although the group had no chapter yet in Virginia, it did in the metro DC area, the National Capitol Area Civil Liberties Union, organized just two years earlier, in 1961, with David Carliner (attorney in the *Naim* case from Virginia in the mid-1950s) a founding member and the first chairman.

Moreover, at least one lawyer in Virginia was associated with the group, Bernard S. Cohen. Cohen, like Carliner, had been a founding member of the metro DC chapter, and he recalls that his wife, Rae, served as secretary, taking notes for the "fledgling board." Cohen had attended City College in New York, majoring in economics, and had then gone to work as a labor economist for the Bureau of Labor Statistics there in New York. Within two years, though, the Labor Department had transferred him to Washington, DC. While continuing to work full-time at Labor, Cohen had attended Georgetown University's "late afternoon session" (as the school preferred to call its evening program), earned his law degree, also in 1961, and in 1963 was practicing in Alexandria, in northern Virginia just south across the Potomac River from the nation's capital.

Larry Speiser was used to fielding inquiries from people with civil rights or civil liberties concerns, and Bernard Cohen was one of the cooperating attorneys to whom Speiser would direct such people. We can imagine Mrs. Loving promptly looking up the ACLU in the DC phone book, finding the number, and phoning Speiser's office, but the letter she received actually supplied her that number. Speiser, immediately understanding her call as far more than just another inquiry, advised her to contact Mr. Cohen. She did.

———

The Lovings Get a Lawyer

As leaders in the ACLU considered how best to proceed in the late 1950s and early 1960s with court cases, they established several criteria for the ideal case for attacking laws against interracial marriage. Far better than a divorce proceeding, such as the one involving the Naims in Virginia in the mid-1950s, was a case involving a criminal proceeding against a couple who wanted to remain together. Wishing not to carry any unnecessary political or cultural freight, they saw as preferable a couple in which the husband was white and the wife not, rather than a black husband and a white wife. Similarly, they saw a white-Indian couple or a white-Asian one as more acceptable than a black-white couple. A couple with considerable reputation, or standing, seemed more promising than one without. And the Deep South was anything but an ideal place to find the ideal case; far better that the test case come from a Western state, a Midwestern one, or perhaps a Border South or maybe even an Upper South state. The Lovings met at least the first two criteria, and Virginia was in the Upper South.

In late June 1963, Mildred wrote Bernard Cohen. Sketching the situation as she understood it, and as she wished him to see it, she wrote from her family's DC address:

1151 Neal St.
N.E. Wash. D.C.
June 20, 1963

Dear sir:

I am writing to you concerning a problem we have.

5 years ago my husband and I were married here in the District. We then returned to Va. to live. My husband is white, I am part negro, + part indian.

At the time we did not know there was a law in Va. against mixed marriages.

Therefore we were jailed and tried in a little town of Bowling Green.

We were [ordered] to leave the state to make our home.

The problem is we are not allowed to visit our families. The judge said if we enter the state within the next 30 yrs., that we will have to spend 1 yr. in jail.

We know we can't live there, but we would like to go back once and awhile to visit our families + friends.

We have 3 children and cannot afford an attorney.

We wrote to the Attorney General, he suggested that we get in touch with you for advice.

Please help us if you can. Hope to hear from you real soon.

Yours truely,

Mr. + Mrs. Richard Loving

She knew herself to be "Mrs. Richard Loving"—that was precisely what was in contest—and so she signed herself. Whether she added "Mr. +" after first signing her own name is uncertain, but of course she intended the letter to represent both of them. Perhaps she did not want to overreach and ask for too much. Yet, despite her concession that "we know we can't live there," the couple surely hoped to be able once again to live in Virginia, not just occasionally visit Caroline County together, without threat of arrest.

Bernie Cohen welcomed the opportunity to take the couple's case. In fact, he found it irresistible. As he has often had occasion to say in the years since then, how could he not want to take the case? Here was a young couple, clearly very much in love, but stymied, in fact threatened, in their private lives by a segregation law. Even the couple's name delighted him, as he foresaw the case taking the name "Loving versus Virginia" when it went to the US Supreme Court, as he guessed it surely would. Moreover, he and Mrs. Loving bonded early on, and he was committed to seeing a challenge to her plight through to a successful conclusion.

Yet, at the same time, Cohen had a divided mind, not as to the importance of the case but whether he was up to it, given his relative inexperience especially in civil rights litigation. He felt assured, though, that he would have the help of David Carliner, who had worked on Ham Say

Naim's case back in the mid-1950s. Cohen contacted the Lovings and arranged to meet with them in an office he kept in the District, so the couple could meet with a Virginia lawyer without having to enter the state they had been banished from. This was five years after they had driven from Virginia to the District to get married.

Richard Loving could not believe that the case might go to the Supreme Court. His brush with the law in 1958 and 1959 over his marriage in no way prepared him to understand how the legal system works or, more particularly, how constitutional law develops. But controversies like his are occasions for an adversarial dance, in which parts are assigned. The premise is twofold: that both parts will be played well and that the right answer will prevail, not only for the case at hand but perhaps also with far broader application. Richard Loving had, most of his life, fixed automotive things—tinker with a tractor to make it go again on the farm, soup up a car so it could go faster in a race. To him, the legal system was an alien universe, but perhaps it too had its tools. Rather than "reach me that wrench," a legal technician might say "the equal protection clause should work here" or, in effect, "hand me that Fourteenth Amendment, and maybe that *Shelley v. Kraemer* too."

Cohen saw "two doors" ahead of him, as he put it many years later, for which he would need "two keys." First he had to find some way to get the case reconsidered in the Virginia courts. Once back in court, he had tremendous confidence the Lovings would secure a victory on constitutional grounds.

Cohen ran into repeated obstacles. How was he to get the case of *Commonwealth v. Loving* back into the courts? More than four years had passed since the case had been resolved—the couple had pleaded guilty, had been sentenced, and now wanted to reopen their case. He had to find some way to obtain a rehearing. Then, some months in, he came across a means that seemed promising: *Fuller v. Commonwealth* (1949), a Virginia Supreme Court decision that addressed reviving a case in which there had been a suspended sentence. The court had ruled that, under the Virginia law "providing for the use of probation and suspension of sentence in criminal and juvenile courts," such cases might be reviewable as "still in the breast of the court." A light bulb went off in his head, he recalls; he had found key number one. With a new confidence that he could get the judge's attention, Cohen took that approach, and though nothing in the record of the *Loving* case directly reveals the *Fuller* case and its significance, Judge Bazile did not clearly reject it, and Cohen has always considered it the requisite means of getting him to reconsider the case. Regardless, it gave Cohen the confidence he needed to push ahead.

On November 6, 1963, Cohen filed a motion in Judge Bazile's court to set aside the Lovings' convictions and the sentence that they leave the state in lieu of spending a year in jail. He said their sentence "constitutes cruel and unusual punishment" under the Virginia Constitution, that it "exceeds the reasonable period of suspension" under Virginia statutes, and that it "constitutes banishment, and is thus a violation of constitutional due process of law." Taking another approach, Cohen attacked the sentence as "improper because it is based on a statute which is unconstitutional on its face, in that it denies the defendants the equal protection of the laws and denies the right of marriage which is a fundamental right of free men in violation of Section 1 of the Virginia Constitution and the Fourteenth Amendment of the Federal Constitution." In addition — reaching now — he argued that the statute and the sentence were "unconstitutional burdens upon interstate commerce" and that, moreover, the sentence had "worked undue hardship upon the defendants by preventing them from together visiting their families from time to time as may be desireable [sic] and necessary, to promote domestic tranquility."

Nothing happened. Judge Bazile was in no hurry to second-guess himself, and Cohen had no way to force him to. Having run into a second major obstacle, he again for a time saw no way to make his way around it. Seven months had passed since he filed his motion in Caroline County, and a year since Mildred's initial letter to him, when she wrote him again:

July 6, 1964
1610 10th St.
N.W. Wash. D.C.

Dear Mr. Cohen,
    Hope that you remember us.
    You took our case from Bowling Green, Va.

We haven't heard anything from you for so long, we had given up hope.

Now once again we have something to hope for. Since the "Civil Rights Bill" have become a Federal Law is there anything that can really be done for us?

Can they really stop us from visiting Va?

Do you think it would help if I wrote to the President Mr. Johnson, or got in touch with the N.A.A.C.P.?

Please write to us and let us know what you think. We will be looking to hear from you.

Thank you for your time and consideration.

Very truely,

Richard + Mildred Loving

P.S. Please note that we have a new address.

———

And Then There Were Two Lawyers

Cohen knew he had to do something but still couldn't see what, or rather how. The first door required two keys, it seemed, so he stopped by to brainstorm with his constitutional law professor at Georgetown University, Chester James Antieau. That same afternoon, so did another of Professor Antieau's former students, an even more recent one, Philip J. Hirschkop, who had stopped off in DC on his way to New York from the Deep South, where he was working on civil rights cases in federal district courts. Hirschkop had gone into the military right out of high school in 1954, spent two years in the Green Berets, and then had gone to Columbia University thinking he might study music but instead—after lettering in soccer and serving as class president—had earned a degree in mechanical engineering in 1961 (the same year Cohen finished law school). After that, he worked at a "day job" at the US Patent Office in DC while attending law school at Georgetown (like Cohen, in the "late afternoon session"). By 1964, the year he earned his law degree, he had become immersed in the Civil Rights Movement.

Professor Antieau introduced the two to each other, and Hirschkop asked Cohen what he was working on. By the end of their visit, Hirschkop had introduced Cohen to a means to bring leverage to bear on Judge

Bazile's trial court or perhaps even bypass it entirely. Hirschkop advised Cohen to file a "2283 motion" seeking a panel of three federal judges to address a matter of constitutional law. No longer dead in the water, the case came back to life and veered toward federal court.

That meeting in summer 1964 had tremendous impact. Antieau and Hirschkop are, in different ways, vital parts of how the story of the Lovings unfolded the way it did. Antieau did more than teach, research, and publish, for he was active, too, in civil rights litigation, and the teaching no doubt aimed to promote social change. As for Hirschkop, he appeared fearless, and working on the civil rights front lines he had to be. He was a force of nature in his approach to courtroom tactics, and he was absolutely committed to change on the racial front. Antieau and Hirschkop each brought a profound commitment, considerable experience, and a firm knowledge of the relevant law. They had worked closely together the preceding summer, in 1963, when racial conflict in Danville, a city in Virginia's Southside, bubbled into violence directed toward black protesters, as well as mass arrests of them, and they had proved creative in retooling the law to permit the protests to keep going. By soon after the time of Hirschkop's visit to see Antieau, together with William Kunstler he was litigating *Johnson v. Branch*, a case from North Carolina that eventually gained recognition of public schoolteachers' right to engage in civil rights activities.

Cohen and Hirschkop joined forces to prepare for the next step. The two young lawyers, both from Jewish families, had both grown up not far from Manhattan, one a native of Brooklyn, the other from Hightstown, New Jersey. Both had attended college in New York City, one at City College, the other at Columbia, barely a mile away. Both had made their way to the nation's capital, working for the US government, and both had also attended Georgetown University's evening law program, one beginning there a few months after the other had finished. Their lives converged spectacularly in the office of their former constitutional law professor, after which they embarked on making the world safe for Mildred and Richard Loving to marry and live freely wherever they wished.

On October 28, with Judge Bazile still silent, the two attorneys began a class-action suit in the US District Court for the Eastern District of Virginia. Cohen and Hirschkop requested that a three-judge court convene, first, to determine the constitutionality of Virginia's miscegenation statutes and, second, to prohibit the enforcement of the Lovings' convictions and sentences under those laws. Pending a decision by such a three-judge panel, they requested a temporary injunction against the enforcement of those laws, which they said were designed "solely for the purpose of keeping the Negro people in the badges and bonds of slavery." Seeing no "irreparable harm" to the Lovings while they awaited the panel's decision, however, District Judge John D. Butzner Jr. rejected a motion for a temporary injunction. But he did ask for the three-judge court to hear the couple's case.

Two weeks earlier, the Supreme Court had heard argument on a case, *McLaughlin v. Florida*, in which a couple had been charged with interracial cohabitation. In this case, the NAACP did the heavy lifting, finally making its entry as a major player in the fight against miscegenation laws. On December 7, the Court ruled against the statute. Addressing the precedent from 1883 of *Pace v. Alabama*, the Court declared: "*Pace* represents a limited view of the Equal Protection Clause which has not withstood analysis."

Pace v. Alabama was no more. But if they were prosecuted for interracial cohabitation, the Florida couple did not have the option of marrying, and the Court was not prepared to go there. (They and their attorneys suppressed evidence that they were, in fact, married, since the penalty for marrying exceeded the one they were challenging, so they did not gamble on taking the challenge still further.) Taking a narrow approach, the Court threw out the convictions but did so, in the language of the opinion, "without expressing any views about the state's prohibition of interracial marriage." Justices William O. Douglas and Potter Stewart, although in agreement with the outcome, stated their objection differently in a short concurring opinion: "I think it is simply not possible for a state law to be valid under our Constitution which makes the criminality of an act depend on the race of the actor."

Later that month, with the three-judge hearing coming up, Hirschkop and Cohen filed an eighteen-page brief detailing the Virginia laws and arguing that they should be struck down on grounds of both equal protection and due process. They reviewed the Lovings' situation, including their punishment and exile. And they noted that white-Asian marriages did not carry the same penalties under the Virginia laws but were nonetheless also void.

Waiting on Judge Bazile

In early January 1965, less than two weeks, as it turned out, before the judge finally acted, the Lovings met with reporters in their lawyers' Alexandria office. Demonstrating a combination of determination and frustration, both were more outspoken than usual about their situation and their hopes, Mildred as usual somewhat more so, Richard sometimes saying he had nothing to add. Mildred explained: "All we want to do is go back to Virginia, build a home, and raise our children." She went on: "We loved each other and got married. We are not marrying the state. *The law should allow a person to marry anyone he wants.*" Richard, in one of his rare moments of downright loquacity, asserted: "They said I had to leave the state once, and I left with my wife. If necessary, I will leave Virginia again with my wife. But I am not going to divorce her."

"Leaving home was the hardest part of it for me," Richard observed that day. His tenacity in his commitment to Mildred particularly struck his lawyer Phil Hirschkop. Why would a man, a white man at that, put up with all the wrenching experiences he had endured — unless, as Hirschkop could see, he really was devoted to her. Then again, getting divorced would have been a tricky maneuver in its own right. They would have to do that back in DC. The state of Virginia wouldn't recognize Mildred Jeter as Mrs. Loving for any purpose, including permitting them to divorce. This the Virginia Supreme Court had made clear enough — despite an alternative possible scenario, like the one that unfolded in a Norfolk courtroom in Ham Say Naim's case a decade earlier — in another case, just months before Mildred wrote to Kennedy and then to Cohen. That case, *Calma v. Calma* (1962), involved a Caucasian woman and a Malay man, that is, Filipino. They had married in New Jersey in 1954 and later had come to Virginia under his military orders, but she now wanted to divorce him, and yet they could not get the state courts to agree that they even had a marriage they could dissolve. The Lovings would have had to stay married until they could get their marriage recognized. Then again, under Virginia law their marriage had always been void.

As for where they were living by that point, Richard gave a clue when he noted that, "if necessary, I will leave Virginia again with my wife." In fact they had been spending a lot of time in Virginia since late 1963, when Bernie Cohen had first moved to get their case back into court. They were understandably hesitant about returning to Caroline County together, though, so they made other arrangements. For a time beginning (as Mildred later recalled it) in June 1964, so shortly before she wrote her follow-up letter to Cohen, she stayed in Essex County with her sister, while he stayed with his parents in Caroline. After a while they found a place for the entire family in Essex County, where they stayed until the first of 1965, and then they settled in a place in King and Queen County, also right next door to Caroline (just south of Central Point, rather than just east of it), but remained mindful of their sanctuary in Washington, DC. Sidney began attending school in Virginia, and in turn his younger siblings did as well.

––––––

Back in the Court of Judge Bazile

The three-judge federal court had set a date of January 27, 1965, when it would rule on the case. As the winter days of January went by, Judge Bazile was running out of time to have his say, so he finally acted on Bernard Cohen's motion from back in November 1963. We have no transcript that details the arguments that took place in Bazile's court on January 22, 1965, six years after the original trial, because, according to Philip Hirschkop, no such actual meeting ever took place. What we have is what Cohen had said in his motion, as well as what the two sides argued later on, and we have what the judge, when he issued his ruling that day, wrote to justify the disposition he had made of the case all those years earlier. He took twelve pages, in longhand on a yellow pad, to develop his argument. The case might soon leave his jurisdiction, but before it did he would reach for his megaphone while he had one and broadcast his version of the story of the Lovings and the law.

Was the Virginia statute of race and marriage constitutional? Bazile wondered how it could even be a question. In rejecting the Lovings' motion, and explaining his decision, the judge had various materials to work with. He had had ample time to review various cases on miscegenation across the previous hundred years. So he called a meeting of some old friends, cases in which the Virginia Supreme Court and other courts had upheld laws like the one—and even the very one—being contested by the Lovings. Other cases might have joined him, but those that did seemed sufficient, even compelling witnesses on his behalf. One can imagine *Green v. State* stopping by from Alabama, together with a host of other cases from there and other states, and nodding with approval as they watched two cases from the Virginia Supreme Court, one from 1878, the other from 1955, bookend a series of witnesses all pointing in the same direction.

The judge cited to good effect the 1883 decision by the US Supreme Court in *Pace v. Alabama*, and he also brought in *Jackson v. State*, an Alabama case that also went to the US Supreme Court, as recently as 1954, but had been denied a hearing there. And he put the 1871 decision by a northern court, *State v. Gibson*, on parade: "If the Federal Government can determine who may marry in a State, there is no limit to its power."

But mostly he deferred to the only authority he truly recognized in either education or marriage, so he cited earlier cases from the Virginia Supreme Court. He quoted *Kinney v. Commonwealth*, a ruling by the court upholding the then new 1878 miscegenation statute: "If the parties desire to maintain the relations of man and wife, they must change their domicile and go to some state or country where the laws recognize the validity of such marriages." In Virginia, a marriage like that of the Lovings was—and here he quoted from another Virginia ruling, *Greenhow v. James Executor*—"not only absolutely void but criminal."

He quoted with particular enthusiasm some of the Virginia court's more exuberant language in the 1955 case of *Naim v. Naim*: "Regulation of the marriage relation is, we think, distinctly one of the rights guaranteed to the States and safeguarded by that bastion of States' rights, somewhat battered perhaps but still a sturdy fortress in our fundamental law, the tenth section of the Bill of Rights." *Naim v. Naim* termed marriage "a subject which belongs to the exclusive control of the States," and the US Supreme Court had done nothing to overturn that Virginia decision from 1955 or, Bazile was quite sure, to undermine any state's laws against interracial marriage.

As for the matter of banishment, Bazile rejected any such character-ization of the sentence he had handed down six years earlier. Simply put, they had not been banished at all: "Each one of them can come to Caroline separately to visit his or her people as often as they please." But both were "guilty of a most serious crime," and if they ever came to Virginia at the same time, "they would be subject to prosecution for unlawful cohabitation."

Explaining the original disposition, he elaborated the rationale. Quite aside from the terms he had imposed, had they returned, or if they ever returned, "to Caroline County or to the State of Virginia together" and resumed their "cohabitation," they would be "subject to prosecution," just as before. Implying that the twenty-five-year suspension hardly pointed to a time in the future when they might return together, he ob-served that they could not—that is, could never—"cohabit in Virginia without incurring repeated prosecutions."

His ruling did not merely reflect his personal whims, or his judicial idiosyncrasies, but rather summed up very well the law as he and most, if not all, other southern judges understood it in the middle 1960s. For him, there had been no relevant change in the constitutional status of miscegenation laws since the classic cases of the 1870s, 1880s, and 1890s. For science as well as law, he reached back to the nineteenth century. In his distinctive penmanship, he wrote out his opinion, a printed version of which appeared the following year in the case file before the Virginia Supreme Court.

McLaughlin v. Florida, ruled on in late 1964, so some weeks before Judge Bazile released his ruling: was it even on the judge's radar? The case had been argued in October and the decision announced on the first Monday in December. Maybe the judge hadn't heard about it? Very unlikely. Maybe he saw it as irrelevant, since the Court had expressly declined to rule on interracial marriage? Maybe, but of course the Court had expressly overruled *Pace v. Alabama*, one of those old friends and faithful allies in the congregation when Judge Bazile wrote out his opinion on the Lovings' challenge to his handling of *their* case. Far more likely is that the judge saw *McLaughlin v. Florida* as no more legitimate than *Brown v. Board of Education*. The federal government had no busi-ness, under the US Constitution he knew and abided by, to interfere with a state matter like marriage any more than it did a state matter like education. So he ignored it, willfully, blatantly, in defiance, and with exasperation.

By way of conclusion, Judge Bazile wrote out, again in his longhand: "Almighty God created the races white black yellow and malay [interpolated: red] and he placed them on separate continents. And but for the interference with his arrangement there would be no cause for such marriages. The fact that he separated the races shows that he did not intend for the races to mix." Here he was drawing on ideas, even expressions, that had appeared in court rulings often before, but would bring ridicule this time.

From One Court to Another

Judge Bazile had spoken, yet his was not the final word. But where would the case go next? Back into federal court or continue on in the state court system?

The case first went back to the three-judge federal court, comprised of District Judge Butzner joined by another district judge, Oren R. Lewis, as well as Fourth Circuit Court of Appeals Judge Albert V. Bryan. There, as scheduled on January 27, lawyers for the state argued that the case should next be heard in the Virginia Supreme Court. Lawyers for the Lovings insisted that the state court had, in the *Naim* case, already made its position abundantly clear on such matters, and the federal court should rule on the case. On February 12, the judges rendered their opinion. The case would next go to the state's highest court, but it must address the constitutional question.

Mr. and Mrs. Loving had not yet won their case, nor could they know when they might win, or be sure in fact that they ever would. Their trials would continue. But now they could legally return to Virginia, or actually stay in Virginia, said a court order from the three-judge federal panel, in February 1965, good for as long as the case continued in the courts, state or federal. So the couple and the three children continued living in the country — Mr. and Mrs. Loving once again after their years in exile, Sidney for the first time since he was a toddler, and Donald and Peggy for the first time ever — not far from friends and family, with Richard and Mildred now more sure than they had been in a long time that they would not be arrested, or would be bailed out in short order if arrested.

During that time, two kinds of pictorial images were taken that can give people far away in time and space many glimpses into their family life at their new place. Grey Villet took photographs for a story that appeared as "The Crime of Being Married" in *Life* magazine in March 1966, and the family has always possessed proofs of a great many images that did not make it into the story. Hope Ryden camped out in their hideaway house in King and Queen County, shooting film as the family went about their business, including a scene in which Richard nervously shuffled a stack of the proofs that Villet had given the family.

Hardly just a fly on the wall, or for that matter on the scene just a short while, Ryden had contacted Cohen, as he recalls, shortly after the story made news when the Lovings challenged their convictions and sentences. She recognized the case as significant, and the story compelling, and she hoped to make a documentary film about it all as it unfolded. Agreement reached, she would "protect the secrecy" of the lawyers' "strategy and discussions" until after the case was concluded. Over the course of several years she filmed such scenes as the two lawyers in their Alexandria office huddling on the case; the Lovings at home in one place or another, and Mr. and Mrs. Loving together with Hirschkop and Cohen outside the federal courthouse in Richmond after a session with the three-judge court. Footage shows that from time to time Ryden asked Mildred or Richard a question that occasioned a response as to their feelings and thoughts, while her cameraman Abbot Mills went about his business. The documentary film that she had in mind did not come to pass, and she stashed the footage in a closet at her place in New York City, went about her own life and her varied other projects, and for many years pretty much forgot about it.

The Virginia Supreme Court

Back in Richmond, lawyers for both sides rehearsed arguments at the Virginia Supreme Court that, everyone understood, were likely to be heard again before long at the US Supreme Court. The state argued along the lines that Judge Bazile had outlined. Cohen and Hirschkop quoted from *Perez v. Sharp*, the 1948 California Supreme Court decision on such laws: "If the right to marry is a fundamental right, then it must be conceded that an infringement of that right by means of a racial restriction is an unlawful infringement of one's liberty." They continued: "The caprice of the politicians cannot be substituted for the minds of the individual in what is man's most personal and intimate decision. The error of such legislation must immediately be apparent to those in favor of miscegenation statutes, if they stopped to consider their abhorrence to a statute which commanded that all marriages must be between persons of different racial backgrounds." Such a statute, they claimed, would be no more "repugnant to the constitution"—and no less so—than the law under consideration. Something "so personal as the choice of a mate must be left to the individuals involved," they argued; "race limitations are too unreasonable and arbitrary a basis for the State to interfere."

Members of the Virginia judiciary, whether circuit court judges (like Leon Bazile) or members of the Virginia Supreme Court, are elected—and periodically reelected—by the legislature, though sometimes those on the state supreme court initially get there by gubernatorial appointment. All made their way through an approval process that depended on a prediction that they would prove safe on policy issues that came before them. At both levels, therefore, any judge the Lovings encountered had been carefully vetted by a legislature that itself was recruited through a small and overwhelmingly white electorate. Anyone tinged as a renegade, an apostate from Harry Byrd's orthodoxy, need not apply.

Among the Virginia Supreme Court's seven justices, Harry Lee Carrico, who was appointed in 1961 to the vacancy that Judge Bazile had yearned to fill, was born in Washington, DC, and earned his undergraduate and law degrees at George Washington University there. None of the other justices had been born outside Virginia, nor had any attended an institution of higher education outside the state. They had grown up in a world that looked a lot like Judge Bazile's, and their worldview was scarcely distinguishable from his, though they had split in January 1959 over the question of whether the state constitution mandated a system of public schools even if those schools might be desegregated. Chief Justice John W. Eggleston, with a fairly typical background, was born in Charlotte County in the Southside and attended Hampden-Sydney

College in next-door Prince Edward County, as did Archibald Chapman Buchanan, who had authored the court's unanimous 1955 opinion in *Naim v. Naim*. But Buchanan did not write the state supreme court's unanimous opinion in the *Loving* case. Carrico did. The ruling came on March 7, 1966.

Justice Carrico tagged *Naim v. Naim* as the place to begin. That decision by the court had been sound in 1955, no question about that, and it cited at length the many authorities that supported it then. Had anything happened since then that the court should see as requiring a reconsideration of its stance on the Virginia law? The Lovings' attorneys argued that *Naim* rested on *Plessy v. Ferguson*, but that *Brown v. Board of Education* had overruled *Plessy*, so *Naim* should fall too. To the contrary, according to the court, *Brown* had to do with education, not marriage. Six months after the 1954 decision in *Brown*, moreover, the US Supreme Court itself had refused even to hear the miscegenation case *Jackson v. Alabama*, in which a multiyear prison sentence was at issue. As to the challenge to *Pace v. Alabama* made in light of *McLaughlin v. Florida*, decided just a year or so earlier, there the Supreme Court had ruled only on a conviction for cohabitation, not marriage, and had decided the case, as it had said, "without reaching the question" of whether the Florida law against interracial marriage was valid.

In short, none of these cases, according to Virginia's highest court in 1966, "deals with miscegenation statutes or curtails a legal truth which has always been recognized—that there is an overriding state interest in the institution of marriage." So *Plessy* lived on as regarded segregation (except in the public schools), as did *Pace* with regard to race and marriage, as well as *Maynard v. Hill* as to the state's great interest in and authority over the regulation of marriage. The great trilogy of cases from between 1883 and 1896, said the court, had in no way been undermined or overruled with regard to marriage. So how could it be said that the nation's highest court had ruled in such a way as to require throwing out the Virginia statutes of race and marriage?

Thus the Virginia Supreme Court's opinion largely adopted the position taken by the state of Virginia. Its reasoning and conclusion from the case of Ham Say Naim remained as sound in 1966 as it had a decade earlier. As far as the court was concerned, in fact, the Virginia law against interracial marriage was as sound in the 1960s as the earlier version had been back in the years around 1880. On March 7, 1966, a unanimous court declared:

> Our one and only function in this instance is to determine whether, for sound judicial considerations, the *Naim* case should be reversed. Today, more than ten years since that decision was handed down by this court, a number of states still have miscegenation statutes and yet there has been no new decision reflecting adversely upon the validity of such statutes. We find no sound judicial reason, therefore, to depart from our holding in the *Naim* case.

But one significant part of the case did cause the court pause: Judge Bazile's directing the couple to leave for twenty-five years and not return together at any time. Here the court differed with both the state and the Lovings. They had not actually been banished, it told the Lovings, since — as Judge Bazile had pointed out — they could come back anytime they wished, just not both together. The sentence was nonetheless void, it held. The sole objective of the suspended sentence should have been keeping the couple from continuing to violate the Virginia statute (though of course their nonbanishment accomplished that): "The condition reasonably necessary to achieve that purpose was that the defendants not again cohabit as man and wife in this state." So the supreme court remanded the case back to Judge Bazile's court for resentencing. Meanwhile, Richard and Mildred, not yet "Mr. and Mrs. Loving," were free to come and go in Virginia, so long as they did not "cohabit as man and wife in this state."

Oh, one other thing, the court said. "Although it has not been alluded to by either side to this controversy," the law in question "provides for a sentence in the penitentiary, and not in jail." So the sentence had to be reconfigured. First, the sentence of spending time in confinement had to be altered to state prison, not the Caroline County jail. Next, if a new suspension took the shape of simply directing the couple to cease acting like a married couple living together, then all right, so long as said married couple was prepared to comply, but that was hardly going to happen. If it took the shape of an actual prison sentence, with no suspension, then they were far worse off than before, a possible outcome that had troubled Hirschkop in particular. A new sentence of time in prison, whether for a year, as before, or five or something in between (just as the couple had faced seven years before, when they first went on trial), could put them behind bars and away from their children rather than out of prison and together with them, whether in Washington, DC, or in Virginia.

Then again, it appeared that the case would not go back to Caroline County at all, but rather back into the federal court system. The Lovings had exhausted their appeals in the Virginia courts, and their convictions remained intact. They were still not allowed to "cohabit as man and wife" in Virginia. Of course they would appeal their case to the US Supreme Court. And if they were turned down there? Then they would be in Virginia awaiting Judge Bazile's choice as to how to reconfigure their sentence, or back in the nation's capital. Back in DC, they would be in exile much as they had been before Mrs. Loving wrote Bobby Kennedy.

Other People Write Letters

News came nine months later, in December 1966, that the US Supreme Court would hear the case. The news stories typically repeated Judge Bazile's pronouncements concerning the five races and God's intention that they remain separate and unmixed. The news promptly elicited one New Yorker's spirited reply. Writing to the judge on December 14, from Great Neck, on Long Island, Harold S. French referenced the authority of the Fourteenth Amendment and then made a suggestion: "Now, if you are sworn to uphold the Constitution of the United States, I suggest that you take the first boat back to whichever continent your ancestors came from and from which surely God did not mean them to migrate to this new land," either that or, he proposed, "resign your office for you are not upholding the constitution but your own southern born bigotry."

Going on to quote Thomas Jefferson's language in the Declaration of Independence about "all men . . . created equal," French indicted Bazile for privileging the people he identified with and excluding all others: "But not red, Malay, green or polka dot people because you are not red, Malay, green or polka dot." French closed with: "Sir, for shame, for shame. You surely did not mean what you said. Not in 1966; 1866 or 1766, yes, but not 1966. Don't you want to retract? You'll become the laughing stock of the country. Call the press and retract or deny; it's just too ludicrous."

According to the "cc" at the end of the letter, French also shipped his missive to two justices of the US Supreme Court: Byron White, "whom I knew," he noted, "as 'Whizzer' in the basketball days of the '30s" (when White had been a multiple-sports star at the University of Colorado); and Abe Fortas. To his credit, or reflecting his own amusement at the benighted whims of an alien world, the judge kept the letter for his files.

By that time, Bazile had come down with a serious illness. He had major surgery in October 1965, and week after week he received well-wishers' notes and cards at the Johnston-Willis Hospital in Richmond. From a woman in Louisa County: "We all think so much of you up here." From nearby Ashland, another woman wrote for herself and her husband: "Tom says everywhere he goes he hears such wonderful things said about you.... You are loved and admired." She spoke with great warmth of "your loving heart accompanied by a brilliant mind, strong will for right, your loyalty + devotion to friends + family . . . all whose lives you have touched." An old friend wrote with fondness and regret, recalling a time, more than half a century before, that would never come again: "My earliest recollection of you is seeing you vigorously walk-ing up Broad Street from the Ashland Car Line Terminal to old Rich-mond College." (The school's move west of the city from downtown took place in 1914.)

Hanover County's board of supervisors passed a resolution tout-ing his virtues as a constitutional lawyer, an adherent of the Catholic Church, a judge, and a family man, and the occupant for a time of the legislative seat once held by Patrick Henry. Actually, Henry had rep-resented Hanover County in the old House of Burgesses in the years before the American Revolution, but the connection is nicely drawn, for Leon Bazile had long echoed Patrick Henry's profound distrust of national authorities, a distrust shared by the people passing resolutions about him at his retirement from the fray. The pair embodied the con-siderable continuity, from eighteenth century to twentieth, of political culture among elite Virginians.

Judge Bazile was no longer young, no longer vigorous, no longer in-nocent of knowledge of all he might accomplish, or for that matter of the single image that would come to dominate faraway observers' sense of him. In the other side of that split image of him, he was neither loved nor admired, and he was seen in any light but having a "strong will for right." And of course his devotion to "family" did not extend to the Lovings' family.

In November 1965, just ten months after releasing his ruling on the Lovings' appeal—including the statement in which he had voiced the nineteenth-century anthropological language of five races, as well as his certainty of their separateness and God's intent that they stay that way—he declared his intention to retire.

One More Court

Bernie Cohen had found a means to get over one hurdle, through one door, getting the case back into court, years after the Lovings had agreed to plead guilty and Judge Bazile had handed down his sentence. Whether the original trial judge accepted the approach Cohen took is hard to say, since the judge never got around to acting until the federal courts were about to intervene if he did not, but it gave Cohen some assurance he would get a hearing, and he got the process under way. Months later he was still trying to move it along, or he would not have stopped by his old law professor's office to consult on it. Phil Hirschkop, after meeting Cohen on that occasion, came aboard with a plan to get the case past the next obstacle, Judge Bazile: lean on Bazile, by bringing the case into federal court, to respond to the petition for a rehearing in state court, so they could get beyond his court. From Judge Bazile's court, the Lovings had gone next to the Virginia Supreme Court. They were not yet done.

The case of the Lovings versus the state of Virginia headed toward the US Supreme Court. How would those nine justices rule on the Virginia law of race and marriage? How narrow or broad might their ruling turn out to be? What would it mean to Mr. and Mrs. Loving, their children, and their friends and relatives? What would it mean to people throughout the state, the region, the nation?

Loving v. Virginia and the
US Supreme Court

Richard Loving, a private and taciturn man, put more words together for public consumption than usual after the Virginia Supreme Court ruled against him and Mildred in March 1966. Now they would have to take their appeal to the nation's highest court. "We have thought about other people," he told a reporter in Richmond, "but we are not doing it just because someone had to do it and we wanted to be the ones.... We are doing it for *us*—because we want to live here," in Virginia. He was not discounting the broader significance of their action and its possible success, but that was not what animated him or his bride, although Mildred Loving told Hope Ryden that her family could always go back to DC but she saw the importance to others of their pursuing "the principle" of it all. This was no contrived case. It came, as great constitutional cases generally do, out of real world concerns, in which someone's life, liberty, or property turned on the outcome.

First the Lovings had to convince the nation's highest court even to hear their case. In their jurisdictional statement to the Court, attorneys Bernard Cohen and Philip Hirschkop began with facts that would have been unavailable even three years earlier. The Civil Rights Act of 1964 and the Voting Rights Act of 1965 were both on the books, they noted, so "the elaborate legal structure of segregation has been virtually obliterated with the exception of the miscegenation laws." As for those remainders from the panoply of Jim Crow statutes, they went on, "There are no laws more symbolic of the Negro's relegation to second-class citizenship. Whether or not this Court has been wise to avoid this issue in the past, the time has come to strike down these laws; they are legalized racial prejudice, unsupported by reason or morals, and should not exist in a good society."

As the Court considered whether to hear the case, Justice John

Marshall Harlan's clerk said it another way. "The miscegenation issue . . . was left open in *McLaughlin*," the 1964 Florida case, he wrote his boss, "and appears ripe for review here. If the Court's traditional test that discrimination based on race must be examined carefully for any justifiable state interest, I doubt whether this statute can stand."

Indeed, on December 12, 1966, the Court agreed to hear the case, and oral argument took place four months later, on April 10. The Court would act out of necessity as something of a legislature, making policy no matter how it ruled, and interested groups not directly involved in the case weighed in to help shape the outcome. Some, as we will see, did do with a focus on the Loving case. But other actions eased the way as well. Among key indicators of a shift in Americans' center of gravity on interracial marriage, a significant straw in the wind came in Maryland, a Border South state where, with a newly reapportioned legislature as well as enhanced black enfranchisement and new black legislators, the laws against interracial marriage were repealed in 1967. Enacted in March 1967, the new Maryland law went into effect on June 1.

Lobbying the judiciary in general and the Supreme Court in particular takes two forms. One is in the shape of journal articles in law reviews, and the other is playing the role of amicus curiae, "friend of the court." So, for example, from the Loving side, there are the written arguments, or briefs, as well as the oral argument before the justices, of the Japanese American Citizens League (JACL) and the National Catholic Conference for Interracial Justice (NCCIJ).

As for essays in law journals, Alfred Avins published "Anti-Miscegenation Laws and the Fourteenth Amendment: The Original Intent" in the November 1966 issue of the *Virginia Law Review*. Avins asserted that the amendment's framers had not meant to include miscegenation laws among those that the equal protection clause would invalidate. Moreover, while neglecting some major court rulings that would have supported his side, Avins listed many that showed a judicial history of upholding such laws against constitutional challenges, though he also ignored all that went the other way. He was adamant that the traditional police powers that states had exercised over matters of race and marriage ought to continue, unless the Constitution were formally amended to make a change.

The same issue of the *Virginia Law Review* carried an opposing piece by Walter J. Wadlington, a young professor at the University of Virginia Law School, "The *Loving* Case: Virginia's Anti-Miscegenation Statute in Historical Perspective." After a careful review of the long history, Wadlington observed that, "if we should not fault our forefathers for enacting miscegenation laws under the circumstances confronting them, neither can we justifiably perpetuate those laws under the changed circumstances of our world." Then, pointing out that "a constitutional attack in the federal courts" seemed the only potentially effective "avenue" for terminating Virginia's participation in the antimiscegenation regime—in fact, he might have observed, for bringing that entire regime to an end—Wadlington concluded that "the whole of Virginia's miscegenation machinery should fall."

Though obtaining crucial support from experienced hands at the ACLU and elsewhere, the two young lawyers for the Lovings did the heavy lifting. They had to get it right. As they saw it, after the Civil Rights Act of 1964 and the Voting Rights Act of 1965, this was the last great fight in the struggle for racial justice under the law. As they saw it, a white man and a black woman had been caught in the toils of an ancient legal effort, sustained through the years, adapted to changing circumstances, but always with the primary purpose and function of demeaning one group of people, artificially subordinating them, keeping them available to do others' bidding, to remain marginal players in the economy and largely excluded from politics and policymaking. The attorneys' job, though they only partly understood this, was to wrestle into alignment two story lines, the everyday texture of multiracial life in Central Point and the great struggle to end legally enforced racial separation and black subordination. They sought abundant assistance from some very able and experienced attorneys and law professors associated with the ACLU. Supporters from various other sectors weighed in as well.

Friends of the Court

Two groups had for some years been seeking a test case to bring down miscegenation laws, and additional groups signed on in 1963 and 1964. The ACLU had been on the lookout for a test case ever since its involvement in the California Supreme Court's 1948 ruling in *Perez v.*

Sharp, and it had supported the losing side in the Virginia case from the mid-1950s, *Naim v. Naim*.

As for the JACL, that group had pushed successfully for an amendment to the Soldier Brides Act in 1947, which permitted immigration by the Japanese wives and biracial children of American servicemen stationed in Japan. Since then, it had been looking for a test case, particularly one involving a "war bride" from Japan or Korea, where so many American GIs were stationed. But no promising case had materialized; the JACL could not even unearth a single situation where a white-Asian couple had been prosecuted for their interracial marriage, even though a number of states, especially in the West, had banned marriages with whites that involved "Mongolians." Then again, the most populous such state, California, included no criminal penalty in its ban, and anyway its law had been overturned in 1948. Not generally having been much involved in the struggle to get rid of antimiscegenation laws, the JACL had, however, helped obtain repeal of Idaho's miscegenation law in 1959.

The JACL entered the *Loving* litigation once the case reached the Supreme Court. Appearing at the Court for oral argument was William M. Marutani, who as a young Nisei (second-generation Japanese American) was forced to abandon his studies at the University of Washington after the United States entered World War II and the order came down to evacuate all ethnic Japanese residents along the Pacific Coast. For a time he lived at the Tule Lake internment camp in far northern California, before he was allowed to resume his higher education, this time in South Dakota. Later he served in the US Army, was assigned to the Military Intelligence Service, and spent time with the army of occupation in early postwar Japan before attending law school at the University of Chicago. For the rest of his life, he maintained a deep involvement with the JACL in its evolving effort to address discriminatory laws that curtailed the rights of Asian Americans.

In the 1960s, various religious figures and groups of church people voiced a growing opposition to laws and attitudes alike that would bar interracial marriages. In November 1963, for example, some months after the Lovings' plight came to the attention of Bernie Cohen and the ACLU, the board of the NCCIJ resolved to attack miscegenation laws, seeking either legislative repeal or judicial rulings against their constitutionality.

Across the 1950s and into the 1960s, success was had, whether with these groups' involvement or not, in securing repeal of miscegenation laws in states outside the South. Just between the 1958 arrest of the Lovings and the end of 1963, the number of states with such laws dropped from twenty-four to nineteen, leaving just Wyoming, Indiana, and the seventeen southern states, and in 1965 Wyoming and Indiana both peeled away from the antimiscegenation regime. Finally, in a miscegenation case that the US Supreme Court decided in 1964, *McLaughlin v. Florida*, the National Association for the Advancement of Colored People (NAACP) Legal Defense and Educational Fund (LDF) finally got very involved in the issue.

As the words and deeds of the NCCIJ made clear, Judge Bazile's Catholic coreligionists did not by any means all share his racial orientation. He was of necessity responding primarily to the legal issues that the Lovings' case raised, not only in his disposition of their case at the January 1959 trial but more especially in the rhetoric he deployed in explaining his refusal to reconsider matters in January 1965. And he was doing so as a white southerner distinctly uncomfortable with the unfolding Civil Rights Movement, in fact feeling embattled as the federal government increasingly raised its level of activity and commitment, intervening to transform the historical racial ways of the South.

The NCCIJ originated in 1960, with the federation of Catholic Interracial Councils, the first of which dated back to the 1930s. It reflected the initiative of lay Catholics, in particular Mathew H. Ahmann, but it also served as an arm of the church hierarchy. Ahmann embodied, as he promoted, a pair of significant developments in American religious life beginning especially in 1963. One was linking leaders of the Protestant, Catholic, and Jewish communities into a combined force seeking progressive social change on the racial front. The other, in particular, was challenging state laws against interracial marriage. The resolution approved by the board in November 1963 began with a declaration that this particular initiative lay at the center of the civil rights struggle and must therefore be addressed:

> Since we are aware that for white Americans, the most emotionally charged aspect of the struggle for racial justice is the question of intermarriage, and since we are aware that the fear, apprehension and

anxiety which surrounds this question have their roots in past conduct, false philosophies and sheer myths, we feel that the clear witness of Catholic doctrine and canon law concerning marriage must be brought to the attention of Catholic and other Americans. . . .

The Catholic conscience condemns, abhors and rejects the underlying racist philosophy which speaks of interracial marriage as "depreciating a racial strain." Human beings are not cattle. The Catholic dogma, revealed by God, of the unity of the human family cries out against this pagan ideology.

We will join in an effort to repeal or have ruled unconstitutional those remaining state laws banning marriage across racial lines.

Two months later, in January 1964, Mathew Ahmann wrote John Kenna of the National Catholic Welfare Conference's (NCWC) Family Life Bureau, raising the possibility of an "interreligious" assault on miscegenation laws in each state, an initiative, he said, that might "provide some useful service, and also be an educational social action project." The first opportunity to get involved appeared to come in Maryland, where a license had been denied to a couple because one party appeared to be a "Malay." John P. Sisson, assistant to Ahmann in the NCCIJ, wrote John J. Sweeney Jr., counsel for Elizabeth Medaglia, the white prospective bride of this "Malay" man, asking whether issuing a statement or preparing an amicus curiae brief might be helpful. The offer was turned down, however, as the judge ruled that the person alleged to be Malay in fact had "some 'Spanish blood'" and therefore could qualify as white and obtain the marriage license without further proceedings. (Had a Maryland judge discovered a one-drop rule of *white* racial identity?) Nonetheless, lawyer Sweeney, while noting that he had closed his file on the case, ended his reply with these words:

This is not to say, of course, that I think the statute is equitable, moral or constitutional[,] because my thoughts are to the contrary. The morality of interracial marriage has, of course, long been clear to most Christians and the unconstitutionality of the miscegenation statutes has been clear to most lawyers since the Perez case in California in 1948. I trust that our particular statute will be thoroughly tested in the not too distant future so that this odious prohibition may be removed from our statutes.

By March 1965, weeks after Judge Bazile's words about how "Almighty God created the races," the activists had found the embodiment of their cause and were seeking to assist with the *Loving* litigation. In August 1966, with the Lovings' case going to the US Supreme Court for consideration, Sisson wrote William C. Lewers: "I will try to enlist the Family Life Bureaus and/or bishops of the dioceses in all the states where miscegenation laws are on the books." The group had some difficulty identifying just which states still had such laws, confused for a time about some that had in fact already repealed theirs, but they had all the states of the South right. More particularly, it was seen as simply essential to secure the support of the bishop of the diocese of Richmond, Virginia, and much effort was directed toward making that happen. The Bishop of Richmond to whom Sisson was referring was John Joyce Russell, whose diocese included Hanover and Caroline counties, the home places of both Judge Bazile and the Lovings.

In October 1966, the NCWC's John Kenna wrote John J. McMahon in Richmond: "We are a peculiar institution in that we aren't able to move on such a matter unless the 'Bishop of the place'" approves it, "or so I'm informed." As Kenna put it, "This is a matter in which the Roman Catholic Church has a vital interest which, strangely, coincides with that of the American Civil Liberties Union": "Can you persuade Bishop Russell to exert leadership in swinging NCWC on this? The Lovings will probably win the case. . . . This means that without taking way-out chances the Church would be able to strike a blow for freedom by helping to establish the unconstitutionality of state anti-miscegenation laws in the name of religious liberty."

The NCCIJ drafted the letter that Bishop Russell sent out on November 28, 1966. In that letter, the bishop explained about the Lovings to his peers in other southern states, in fact all twenty states that were thought still to have miscegenation laws: "After five years of exile, they were re-arrested while on a visit to family in Virginia, and began the process of appeals. All Virginia courts have upheld the miscegenation statutes, and the Supreme Court of the United States is now considering whether or not to accept the case for review." Should the case be accepted for review, then the NCCIJ would be filing a brief as a friend of the court. Bishop Russell specified that the Lovings' attorneys would be emphasizing Fourteenth Amendment considerations, whereas the

NCCIJ would be emphasizing the First Amendment: "If your reflections lead you to believe this matter deserves your support, will you join in the amicus already being prepared; it is merely necessary to send Father Lewers written authorization to represent you."

Lewers, reporting back to Sisson in mid-January, observed that "perhaps" his "confidence in this matter springs from the fact that Justice Roger Traynor of the California Supreme Court, in striking down the California miscegenation statute, used, among other arguments, that which we are following."

Bishop Russell participated in August 1963 in the March on Washington for Jobs and Freedom. In 1967 he joined in a brief, as a friend of the court, in support of the effort by the Lovings' attorneys to dismantle miscegenation laws in all the states that continued to maintain such bans.

Briefs

The time had come for Hirschkop, Cohen, and the ACLU to prepare a written argument to convince the Court to invalidate the Virginia laws under which the Lovings had been indicted and convicted. Yet the power of miscegenation laws to affect interracial couples in the United States went far beyond the Virginia laws and far beyond the Lovings. The ACLU wished to secure a ruling from the Court broad enough to address the wider issues and invalidate every state's miscegenation laws.

Hirschkop and Cohen played important roles in crafting the ACLU brief in *Loving*, but they were not alone. For example, William D. Zabel wrote Arthur L. Berney at the Boston College Law School about his thoughts on how to proceed. The ACLU attorneys were in agreement that the Lovings' case should provide a vehicle for attacking all miscegenation laws. *McLaughlin* had produced only a narrow ruling, and Zabel warned, "We should not assume that the Court will try to avoid a narrow holding" in *Loving*. Zabel argued, however, against stressing the kind of sociological evidence that had been deployed in *Brown v. Board of Education*. In *Loving*, he said, "there is no separate but equal problem": "Two consenting, competent adults ought to have the right to marry regardless of race and there can be no separate but equal opportunity for them."

David Carliner commented years later that his name had been put on the ACLU brief even though he had had no specific involvement in the *Loving* case. Then again, he had done foundational work along these lines back during his involvement in the *Naim* case, not to mention he was also chair and founding member of the DC chapter of the ACLU, which had first taken up the *Loving* case.

The written arguments brought the two sides of the controversy into clear focus. Where the ACLU emphasized the Fourteenth Amendment as interpreted in *Brown v. Board of Education* and in *McLaughlin v. Florida*, the state of Virginia emphasized the doctrine in *Maynard v. Hill* that states had authority over the regulation of marriage. One side emphasized how far the Fourteenth Amendment could reach, the other the limited intent of its framers. One side recounted the history of privacy cases from the 1920s into the 1960s. The other spoke instead of an unbroken string of federal cases in which statutes banning interracial marriage had been upheld, including the 1940s case *Stevens v. United States*. Rejecting all such precedent, the ACLU brief reviewed the history of Virginia's miscegenation laws from the seventeenth century to the twentieth and characterized those statutes as "relics of slavery" and, at the same time, "expressions of modern day racism."

Revealing an interest in the question that went beyond black-white marriages and the law, the JACL also submitted a brief as a friend of the Court. Regardless of the number of people of Asian ancestry living in Virginia at the time the Lovings brought their case back to court, the Racial Integrity Act of 1924 made it clear that none was a viable candidate for a matrimonial alliance with any white Virginian. The JACL noted that there were 1,133 "Japanese" residents of Virginia according to the census of 1960, not such a big number, yet then again not small—even the four who lived in Caroline County had rights, too—but nearly eighteen thousand people of Japanese ethnicity lived in the seventeen states that continued to maintain miscegenation laws.

In Georgia and Virginia, ethnic Japanese people were "colored," in Texas and Oklahoma apparently "white," but not everyone could know with certainty elsewhere which they were, who they could or could not marry. As for Richard Loving, the JACL maintained that the state could in no way have proved that he had nothing but Caucasian ancestry, so he could be found guilty only because he confessed to a fact he could not know. Just on the basis of racial classifications' vagueness, inconsistency, and uncertainty, said the JACL, the statutes must be toppled as failing to meet the requirements of due process under the Fourteenth Amendment (the JACL stipulated other grounds as well). The JACL also wrote about citizens' constitutional right to move from one state to another.

The NAACP asserted regarding the unfinished legal business of the Civil Rights Movement: "Negroes cannot be considered to have obtained equal rights or to have gained full freedom as full-fledged citizens of the United States until they are free to make the individual decision as to whom they will marry without legislative interference or proscriptions based solely on the accident of their color." As for the contentiousness that the issue of interracial marriage generated among many Americans, the Constitution had to govern public policy: "Desegregation of the schools, housing, and public facilities, and freedom to vote are being required despite the violence of the opposition."

As an organization separate from the NAACP, the NAACP Legal Defense and Educational Fund—which was very much involved in the case when it reached the Supreme Court—homed in on the Virginia court's 1955 statement in *Naim v. Naim* that the 1924 law aimed to "preserve the racial integrity" of Virginia's white residents so there would be no "mongrel breed of citizens." In rebuttal, the NAACP argued that "there is no rational or scientific basis upon which a statutory prohibition against marriage based on race or color alone can be justified as furthering a valid legislative purpose." It noted that the Fund had "litigated a great many cases involving the civil rights of Negroes which have sought to eliminate racial segregation and discrimination," among them *McLaughlin v. Florida*. Making its major point, it stated: "We urge that racially discriminatory state laws are no longer only 'constitutionally suspect' ... and merely subject to 'rigid scrutiny.' ... The decisions which have invalidated every state segregation law or practice to come before this Court establish that there can be no justification for such laws and that they are all invalid *per se.*"

Finally, the Catholic brief —representing many Catholic bishops from the South, including Virginia's Bishop Russell, as well as the NCCIJ and other organizations—argued mostly from a freedom-of-religion stance premised on the theology of the Catholic Church regarding marriage, largely shared, it insisted, with Protestants and Jews. It took care to explore—and demolish—the relevance of *Maynard v. Hill*'s broad assertion of the primacy of legislatures in establishing the law of marriage. Then it attacked the conflation of polygamy and interracial marriage to reject the relevance of *Reynolds v. United States*, a nineteenth-century ruling by the Supreme Court that permitted states to ban Mormon plural marriage even though it was an "exercise of religion." It addressed the Supreme Court's having spoken to people's constitutional right to have children—legitimate children, the Catholic brief insisted. And of course it drew upon Justice Traynor's 1948 ruling in the California case *Perez v. Sharp*.

Oral Argument

In oral argument on April 10, 1967, the state of Virginia had the task of convincing the Court that miscegenation laws should continue to be left up to the states. Once again, a state mounted the old steed, the Tenth Amendment, to joust with its adversary, mounted on the Fourteenth. The Tenth Amendment, Virginia argued, and not the Fourteenth ought to govern marriage. But while *Maynard v. Hill*, which declared marriage to be subject to state legislation, could be trotted back out for another fray, its twin from the 1880s, *Pace v. Alabama*, had died three years before in *McLaughlin v. Florida*, and so was no longer available to assist. And talk about the need for racial purity sounded even less convincing in 1967 than it had in oral argument before the California Supreme Court in 1948.

Representing the state of Virginia, assistant attorney general R. D. McIlwaine did what he could in an arena that appeared inhospitable to previous conventional wisdom on race and marriage. Drawing in part from a book by Albert I. Gordon, *Intermarriage: Interfaith, Interracial, Interethnic*, published in 1964, he brought in the kind of sociological material that had been derided by opponents when the Court used it in *Brown*: "intermarried families are subjected to much greater pressures and problems than those that are intramarried." Chief Justice Warren was skeptical; for the past twelve years a daughter of his, raised a Protestant, had been married to a Jewish man, and he interrupted McIlwaine: "There are those who have the same feeling about interreligious marriages." Would you then, he asked, "prohibit people from having interreligious marriages?" McIlwaine tried to claim that the pressures were greater when the couple married across racial lines than when they crossed religious boundaries, and he tried to point toward the children in such families as the "victims" that the state was trying to protect. Hirschkop later exploded at the memory of this "immoral" posturing by the state, as if the purpose behind the Racial Integrity Act was more akin to a Children's Protection Law.

The ACLU lawyers argued, of course, that Virginia's miscegenation laws could not pass constitutional muster. Phil Hirschkop focused on the equal protection clause, Bernard Cohen on the due process clause. Hirschkop argued from the legislative history of the Virginia laws that their intent to secure the racial purity of the "white" race, and their intent to demean and control black Virginians, violated the Fourteenth Amendment. Cohen concentrated on the personal impact of the laws on the Lovings. He spoke of their "right" to marry, as he and they saw it, and their wish to live together in peace in Virginia. And he referred to their terror and humiliation at being dragged out of bed and off to jail for presuming to live as husband and wife.

Cohen summarized some of the civil penalties (quite aside from the criminal penalties) that automatically attached to the couple under Virginia's laws. "The Lovings have the right to go to sleep at night," he declared, "knowing that should they not awake in the morning their children would have the right to inherit from them, under intestacy [in the absence of a will leaving them their parents' property]. They have the right to be secure in knowing that if they go to sleep and do not wake in the morning, that one of them, a survivor of them, has the right to social security benefits." The "injustices" that necessarily followed from the Virginia law, Cohen argued, "amount to a denial of due process," for those rights were being arbitrarily denied to the Lovings.

Cohen highlighted his argument by conveying to the Court the words of Richard Loving: "Mr. Cohen, tell the Court I love my wife, and it is just unfair that I can't live with her in Virginia."

After oral argument had concluded, the two attorneys and their small entourage made their way out of the Supreme Court building. It was time for secretary Martha Lee to fetch the car, time to head back to the office in Alexandria. First, Phil Hirschkop would remember many years later, he "received a hug from my father on the steps of the Supreme Court."

Reporting on the oral argument for the *New York Times*, Fred Graham observed that most justices had participated in the back-and-forth between bench and attorneys and not a one of them seemed inclined to rule in favor of the Virginia statutes. That observation did not, however, give a clear picture of the Court's probable ruling: "A central issue in today's arguments was whether the Supreme Court could strike down the entire system of Virginia's antimiscegenation laws, or merely the criminal penalties invoked against the Lovings." Either way, the Lovings would win their freedom. But which kind of ruling came down would still make a great difference.

The Supreme Court Speaks

Soon after oral argument, William Lewers reported in to his fellow Catholic Mathew Ahmann:

> The arguments before the Court . . . last Monday went very well. I think that the only real question concerns the possible reach of the Court's decision when it comes. That is, will the Court strike down only those sections of the Virginia law declaring interracial marriages to be criminal, or will it also invalidate those sections declaring such marriages to be void?
>
> Also, I was glad to note that counsel for the Lovings used two arguments taken from our brief — the analyses of *Maynard v. Hill* and of *Reynolds v. US.*

As chief justice, Earl Warren assigned to himself the task of writing the Court's opinion in *Loving v. Virginia*. In the way that law clerks often do much of the actual drafting, however, Warren's clerk Benno Schmidt did so in the *Loving* case, with his boss's directions as to the reasoning (racial discrimination, the right to marry) and also some of the content (definitely include Judge Bazile's language about how God had created the separate races and wanted to keep them separate).

Warren was not new to issues related to the law of race and marriage. As state attorney general in California back in 1939, he had occasion to interpret the racial restrictions on marriage there. And in 1948 he was serving as governor when the California Supreme Court struck down that state's law against interracial marriages. Within three years of his appointment as chief justice, two cases regarding the constitutionality of laws against interracial marriage had come to the Court, and in each—one from Virginia, one from Alabama—he had been in the minority when the Court declined to hear the case and, perhaps, overturn the law that had given rise to it. As late as 1964, in *McLaughlin v. Florida*, though ruling in favor of an unmarried interracial couple, the Court had not been prepared to overturn laws against interracial marriage. Now he had the perfect case and the perfect occasion for ruling against them everywhere.

As for his brethren, the Warren Court had been relying on the equal protection clause to chop away at the edifice of Jim Crow all the way back to *Brown v. Board of Education*, with considerable preliminary work along those lines having been accomplished even before Warren came on the Court. Quite aside from race, the Warren Court had been attacking impediments to human freedom that state authorities often imposed, whether state failure to provide defense lawyers to indigent defendants or state laws restricting access to birth control even for married couples. *Loving v. Virginia* reflected both impulses.

A strong inclination among at least a majority of the justices did not, however, guarantee clear sailing in crafting a ruling to dispose of the case and dispatch the Virginia law of race and marriage. Hugo Black was hard-pressed to find a right of marriage in the Constitution. In any case, both he and Byron White thought the equal protection clause sufficed to reach the conclusion the chief justice was pointing toward. So why include the due process clause? Justice White thought he might just "concur in the result." Justice Black conceded that maybe he could support Warren's draft ruling if the due process section were divided from the equal protection section, and so it appears in the final version. Justice White's concerns led to a clearer statement than in the original draft as to how, given the lack of a constitutionally acceptable purpose in criminalizing interracial marriage, the state utterly failed to meet the demands of the equal protection clause.

The Court announced its ruling on June 12, four years after Mildred wrote Attorney General Kennedy and then Bernie Cohen, and nine years after the day trip to get married in DC, within a few miles of the Supreme Court building. Chief Justice Earl Warren declared in his opening sentence, as he began reading the decision that the Court had made—the opinion that he had authored—in *Loving v. Virginia*: "This case presents a constitutional question never [previously] addressed by this Court." At the same time as he was pointing up the novelty of the question, and of the position the Court was taking that day, the chief justice may have been apologizing for the Court's failure to address the question of interracial marriage at any of several earlier opportunities, including those three on his watch—*Jackson v. Alabama*, *Naim v. Naim*, and *McLaughlin v. Florida*.

He specified the question: did state laws against interracial marriage violate the equal protection clause and the due process clause of the Fourteenth Amendment? He did not reserve the punch line: indeed they did conflict with the Fourteenth Amendment, so they must fall. He then recounted the long journey the Lovings had taken, from their wedding nine years earlier to their triumph as he read the Court's unanimous ruling that day that their convictions could not stand. And he quoted Judge Bazile's language about how God had "created the [different] races" and wanted them not "to mix," though he misdated the trial judge's comments as if they came from the original trial in 1959 rather than the actual occasion, in 1965.

The chief justice quoted the statutory provisions in full that made it a crime for an interracial couple in Virginia to marry (if only one was "white"), not only inside the state but also outside of it if they planned to return to Virginia and live as a married couple there, as the Lovings had. He also supplied (in a lengthy footnote) the exact language that defined "white persons" and "colored persons" in Virginia. And he noted that the Lovings had never contested their being classified, one as "white" and the other as "colored," under those legal provisions—an approach sometimes taken by other interracial couples, who claimed both to be white or both nonwhite and therefore not subject to prosecution under the law. The Court mentioned the extraordinary antiquity of Virginia's law, and the fact that "penalties for miscegenation arose as an incident to slavery and have been common in Virginia since colonial times." But, he observed, "the present statutory scheme dates from the adoption of the Racial Integrity Act of 1924," whose key provisions he recounted. A footnote listed the laws of the fifteen other states, all in the South, that still had such laws as Virginia's, and it also listed the fourteen states that, in the previous two decades, had done away with their miscegenation laws, beginning with the California court ruling in 1948 and ending with Maryland's very recent legislative action, which had gone into effect just days before.

The chief justice reviewed the leading arguments that the state of Virginia had offered in its defense of its laws and of the charges against the Lovings, and he rebutted each in turn. The Virginia Supreme Court, whose ruling was under appeal in this case, had, as one of its arguments in support of the constitutionality of its miscegenation laws, reached for a ruling by that same court a decade earlier, *Naim v. Naim*, regarding a Chinese man and a white woman. The Virginia court had declared that the state's "legitimate purposes" in enacting, enforcing, and upholding such laws, as the Supreme Court now reported, "were 'to preserve the racial integrity of its citizens,' and to prevent 'the corruption of blood,' 'a mongrel breed of citizens,' and 'the obliteration of racial pride,' obviously [said Warren] an endorsement of the doctrine of White Supremacy." As the chief justice noted a little later, Virginia banned not all interracial marriages, but "only interracial marriages involving white persons." The Court went on, in a footnote, to assert, "we find the racial classifications in these statutes repugnant to the Fourteenth Amendment, even assuming an even-handed state purpose to protect the 'integrity' of all races." So neither white supremacy nor racial integrity passed muster as a defense of the Virginia laws.

Chief Justice Warren had seriously undercut the state's reliance on the Tenth Amendment to deflect arguments based on the Fourteenth. But such an argument still had to be addressed. The state of Virginia had drawn upon a Supreme Court ruling from 1888, *Maynard v. Hill*, in which the Court had baldly stated about marriage that, having "more to do with the morals and civilization of a people than any other institution," it "has always been subject to the control of the Legislature." The Court chided the state of Virginia for mounting such an argument in support of its laws of race and marriage: "While the state court is no doubt correct in asserting that marriage is a social relation subject to the State's police power, . . . the State does not contend in its argument before this court that its powers to regulate marriage are unlimited notwithstanding the commands of the Fourteenth Amendment. Nor could it do so," the chief justice went on, in view of some important cases from long before the 1960s, but long after the 1880s, including *Meyer v. Nebraska* (1923), in which the Court had spoken expressly of "the right . . . to marry."

The state also argued that the equal protection clause should be understood as reflecting an intent by the framers that, so long as punishments visited upon people, both black and white, were the same for violating a law such as Virginia's against interracial marriage, then the requirements of equal protection were satisfied. Indeed the Supreme Court had accepted that very argument in 1883 in *Pace v. Alabama*, a case that arose when a man classified as black and a woman classified as white had, upon conviction for living together without being married, suffered a more severe sentence than they would have had they both been white or both black. Judge Bazile, in writing his opinion in 1965 in support of the original outcome for the Lovings at trial six years before, had called upon a wide range of precedents that supported him, but he had ignored a 1964 ruling by the Supreme Court to the contrary, viewing it as no more legitimate than he had perceived *Brown v. Board of Education* from a decade earlier. That 1964 ruling Chief Justice Warren now trotted out, quoting from *McLaughlin v. Florida*: "*Pace* represents a limited view of the Equal Protection Clause which has not withstood analysis in subsequent decisions of this court."

Did the Fourteenth Amendment protect against "classifications drawn by any statute" that constituted "an arbitrary and invidious discrimination"? Yes, the Court had ruled in *McLaughlin v. Florida*, and yes, the Court ruled again in *Loving v. Virginia*. *Pace v. Alabama* helped the state's case no more than did *Maynard v. Hill*.

The equal protection clause sufficed to strike the Virginia laws and the Lovings' convictions. But their attorneys had also argued on the basis of the due process clause, and this portion of the Fourteenth Amendment the Court also considered. Doing so, the Court went back to *Maynard v. Hill*, one of the key props in the state's case. That long-ago case from 1888, which on its face had nothing to do with race, had spoken in very strong terms not only of legislative prerogative in the law of marriage but also of the supreme importance of marriage as an institution. So in the short final section on the due process clause, the chief justice spoke of "this fundamental freedom" and the miscegenation law's utter denial of "all the State's citizens of liberty without due process of law."

In short, though the Court did not use this precise language, Richard Loving had been denied, as a white man (not despite his being a white man so much as precisely because he was a white man), the right to marry Mildred Jeter, and she had been similarly deprived of the right to marry him. This deprivation, and their punishment for the crime of trying to be a married couple, constituted a denial of both "equal protection" and "due process of law."

So, the Court concluded: "These convictions must be reversed."

One lone justice, Potter Stewart, had yet to speak his mind. Not that he differed with his brethren as to whether the Court should overturn the Lovings' convictions, but he merely repeated his stark observation from three years earlier, in *McLaughlin v. Florida*: "it is simply not possible for a state law to be valid under our Constitution which makes the criminality of an act depend upon the race of the actor."

The chief justice would surely have preferred that the Court speak with one voice, but in this case all he seemed able to get was unanimity on the Lovings' convictions under a criminal law. Justice Potter Stewart had appeared to be going beyond most of the Court in *McLaughlin v. Florida* with this language, but by the time of the *Loving* ruling, it appeared he was unwilling to go as far as his brethren, a measure of how much had changed in three years. Justice Stewart appeared to be giving the narrow ruling that the proponents of a constitutional end to the antimiscegenation regime hoped for at a minimum; but had the Court ruled in accordance with the stance he took in his concurring opinion, the ACLU would have been disappointed, and much of the apparatus of the antimiscegenation regime might have remained in place.

Absent a criminal component, states might have persisted, as California long had, in simply denying marriage licenses to couples defined as interracial. *Loving v. Virginia* would have been far less a breakthrough ruling. Moreover, with such a limited decision, Virginia authorities would still not have recognized the Lovings' DC marriage.

Two young lawyers, the older of them thirty-three, had won the first case they ever argued at the Supreme Court of the United States, and what a case it was. It was time to try to reach the Lovings with the extraordinary news.

Catholics and the *Loving* Decision

In late 1969, Chang Moon Sohn, a lecturer at Hunter College in New York City working toward completion of a dissertation in political science at Columbia University, wrote to the NCCIJ's John P. Sisson with some questions. Sisson replied at length in terms that illuminate the role and perceptions of Catholics who involved themselves in the *Loving* litigation:

> Our intervention in the Loving case was for the most part a matter of my own interest. As a longtime member of ACLU I am somewhat oriented this way. The matter of family life has been a major stated concern of the Catholic Church, and certainly was affected by the miscegenation statutes.
>
> However, the amicus entry was anything but an easy matter [but rather] took about two years of persistence before the brief could be written, the various parties brought in to co-sign. . . .
>
> I finally felt it necessary to go back to Bishop Russell. He was then willing. After he agreed to enter the case we wrote the letter for him by which he invited other bishops to co-sign. This method of invitation is very much in keeping with Church practice. As resident bishop of the place where the action was going on, it was proper for him to invite the other bishops.
>
> By this time the "hearing" date was approaching and we wound up being very rushed. Given enough time, I think we could have induced all the bishops from the twenty-odd states which then had miscegenation statutes to join us. . . .
>
> Entering *Loving* set the stage for our going into the *Jones* housing case a year later, and joining the *Red Lion* fairness in broadcasting case. . . .
>
> I felt the whole program was valid as social action, since it involved Church leadership in a non-Church issue; it joined the official Church with an ACLU case probably for the first time; and it raised the issue of injustices in regard to mixed marriages with Church leadership and Catholics generally.
>
> Although some of our reasoning may have been used in the

decision reached by the court, I do not believe that our intervention played a decisive role in the decision; but the intervention was important to many people outside the court.

The Catholic participation was important in broadening the argument to include freedom of religion, a First Amendment approach, and to make it clear that large numbers of white Americans supported a change in the traditional laws of race, even in marriage. The Japanese-American participation was important in making clear that this was more than a black-white question, and that people who were neither white nor black, and who hailed from states great distances from Virginia, had a profound interest in the outcome of the Lovings' challenge to the Virginia statute. Whatever the state of public opinion in the years around 1870, or even as late as 1960, by the middle and late 1960s the times they were a-changing.

After the Court handed down its ruling, Bishop Russell wished to be clear that he was not promoting interracial marriage. He just believed there should be no law against such marriages. He wouldn't encourage people to marry across racial lines, he said, "any more than I would encourage people of different religions to marry." Given the Catholic opposition to marriages between Catholics and non-Catholics, this was no ringing endorsement of interracial marriage, but the point was to bring down the laws that prevented them. And *that* he had seen happen, had helped make happen. Church authority in matters of theology must be preserved, but secular laws in support of racism should be terminated.

A Virginia Editorial Endorses *Loving*

Ever since World War II, and especially during the 1960s, public opinion had been shifting in favor of interracial marriage, or rather becoming ever less hostile to such. Maryland's action in repealing its laws against interracial marriage, and thus breaking the Solid South, offered a strong example. This shift, demonstrated by the ever diminishing roster of states remaining true to the antimiscegenation regime, is one reason the Supreme Court could move as it did from the *McLaughlin* ruling in 1964 to *Loving* in 1967.

By 1967, though the state had stoutly defeated its antimiscegenation laws, many white Virginians could accept with equanimity a decision that would surely have ignited a firestorm in earlier years. Even in western Virginia, where the black population was generally much smaller than east of the Blue Ridge, the new constitutional order would be of vital significance to some couples. In an editorial response to the ruling, titled "Wedlock: A 'Fundamental Freedom,'" the *Roanoke Times* had this to say about the decision's tremendous historical significance:

When the infamous *Dred Scott* case was decided by the Supreme Court in 1857, Chief Justice Taney observed that the country's attitude toward Negroes was indicated by its laws against interracial marriage. Those laws, he concluded, put "a stigma of the deepest degradation upon the whole race." In part, the court used that evidence of public attitudes to justify its decision that Negroes could not be American citizens.

Before the ink was barely dry on the *Dred Scott* decision, the nation was caught up in a tragic Civil War that ultimately would reverse the Supreme Court's non-citizenship sentence for Negro Americans. But for more than 100 years, there remained the "stigma of the deepest degradation."

This week that stigma finally was shattered. Appropriately enough, it was the Supreme Court that again was called upon to right a [grievous] wrong that still symbolized second-class citizenship for over 20 million Americans. Twelve years ago [in an earlier case from Virginia, *Naim v. Naim*] the court declined to take such action, desperately seeking to prevent a further outbreak of racial antagonism in Old Confederacy states still reeling from the previous year's historical school desegregation decision. . . .

To most Americans, marriage between whites and Negroes will continue to be viewed as wrong. If only because of social inhibitions, intermarriage will not occur except in a small percentage of cases. But the legal obstacle to such marriages has been erased . . . and so too the "stigma of the deepest degradation." The sensitive issue of race and sex will remain dominant in Negro-white relations for the foreseeable future, of course. But a state-administered caste system has been laid to final rest. . . .

{ *Chapter 6* }

"The law," Mrs. Loving once said, "should allow [people] to marry anyone [they want]." Because of *Loving v. Virginia*, the law so allows.

Three Audiences

The Supreme Court had three audiences for its ruling against laws that prevented couples defined as interracial from getting married. First was the Lovings themselves. They wanted to have their marriage legally recognized. They sought an end to their liability for prosecution for publicly living together as husband and wife in Virginia. They yearned for an end to the enforcement of the terms of their plea bargain preventing their even visiting their families together back in Virginia.

At the same time, the Court's audience consisted of public authorities in all sixteen states in which antimiscegenation laws had persisted as late as the time of the ruling. In light of *Loving*, those officials no longer had the authority to enforce such laws, whether in denying marriage licenses to interracial couples, prosecuting married couples under a criminal statute against interracial marriage, or denying inheritance benefits on the basis that a marriage, because defined as interracial, had never been valid in that state.

The third audience was all of America, and indeed the world, with the opinion announcing that new rules of race and marriage were now in place — whereby African Americans might in every state be suitable marriage partners for Caucasians, and vice versa — and that the last wall in the edifice of American apartheid had been taken down.

But history did not end when the Court issued its ruling on *Loving*. The notion of a color-blind approach to public policy could point, as things soon turned out, in a very different direction as well: it could be deployed as an attack on affirmative action and other race-conscious policies designed to undo some of the effects of previous discrimination. Further ahead, the ruling's sweeping language about "the freedom to marry" would resonate into the twenty-first century, as in state after state, same-sex couples sought to have the language and logic of *Loving v. Virginia* about "equal protection" and "the freedom to marry" applied to them.

The more immediate impact of the landmark ruling in *Loving v. Virginia* can be traced in two central ways. One is by taking a series of glimpses at the post-*Loving* lives of the Lovings, the post-*Loving* careers of their attorneys, and ongoing changes in the Lovings' community in Caroline County, Virginia. The other tracks the consequences that flowed from *Loving v. Virginia* in the law of race and family across America, post-*Loving* shifts in family formation, and depictions of the Loving story, as well as other "interracial" stories, in films and other media.

CHAPTER 7

After *Loving*

The Lovings, Their Lawyers, and Caroline County

Nine years had passed since Mildred Jeter and Richard Loving drove from Central Point in Caroline County to the nation's capital to get married. Four years had passed since she wrote a letter to Robert Kennedy and then one to Bernard Cohen.

News of the Supreme Court's ruling reached Mildred and Richard Loving on Monday, June 12, 1967, ten days after they celebrated the ninth anniversary of their DC wedding. The couple made another drive north toward the nation's capital, this time not to get married, and not to find a new home in exile, but to greet their attorneys and be met by members of the broadcast media. In Alexandria, where Bernie Cohen kept his law office throughout those years, and where Phil Hirschkop had joined him, the couple sat for a picture. In it she exudes pleasure and relief, he a gruff satisfaction that he can wrap his arm around her in public and not fear being picked up for a crime against the state. She's not entirely comfortable with this public display of affection, but his expression reveals his fierce intent to be her husband.

In sharp contrast to the other of the two best-known photographs of the couple—one from yet another in their pre–Supreme Court series of losses in court, two and a half years earlier, that displayed their fury, their resignation, their despair—they sat this time in quiet triumph, satisfaction, relief, anticipation. Also in sharp contrast to the scene four years earlier, when Bernie Cohen had arranged to meet them at his office in DC—since they could not legally meet with him together in Virginia, whether in that same law office or elsewhere—they could go public to a national, even international, audience, having finally achieved victory in court.

The Court had heard Bernie Cohen recount what he said were Richard Loving's final words to him: "Mr. Cohen, tell the Court I love my wife, and it is just unfair that I can't live with her in Virginia." The justices thought they understood his love, and regardless they agreed that the couple's conviction and their exile were unfair—more to the point, unconstitutional. A unanimous Court had concluded that no couple, anywhere in America, should face such an experience as the Loving newlyweds had faced, charged with the crime of interracial marriage, the felony of living together as though they were married, in the face of a law that defined them as of different races and then, on that basis, prevented their legally marrying.

Beginning on June 12, 1967, Mr. and Mrs. Loving were free to live their lives and raise their children in eastern Caroline County. Mildred observed: "I feel free now." She expressed a realization of the hopes that had animated Annie Gray in her petition for freedom in 1808. She expressed, too, the hopes of the many thousands of slaves in Caroline County, before 1808 and for nearly another half-century. And she declared exactly what they might have said in 1865 when freedom finally came, in fact what former slave Louise Bowes Rose recalled in the 1930s about her father jumping in the creek and yelling with joy: "I'se free, I'se free! I'se free!"

As for Richard, he used more words than he often did: "We're just really overjoyed," he said. "My wife and I plan to go ahead and build a new house now." The three children would go to school in Caroline. The family could, if they wished, attend St. Stephen's Baptist Church on a regular basis. The couple could visit with their parents and siblings, and the children could spend time with their grandparents and cousins. They could be an American family, in Virginia, no matter their racial identities. Or at least in most respects they could.

Caroline County faded from view as the locus of a landmark constitutional law case. When in the news outside the area at all after 1967, the place might cross people's awareness because of a quadruped or two that became famous in the 1970s. Born in 1969 at Meadow Farm—near what is today King's Dominion, southeast of Ruther Glen, near the county's southern boundary—was Riva Ridge, winner of two of the horse racing world's Triple Crown races in 1972. Born on the same farm a year later, in March 1970, was Secretariat, a gorgeous reddish-brown horse that in 1973 completed the Triple Crown, setting a track record in the Kentucky Derby, another in the Preakness, and yet another in the Belmont Stakes.

Few horses win one of those races, let alone all three, but Secretariat punctuated the task in emphatic fashion, winning the third race by a reported thirty-one lengths.

Race and Schools in Caroline County

Like the law of race and marriage, the law of race and schooling underwent great change in the 1960s. Even in the 1960s, where the kids went to school in Caroline had a lot to do with their racial identities. For a time at least, even after the Caroline County schools began the process of desegregation, race would play a part in determining where local children, white and nonwhite, took their classes. The barest beginnings of desegregation in the county's schools took place in 1965, a mere premonition of the more robust version that came four years later. In the meantime, Sidney, the oldest, the darkest, would attend school with other people classified as nonwhite, wherever his younger brother and sister might go.

Caroline County held off for ten years after the second ruling in *Brown v. Board of Education*, the one in May 1955, before beginning to desegregate its public schools. As early as the 1965–1966 school year, a few Union High students transferred to white schools, and a few white teachers began teaching at Union. As a relatively new school in a central location, the old high school, when integration came in 1969, lost its identity but continued to be used, under the new name Bowling Green Senior High School. Then it became Caroline Middle School. For a time it was used for gym classes for Bowling Green Primary School as well as activities for the parks and recreation department. Finally, the school board turned it over to the county, and for years now it has been the Caroline County Community Services Center, including the Bowling Green Branch of the Caroline Library.

Like the white residents of Hanover County who established Hanover Academy, a number of their counterparts in Caroline established Caroline Academy. It began operations in 1969, at first in the basement of a parent's home. Two years later, its students — normally close to one hundred of them — were attending school in a new one-story, eight-classroom building on Route 207, at West Broaddus Street, in Bowling Green. Each year, it held commencement exercises that marked the conclusion of another successful year. Each year, the place seemed more settled as one resolution of tensions stemming from the social and cultural changes of the years since *Brown v. Board of Education.*

Students and teachers, black and white, all had their own ways of anticipating the end of the old system as "desegregation" approached. Walter E. Lowe, industrial arts teacher and assistant principal at Union High (and director of transportation and also of athletics), later explained that there were "too many principals" after the consolidation of black and white schools, so "they got rid of the Black principals"; and the Union High principal, George B. Ruffin, given a new position on the school board with "just a title" and "nothing to do," soon retired.

By contrast, Lowe—in part perhaps to prepare to become principal, but largely to prepare for whenever desegregation might come—earned a master's degree in 1967 at George Washington University and went on to complete a doctorate in education there in 1969. He recalled that the state of Virginia had helped with his expenses, under the 1936 act that paid for black Virginians to go out of state to take advanced degrees unavailable at black schools in Virginia: "After school, I would drive to DC and take classes in the evenings and drive back to Caroline County after class." When the decision finally came to end segregation in the Caroline County schools, "I contacted Virginia State College to see if they needed someone with my experience." He joined the faculty there as an associate professor of education, and his wife, guidance counselor Fraulein Coleman Lowe, left Union High as well to direct Virginia State's counseling center.

Union students celebrated completing their education at their old school or pointed toward what they felt they had lost, at least as often as they conveyed the sense that integration had been necessary even if painful. After two years at Union High, Beryl Jackson opted under "freedom of choice" to switch to Caroline High. She "wanted to prove a point that Blacks were just as smart as Whites," and she feared that "if the opportunity was not taken then desegregation might not happen." Yet she was "afraid for my physical safety," apprehensive about being "able to compete," and "sad because I was leaving my friends, the band, and people I had known all my life." She felt she was entering "the enemy's territory." On the one hand, she later stated, "I sacrificed my social life by attending Caroline High"; on the other, "We laid the groundwork for the entire school system to be integrated without violence."

Arthur Sizer attended Union for the eighth and ninth grades; then desegregation came and he was assigned to Ladysmith for his final three years, "but my heart belongs to Union High." Catherine Ferguson, who remained at Union and graduated in 1969, years later wrote: "We knew integration was coming," and "We were so happy we would get to graduate before the end of Union High. We call ourselves 'The Last of the Best.' The baccalaureate service was very emotional. That . . . was the end of Union High, and we were the last graduating class."

Many black residents mourned the end of Union High School, but they did not leave it at that. Dr. Walter Lowe surfaced again, years after his transition out of Union High and onto the faculty of Virginia State College. Retired and living again in Caroline, he had become the Mattaponi District representative on the school board, and in 1995 he initiated a successful effort to have a historical marker placed at the old Union High School building. The board of supervisors was also persuaded to add the words on the sign at the building "Formerly Union High School," as it had been for forty years. Moreover, displayed on the walls inside the main entrance is a collage of memorabilia from the Union High School days, including student photos and sports trophies. In contrast to many black high schools after the end of segregation, not only did the black high school go on to serve for a time as an integrated high school, but its history did not vanish in subsequent years.

A new high school, Caroline High, southwest of Bowling Green, opened in 1974 with students both white and nonwhite. Its first four-year graduates, finishing in 1978, included the two younger Loving children, Donald and Peggy. They reflected the senior class generally, among whom 38 percent planned to continue their studies, with 14 percent receiving a total of $5,200 in scholarships. There were three $100 Bits o' Wood scholarships, and one went to Peggy, who was also one of the three graduates planning to attend Rappahannock Community College, where she expected to pursue secretarial studies.

As for Sidney, he had dropped out of school after the eighth grade and then, at age eighteen, had gone into the military for a hitch. His schooling had been disrupted by the changes of venue in the years after he turned six in 1963, and he moved on after he turned sixteen, as many rural kids did in the 1950s and 1960s.

As for the Caroline Academy, in 1985 it closed its doors. It had worked to address the concerns of local white parents and their children during a transitional period after desegregation began, but diminishing enrollment made it less and less viable. White residents of Caroline County had made some accommodation with desegregation or had made other arrangements. Students who would have been starting classes at the academy in the late summer of 1985 would instead, according to a news account, be attending the local public schools, unless they went to Fredericksburg—or they would join the students already enrolled at Hanover Academy or, as the news report had it, the Grymes Memorial School in Orange. The classroom building that had opened with such hopes and amid much consternation among many in the white community eventually supplied a home for the county's parks and recreation department and then, later, its public utilities department.

After *Loving v. Virginia:* The Lovings' Attorneys

What about the Lovings' attorneys in the years after *Loving?* Bernie Cohen had political aspirations as well as a sense of professional opportunity and responsibility. In 1967, the very year of the *Loving* decision, he was selected chairman of the Alexandria Democratic City Committee and president of the Northern Virginia Trial Lawyers Association. He coauthored a book in 1971, *Environmental Rights and Remedies.* He took a case to court, and won, against excessive nighttime noise at Washington National Airport. And in 1979, the voters of his district sent him to the Virginia House of Delegates, where he served for eight two-year terms before deciding not to run yet again for reelection. In addition, he served on the Virginia Code Commission for several years until 2000. His name recognition from the *Loving* case may well have brought him votes, though in much of the state the memory of that lengthy court fight would no doubt have done him in.

Cohen jumped right into proposing legislation, much of it controversial, yet much of it successful. One of these initiatives, one that, emerging piecemeal, stretched over several legislative terms, called for enhanced 911 mailing addresses, so that emergency vehicles could more readily identify where they were needed in rural areas—such as Mrs. Loving's street address, 18146 Passing Road.

One failed initiative would have decriminalized sodomy (it passed in the House of Delegates but not the Senate); not until several years after he left politics did the Supreme Court rule against the enforcement of such laws against anyone anywhere. Another effort, one whose failure he particularly regrets, would have repealed a law according to which, in personal liability suits, any contributing negligence was a bar to recovery and replaced it with a contrasting approach, the "comparative negligence" rule, a change opposed by insurance companies, he notes, but one that has gone into effect in most American states, though not Virginia.

Looking back on his legislative career, Cohen takes the greatest satisfaction from seeing enacted—it goes by several names—the right to die, the living will, a new legal environment designed to allow "death with dignity" for terminally ill people in Virginia. Another law came directly out of his law practice. Grandparents who wished to be able to visit their dead son's children, but were barred from doing so by the son's widow, had come to Cohen for help, and he sponsored a new law to protect child visitation rights for grandparents and other family members. He sees the successful sponsorship of that bill in his very first term in the legislature as having also bolstered support across the political spectrum in his bids for reelection to the House of Delegates.

So by the time Cohen left the state legislature in 1995, he could look back with pride on legislation he had sponsored and, often, seen enacted. At one point he had considered running for the Virginia Senate, when the incumbent retired, but his decision not to run hinged on his realization that if he moved over to the Senate he would lose his seniority, so he stayed in the House until his own retirement.

Phil Hirschkop took a great many cases during the five decades following his completion of law school in 1964, but he would always remember with fondness and pride and gratitude several from the early years, one of them, of course, *Loving v. Virginia*, into which he had poured so much energy and conviction and creativity in the years between 1964 and 1967. But there were many others of considerable significance, too. He continued to maintain a highly visible presence in the legal arena, and he kept pushing back the legal boundaries he encountered, including in the law of family.

Four months after the Supreme Court decided *Loving,* Hirschkop was still operating out of Alexandria, when the writer Norman Mailer got himself arrested at the great protest march on the Pentagon in October 1967. The Pentagon is actually in Virginia, so Mailer found himself in a makeshift Virginia courtroom, where Hirschkop, who was handling scores, perhaps hundreds, of cases, stepped in to assist Mailer, who had just been sentenced to thirty days in jail, all but five of them suspended. Mailer himself wrote an account in *The Armies of the Night: History as a Novel, the Novel as History* of his lawyer's drive, quickness, and humor: "Hirschkop fought the case for the next twenty minutes as if the hill before him might determine the outcome of the war." His "dark hair and powerful short body put double weight back of every remark. He spoke quickly, clearly, with a mixture of brightness, boyishness, and driving determination." Mailer went on to describe what he perceived as Hirschkop's "love of law as an intricate deceptive smashing driving tricky game somewhere between wrestling, football, and philosophy—what also stood out was his love of winning, his tenacity, his detestation of defeat."

Having earlier worked on the defense of black demonstrators in Danville, Virginia, he subsequently participated in the defense of the "DC Nine," a group who had protested the Vietnam War by destroying property of Dow Chemical Company, which produced napalm for use in the war.

Two years after *Loving,* Hirschkop got involved in a challenge to female exclusion from the University of Virginia's College of Arts and Sciences. The institution had been moving in the late 1960s toward some greater inclusion of female students as undergraduates, but some prospective students lost patience with the slow pace; they needed action on their own applications sooner. Four, having applied and been turned down, went to court. All four lived at the time in Charlottesville and wished to attend college—a state-supported school, and Virginia's most prestigious institution of higher education at that—without having to go elsewhere. Each approached the ACLU in spring 1969 requesting help, and the ACLU filed a class action suit, with a hearing set for September.

By this time, in the immediate aftermath of the victory in *Loving,* a number of Virginia attorneys had established the American Civil Liberties Union of Virginia, thus a state affiliate. ACLU lawyer John C. Lowe, himself a recent graduate of the university's law school, pressed for an injunction that would permit the four to enroll for the fall semester rather than wait an additional year. At the US District Court for the Eastern District of Virginia, Judge Robert R. Merhige Jr. granted the injunction, and all four did enroll, although only Virginia Anne Scott did so in the College of Arts and Sciences and as a full-time student. Neither the daughter of a faculty member nor the wife of a graduate student, she was the first female to take classes who would not have met the institution's previous, narrowly tailored criteria. Meanwhile, ACLU attorneys John Lowe and Phil Hirschkop pursued the class action case, *Kirstein v. Rector and Visitors of the University of Virginia*. At the September hearing, the court directed the university to come up with a plan to admit students without regard to gender; and its governing board adopted a multistep plan calling for full coeducation by 1972.

Another case in which Hirschkop played a lead role had to do with the professional and financial opportunities of public school teachers, women who became pregnant. Continuing to work with the ACLU, and continuing also to operate out of Alexandria, he found himself involved in a case that came out of Chesterfield County, a rural and suburban area adjacent to the city of Richmond. There the school board required that every woman teacher who became pregnant let the board know six months before the expected birth of her child and quit work at least four months before the projected date of the blessed event. The board also stipulated conditions for her return to work afterward.

Mrs. Susan Cohen, described as an "excellent" teacher in her third year with the district, eventually balked at the terms of her forced maternity leave. She dutifully informed the board in the fall of 1971 that she expected a child around April 28 the next spring. She asked at the same time that she be allowed to teach until the first of April, and the board said no. Then she asked to be permitted to teach until January 21, the end of the school year's first semester, and the board said no again, requiring her to quit as of December 18, the end of school before the Christmas holidays. Represented by the ACLU, and by Phil Hirschkop in particular, she took her objection to federal court, claiming that the school board policy "discriminates against her as a woman," in violation of her right to equal protection under the law, in that "it treats pregnancy differently than other medical disabilities."

Judge Merhige concluded that the school board's terms of enforced maternity leave violated the equal protection clause of the Fourteenth Amendment. So, in *Cohen v. Chesterfield County School Board*, ruling in favor of Mrs. Cohen, he directed that she be paid the salary she would have earned had she been permitted to teach through the end of March, as she had requested. He drew in part on the Supreme Court's 1964 antimiscegenation ruling in *McLaughlin v. Florida*, the prelude to *Loving v. Virginia*, to characterize a policy of the sort that the school board had followed as—unless serving a "rational purpose," which he denied —"arbitrary and invidiously discriminating."

But the Fourth Circuit Court of Appeals, in a 4–3 split decision, reversed the district court's ruling. Meanwhile, a similar case out of Cleveland, Ohio, followed that pattern in reverse, as the district court ruled in favor of the local school board but the appeals court reversed that ruling and sided with the two teachers who had brought the case. Each case was, again, appealed. Seeing an issue that ought to be addressed, to bring the two circuits—and indeed the entire nation—into alignment, the Supreme Court agreed to hear the two cases. Hirschkop made his way back to the Supreme Court to argue the case.

A 7–2 Supreme Court majority, in *Cleveland Board of Education v. LaFleur* and its companion case, *Cohen v. Chesterfield County School Board*, ruled in favor of Susan Cohen and the two women from Ohio on their forced maternity leave. It did so in part on the basis of *Loving v. Virginia*, and in part on the basis of the string of privacy cases from the 1920s through the 1960s that had helped the Court rule as it did in *Loving*. Like *Loving* in June 1967, the ruling in the Cohen case in January 1974 reached across the nation.

A piece done on him in 1986, titled "Hirschkop the Horrible: A '60s Lawyer in the '80s" and highlighting his fearless and outrageous approach to serving his clients, spoke of him as "a pugnacious and contentious litigator." He has his gentle and soft-spoken side, but in the legal arena it is something he generally keeps under wraps.

Phil Hirschkop and Bernie Cohen parted ways a few years after completing their work together on *Loving*. The split was partly routine, partly a matter of temperament, partly the result of a movie script. Phil does not tend to work well for long periods in harness with partners. But a tremendous rift took place decades later, in the aftermath of the movie *Mr. and Mrs. Loving*, released in 1996. Among the liberties taken with the facts, the movie depicted Mr. Cohen as the Lovings' sole attorney.

Not only did Mr. Hirschkop take exception to his being ignored in this highly visible account of a major episode in his career and in modern American history, but he sometimes took the position that in fact he, not Bernie Cohen, had turned out to be the lead attorney in the case. He pointed, for example, to his role at the US Supreme Court, where he had gone first and brought the equal protection argument. And in fact it was his key contribution early on, after he came into the story in summer 1964, to redirect the case into the federal courts. Both men, of course, even if in differing ways, had been crucial to the outcome in 1967. Cohen was regretful at the turn of events, Hirschkop furious.

After *Loving v. Virginia*: Key Public Figures in Caroline County Affairs

During those years, a number of important people in the story of the Lovings and Caroline County died. Circuit court Judge Leon M. Bazile died even before the US Supreme Court ruled against him in 1967. The long and happy retirement that well-wishers held out to him in late 1965 had not come his way. He did not recover from the illness that forced his retirement, but rather died in March 1967, at the age of seventy-six, just weeks before the ruling he had rendered about God and interracial marriage, early in the year before his retirement, faced oral argument in the highest court in the land. So he did not live to see the Court hand down its decision in *Loving v. Virginia*. Time had already passed him by. He slipped away, as did the worldview he reflected, embodied, and sought to keep intact and in power.

A prominent obituary, in the *Fredericksburg Free Lance-Star*, noted that this "gentle, scholarly man" had not lived to complete his history of Hanover County. That account did not mention the case of the Lovings, but it did take note of Judge Bazile's response to *Brown v. Board of Education*: "He was a leading judicial foe of the U.S. Supreme Court's 1954 school desegregation decision, and when it became apparent racial bars would be lifted he was among the first to call for repeal of the state's compulsory school attendance laws." His wife, who lived until October 1970, left a daughter, a granddaughter, and a great-granddaughter.

William A. Vaughan died June 24, 1987, at the age of ninety-one, after a brief illness. He had had nearly a quarter-century of retirement after stepping down as superintendent of public schools in Caroline County, a position he filled from 1921 to 1963. He outlived his wife by three months, and the couple left a son, a daughter, seven grandchildren, and two great-grandchildren. The county's schools were fully segregated throughout his tenure as superintendent, and he had stepped down at almost the very moment Mildred Loving wrote her letter to Bobby Kennedy in a quest for permission to return to her native county. Vaughan, also a native of Caroline County but a child of the nineteenth century, lived long enough to see both the state's law against interracial marriage struck down and the county's schools desegregated.

The Loving and Jeter Families

Much closer to home, various members of the Loving and Jeter families died. These included Mildred's father, Theoliver Jeter, who passed away in his eighties in 1968, the year after his daughter was able at last to return permanently to Caroline County. His wife Musiel, much younger than he, married Stanley Parker in 1973.

Some of the photographs that *Life* magazine photographer Grey Villet took while the Loving case was in the courts showed a relaxed and happy couple off for a night out in what passed for the bright lights of Bowling Green (or Fredricksburg, perhaps, or Richmond). The pictures show a relaxed and happy couple. A decade later, on the last weekend in June 1975, the couple went out to Bowling Green one evening, together with Mildred's sister Garnett. At around midnight they all climbed into the car and headed back to Central Point. They turned east off US 301 and were driving down Route 721 when a car at the intersection of Route 627 on the right, as Mildred later put it, "jumped a stop sign" and slammed into them. Actually, the state police description that the other car had "passed through" the stop sign came nearer the mark. The side road comes in at an angle—heading west more than north—and the collision was more head-on, angled somewhat at the Lovings' right front fender, with Richard crushed by the steering wheel and Mildred hitting her head on the windshield.

In that one horrific, relentless moment, Richard died at the scene. Mildred suffered cuts to the face and lost an eye. She and Garnett were both treated at the Richmond hospital of the Medical College of Virginia. Mildred returned to the family's home, devastated by the loss of her beloved Richard.

The local story, in the *Caroline Progress*, gave surprisingly little detail about the accident, but news stories in other papers gave the other driver's name as Floyd Goldman and reported that he had been charged with drunken driving and manslaughter. Goldman was a Caroline County resident, a thirty-something black man. At trial, he pled guilty to the misdemeanor charge of drunk driving, for which he paid a fine of $800, had his license revoked for a year, and was sentenced to jail in Bowling Green for thirty days, though the jail time was suspended. On a felony charge of involuntary manslaughter, again he pled guilty. For that offense, the judge sentenced him to three years in the state penitentiary and suspended the prison time as well. Goldman paid court costs.

Bernie Cohen came back into the picture as Mildred Loving's attorney. He filed a civil suit of wrongful death on behalf of her and the three children, and a settlement in 1976 provided a small pot of money, though it hardly replaced Richard's income potential, let alone his presence in their lives. Each of the three children would receive a share upon turning age eighteen. Cohen had to go back into court afterward to make one change, however, because the three children had all appeared in the suit with the last name Loving, but Sidney went by his birth name, with the last name Jeter.

In addition to Mildred and the three children, Richard left both of his parents as well as his two older sisters, Mrs. Ethel Benninghove of Richmond and Mrs. Margaret Cropper of Caroline County. Richard was buried at the cemetery of St. Stephen's Baptist Church, not far from their home, the church that so many people of color in Caroline County had long called their own. His gravestone was very near that of Mildred's father, who had died seven years before.

So when Peggy and Donald graduated from high school, their dad had already been dead for nearly three years. His three children had been teenagers when he died, Mildred in her thirties. He and Mildred had been married in the eyes of officialdom in their native state for less time, after the Supreme Court ruled in their favor, than they had previously been married according to them and the DC authorities. Mildred had Richard always in her thoughts. "He was my rock," she told one interviewer.

"I married the only man I had ever loved," she once told historian and former neighbor Robert Pratt, "and I'm happy for the time we had together." At another time, she told him, "A lot of my memories are tied to the month of June," and she listed them: "We were married on June 2; the Court decision came on June 12; and Richard was killed on June 29." She never did remarry.

The Three Kids

In the early 1980s, in quick succession, each of the three children married, and they did so according to age and birth order, with Sidney first, Donald next, and Peggy last. Their marriage certificates tell a bit about how they described themselves and what they had been doing in recent years. All three were living in Caroline County. In September 1982, twenty-five-year-old Sidney married eighteen-year-old Lorinda Williams, a recent high school graduate from King George County, north across the Rappahannock River from Caroline. She was identified as "Negro." In April 1983, twenty-four-year-old Donald married Kathryn Anderson, a twenty-two-year-old native of Florida who had grown up in Fredericksburg and was a bookkeeper there whose mother was a long-time editor at the city's newspaper, the *Free Lance-Star*. Kathi was listed as "white." And in June 1983, twenty-three-year-old Peggy — who had gone on to complete two years of community college — married twenty-three-year-old Bruce Fortune. He identified himself as "Indian." Donald's was a civil ceremony, but Baptist minister Christopher C. Lee officiated at the weddings of Sidney and Peggy.

All three of the Loving children identified themselves as "Indian," and one had married a "white" person, one an "Indian," and one a "Negro." They had married the rainbow of possibilities in Caroline County.

In this post-*Loving* world, each could act according to what their mother had said back in January 1965 when all three were young children, "The law should allow a person to marry anyone he wants." Also in a post-*Loving* world, each was free to select a racial identity, rather than have a catchall state-mandated "colored" tag thrust upon him or her.

Peggy would say some years later about her parents' case, "Their struggle gave me the opportunity to marry who I wanted." Speaking not only of her own life but of the far broader effect as well, she said: "I believe that's what they were put here on earth to do." The Supreme Court ruling in the case that Mildred and Richard Loving had brought made all this possible. It ended the couple's banishment, permitting them to live together, out in public, in Virginia, and free from harassment by the law, the law of race and marriage. It brought their children back to Caroline to live their lives there and marry whomever they wished, as a private matter, unencumbered by the law.

More Funerals

In the 1980s, Richard's parents died. Born much later than Mildred's father, they lived nearly another two decades. Their obituaries suggested that they had not been, or were not seen as, maintaining a close relationship with their deceased son's widow. Unlike their son, moreover, they were buried in a white cemetery. Lola Jane Loving died at the age of seventy-five on August 8, 1985. She was buried in the town of Hustle, a few miles east of Central Point, in Essex County, at the Bethlehem Baptist Church cemetery. Her obituary spoke of her survivors as her husband, Twillie Loving; two brothers and two sisters, all of them named; and "five grandchildren and three great-grandchildren," none of them named, nor her grandchildren's mother, Lola Jane's daughter-in-law, Mildred Loving.

Twillie Loving died two years later, at the age of eighty-one. It was one thing for him to be the one who buried a spouse, but years earlier the couple had buried their son, and that never seems right. He, like his wife, was buried at the Bethlehem Baptist Church in Hustle. He left a sister, Mrs. Elizabeth Lett; his two widowed daughters, Ethel and Margaret; and "five grandchildren and three great-grandchildren." His obituary, like his wife's, failed to mention the names of any of the grandchildren, or the name of his daughter-in-law, Mildred Loving, the widow of his son Richard. Pallbearers included neither of Mildred's sons.

Members of Mildred's immediate family, quite aside from her in-laws, left her as well. Her mother, Musiel Byrd Jeter Parker, died in May 1997, at the age of eighty-six, and was laid to rest at St. Stephen's Baptist Church. Three months later, Mildred's beloved sister Garnett—Susie Garnett Hill—died of cancer at the age of fifty-nine. A member of St. Stephen's Baptist Church, she too was buried in its cemetery, after a ceremony at which Rev. William Gibson presided. Aside from her sister Mildred, Garnett left four brothers—James, Richard, Douglas, and Lewis—and two sons, Jerrell, who still lived in Caroline County, and Warren, who lived in Texas. Garnett's passing left Mildred alone, more than ever before, bereft of the people who, for all her life or at least most of it, had been central to her emotional well-being. The house across the road from hers, the place that had often been her refuge, was empty.

Then suddenly Donald died, too, at the end of August 2000. Surviving him were his wife, Kathi, and his young son, Donald Jr. Much as his father had died at forty-one, leaving a wife and three teenaged children, Donald died at forty-one, leaving a teenaged son. Donald Sr.'s gravesite, at St. Stephen's Baptist Church, is very near that of his parents.

———

Family

Difficult as it often continued to be, life went on for Mildred's family. Even as older members peeled off, new arrivals took their places. The house that Richard built, albeit years later than he had wanted to, remained the center of the family's collective life. Mildred cooked up the meals, and the extended family came together, especially on Sunday afternoons. Each of her three children had at least one child, and then those grandchildren grew up and began having their own children. Mildred's children might not remain married, but Peggy's ex remained part of the family, as did Sidney's, and Donald's widow certainly did as well.

Four generations came together on a frequent basis. Mildred's parents were no longer among them, but as she grew older she had more and more grandchildren and even great-grandchildren.

Close to all of them, she had an even greater emotional bond with some. Peggy's son Mark Loving spent much of his babyhood with his grandmother, and the two had a particularly special relationship. The white cinderblock house remained her sanctuary, the physical space where she felt very much at home, whatever the challenges she faced. When parents bury a child, when a thirty-something woman buries the love of her life, heartbreak can overwhelm. But Mildred had never demanded guarantees. She had insisted that arbitrary obstacles not be placed in the way of her carrying through on her sweet, ferocious commitment to her family. She wrote a letter, she and Richard found a lawyer, and then another, and together they took a case to the US Supreme Court and won her family's freedom. She had her faith, and she had kept that faith.

CHAPTER 8

After *Loving*

Race and Family in America

Loving v. Virginia transformed the law of race and marriage across America. The case and the story also helped reshape family patterns and popular culture.

Although the Supreme Court's decision in *Loving* did nothing to change the law within thirty-four of the fifty states, even there it had an enormous impact in changing the situation families found themselves in. Mixed-race families whose marriages would be illegal under other states' laws had every right to change their residence and move to a new state, except that—until *Loving*—their very family might come under challenge. The Calma family discovered this potential challenge in Virginia during the time the Lovings were living in exile. After *Loving*, Patsy Takemoto Mink, a woman of Japanese ancestry elected to Congress for the first of many terms from Hawaii in 1964, could legally move with her Caucasian husband across the Potomac River into Virginia if they chose.

Thurgood Marshall, who argued *Brown v. Board of Education* and many other civil rights cases before the US Supreme Court, and then himself became (shortly after the *Loving* decision) the first African American appointed to the Court, offers a more complex example of the old and new laws of marriage at work. His first wife, who was also African American, had died. In 1955, he was living in New York, and working at the national headquarters of the NAACP, when he married Cecilia Suyat, a Hawaiian-born Filipina, thus a "Malay" in Judge Bazile's world of five "separate" races. New York had no law against any interracial marriage, but when the Marshalls moved to the nation's capital in 1965, so he could take up the post of US solicitor general, they could not live in his native Maryland, which banned any of *three* racial groups from marrying each other: Caucasian, African American, or Malay. They could have lived in Virginia, a state whose laws lumped all non-Caucasians together as "people of color" who could marry freely within that category, but they lived for three years in Washington, DC, which had no restrictions whatever. By the time they moved out of the District in 1968, it could have been to Maryland, but they moved instead into Virginia. Their racial identities for purposes of marriage no longer mattered anywhere.

Yet the transformation in the law did not necessarily translate into transformed behavior by individuals. One way to calibrate this dimension of limited change is to look at the nation's two most populous states, New York, which had never had a miscegenation law, and California, where the law against black-white and Asian-Caucasian marriage had been struck down by the state supreme court in 1948. Black-white and other "interracial" marriages had never been numerous in New York, and after 1948 they had not become particularly frequent in California.

So the impact of *Loving* can be measured in these two very different ways. Yet these are not the only ways, since over time the culture's center of gravity shifted, even substantially. Major movies dramatized race, love, sex, and marriage in America. Historians explored the American past and developed a fuller sense of what the American landscape of race, marriage, and law had looked like at different times and places. Novelists developed stories built around fictional characters in the past or the present. Moreover, people wrote nonfiction books about their own families as the product of interracial connections, whether over recent decades or over the centuries. Examples are Neil Henry, *Pearl's Secret: A Black Man's Search for His White Family* (2001), and James McBride, *The Color of Water: A Black Man's Tribute to His White Mother* (1996).

These genres merged in degree when people combined these roles. Often, for example, it was people in "mixed" marriages or products of "mixed" families who wrote nonfiction works about the operations of the color line (or color lines) and of efforts to surmount it (or them). An example along these lines of authors who explain what drew them to their nonfiction work about other people is Renee C. Romano, *Race Mixing: Black-White Marriage in Postwar America* (2003).

Loving and the Law of Marriage

Loving had no impact on whether couples could marry—and then live together as a married couple—in states that did not have such laws as Virginia's, regardless of whether those other states had never had such laws, as in Vermont or New York, to take two examples, or had abandoned them at some point before 1967, as had happened everywhere else outside the South. In sixteen states, it made a big difference, though mop-up work in the courts might be required. In some of those states, change came very soon. In other states, obtaining compliance took longer.

In a number of cases already in state or federal court at the time of the ruling, the decision in *Loving v. Virginia* quickly determined the outcome, in a way directly opposite to what would have likely emerged in the absence of *Loving*. One, *Davis v. Gately*, had been brought in federal court by an interracial Delaware couple—William Wesley Davis and Sandra Jean Drummond—who had been denied a marriage license in March 1967. On June 26, 1967, the court ruled in favor of the couple, basing the verdict on the *Loving* decision from two weeks earlier:

> Any issue as to the violation of the prohibitions of the Fourteenth Amendment [by Delaware's law of race and marriage] is settled beyond question and in the plaintiffs' favor by the decision of the Supreme Court in *Loving*. . . .
>
> A fundamental civil right, the right to marry, is here involved. . . .
>
> The thrust of the Virginia statutes at issue in *Loving* and that of the Delaware statutes . . . is to prohibit marriage and its consummation on the grounds of race alone. The ruling of the Supreme Court clears the board of all racial barriers to marriage. . . .
>
> Since the decision in *Loving* no substantial constitutional question remains for determination. . . .
>
> The defendant will be perpetually enjoined from refusing on racial grounds to issue a marriage license to the plaintiffs.

In Oklahoma, the *Loving* decision was applied in an inheritance case, *Dick v. Reaves*, in which a person's right to inherit property on the basis of a marriage had been contested. The challenger insisted that the marriage was invalid because it had been between a "person of African descent" and a Native American, someone "not of African descent" and thus "white" under Oklahoma law. The Oklahoma Supreme Court handed down its decision on July 11, 1967, within a month after *Loving*. "In accordance with this clear mandate of the Supreme Court of the United States, we . . . expressly overrule all prior decisions of this Court to the contrary." Therefore, it continued, "the marriage of Martin Dick and Nicey Noel Dick was valid, regardless of the racial ancestry of either party to the marriage."

New cases arose as well. The armed forces are always moving personnel around, and thus local authorities' insistence on traditional ways of sorting out acceptable marriage partners could complicate day-to-day questions of national security. In Alabama, Army Sgt. Louis Voyer, a Vietnam veteran from Massachusetts who was stationed at Fort Mc-Clellan, and his black Alabama-born fiancée, Phyllis Bett, went to get a marriage license in Calhoun County in November 1970 but got turned back. So the federal government, during the presidency of Richard M. Nixon, found that it had to go into federal court in Alabama to get local officials to come into line behind the *Loving* decision, which dated back three and a half years.

The Justice Department—in the person of Attorney General John M. Mitchell, holding the office that Bobby Kennedy had been filling when Mildred Loving wrote him back in 1963—went to court to have the Alabama statute, as well as the provision in the state constitution to the same effect, struck down. Representing the Alabama attorney general's office, John Bookout put up a defense. True, he conceded, the Supreme Court had ruled the way it did in *Loving*, but what did that have to do with Alabama? "The Alabama law is still law until it is stricken down. They don't just wipe these laws off the book all over the United States because of one ruling."

US District Judge Sam C. Pointer promptly obliged both parties—this was exactly four weeks after the failed effort to get the license—and struck down the Alabama law, in *United States v. Brittain*. As he declared, while also citing *Davis v. Gately*: "The matter indeed is so clear since the *Loving* case that no substantial question remains on the question of constitutionality, and therefore it is not necessary to travel the route of a three judge panel."

The state attorney general's office had acted much as it, and its counterparts across the former Confederacy, had with regard to *Brown v. Board of Education*: sue every place you want compliance, the new law there is not yet good here. In the end, Sgt. Voyer and Miss Bett could get married. Despite the promise implicit in Bookout's defense, however, as to what would happen if he lost the case, the miscegenation provision in Alabama's state constitution remained on the books until the end of the twentieth century.

The ability of two people to enter into a lawful marriage, no matter their racial identities, had been established. The federal rulings in the Delaware and Alabama cases exemplified the way that, though further work might be required in some places, interracial couples would soon be able to marry and live in any state. The state court's ruling in the Oklahoma case offered another reminder that ancillary issues, in that case inheritance, had always been part of the legal controversy and social significance swirling about miscegenation laws and their enforcement. A later case, *Sidoti v. Palmore* (1984), which, like *Loving*, went to the Supreme Court, addressed child custody.

A white couple, Linda Sidoti and Anthony Sidoti, got divorced in Florida in 1980, and she obtained custody of their three-year-old daughter, Melanie. Then, though, she married Clarence Palmore Jr., an African American, and her husband filed for custody. He won at trial, when the court ruled that Linda Palmore had "chosen for herself and for her child . . . a life-style unacceptable to the father and to society." She did not give up, and the US Supreme Court agreed to hear her appeal.

Chief Justice Warren Burger wrote for a unanimous Court. After observing that issues of child custody were not the usual fare of his Court, he cited *McLaughlin v. Florida* and *Loving v. Virginia* in declaring the Fourteenth Amendment to have barred "all governmentally imposed discrimination based on race." True, as had been argued by the other side, little Melanie might face prejudice, given her family's makeup, but that could not govern the case: "Private biases may be outside the reach of the law but the law cannot, directly or indirectly, give them effect." Melanie would stay with, or go back to, her mom.

Loving in Films

Within a year of the Supreme Court's ruling in *Loving v. Virginia*, a Stanley Kramer movie dramatized interracial marriage as a matter of social conscience among white Americans. Joey Drayton, a white woman who had been brought up in a privileged and progressive household in which traditional prejudices were considered and discarded, had found her soul mate in Hawaii and was bringing him home to meet her parents. Dr. John Prentice (played by Sidney Poitier) happened to be an African American who also happened to be an absolutely stellar specimen of humanity, a medical doctor and humanitarian of Nobel Prize–winning caliber, a gentleman, and very good looking to boot. Spencer Tracy and Katherine Hepburn played her parents, Matt and Christina Drayton, startled to discover the racial identity of their prospective son-in-law, and forced to consider their one big remaining prejudice. Since there could be no other grounds for serious hesitation, the only possible argument against the young couple's marrying had to be his racial identity, and this they had to confront.

The couple lived in San Francisco, an urban bastion of liberal thinking, where he published a progressive daily newspaper. As the movie was being shot in the early months of 1967, miscegenation laws remained in force in seventeen states, but California had done away with its restrictive law along those lines almost two decades earlier, in *Perez v. Sharp*. Personal attitudes and behavior against black-white marriage evidently persisted, even if no longer backed up by the force of the law. Yet the prospective groom's African American parents revealed similar consternation, as both fathers grasped at every available argument against such a marriage for their children, so the situation didn't appear as simply a matter of white prejudice versus black equanimity. It took the mother of each young person to bring her husband around to see that, as Tracy/Drayton put it at the end: "But you're two wonderful people . . . .who happened to fall in love," and the "only one thing worse" than *getting married* would be if "knowing what you two have . . . and knowing what you two feel . . . you didn't get married."

Spencer Tracy and Katherine Hepburn had themselves been together, living out their own great love story, for a great many years, and this was their last film together. Tracy, very ill during the filming, in fact died on June 10, two days before the Supreme Court handed down its ruling. Released at the very end of 1967, six months and more after *Loving*, the movie did not reach much of an audience until 1968, so it could not help prepare the way for the Supreme Court's ruling, but it could help address concerns that Americans, especially whites but all others as well, might feel and face in the aftermath of that decision. Nominated for a slew of Academy Awards, and the recipient of those for best actress and best original screenplay, it was very well received as well as highly visible, and it no doubt nudged the culture in the direction its creators hoped.

Guess Who's Coming to Dinner, constructed like a play built around a series of scenes in a single day, developed a story line that made its way through to a happy conclusion. Yet the "passion" that the couple reportedly felt for each other was scarcely in evidence, and the couple—he in particular—had expressly decided to postpone sex until after they had married. So moviegoers were not faced with interracial sex as well as interracial marriage. The sizzle that was missing in that show emerged a quarter-century later in the blockbuster movie *The Bodyguard*, released in 1992. Whitney Houston and Kevin Costner discovered their passion for each other, and the kiss that she raced to give him late in the film showed what the hit song she sang as part of the soundtrack was saying, "I'll Always Love You."

The theme could also take a very different trajectory. Spike Lee's movie *Jungle Fever* from about the same time (1991) depicts the cultural politics of race and sex played out in New York City, in particular between a successful (and married) black architect, Flipper (Wesley Snipes), and an Italian-American temp secretary at his firm, Angie (Annabella Sciorra). The title is designed to get at the unhealthy ways in which, according to Lee, people reaching for sex across the color line often do so on the basis of stereotypes more than genuine personal connections. And in a particularly compelling scene midway through the movie—what Spike/Cyrus refers to as a "war council" comprised of Flipper's wife and her girlfriends—several African American women address ways in which they feel threatened, even violated, by the redirection of attention and affection by black men away from them and toward white women, a key answer to the question posed by one of them: "Where are the good black men?"

And then came a remake of *Guess Who's Coming to Dinner*. The new version, *Guess Who* (2005), depicts a young black lady bringing her chosen one, a young white man, home to her folks, with misplaced confidence that his misgivings are unfounded. In this version, there are no white parents to wrestle with, or embrace, the choice their child has made, as the focus is on the black parents, especially the father.

In 1996 a Hallmark movie produced for Showtime purported to tell the story of an actual couple, with the title *Mr. and Mrs. Loving*. The title was excellent, capturing the passion and commitment that drove the nonfictional couple to seek to overcome the biggest of obstacles, one that went much further than a parental expression of disappointment or concern. It captured, too, exactly the central issue: could they, under Virginia law, ever be "Mr. and Mrs. Loving"? Even had the writer-director Richard Friedenberg been intent on telling a nonfiction story, he would have had fairly scant historical writing to draw upon, since scholars had not yet written very much on the subject, though some good work had been done by then. That material would emerge in far more substantial fashion beginning in 2002 from what turned out to be a cottage industry focusing on what one scholar termed America's three-century-long "antimiscegenation regime."

Starring a good-humored but generally taciturn Timothy Hutton as Richard Loving and a luminous Lela Rochon as Mildred Jeter, the movie did a fine job of evoking both their love and their agony. But it did strange things with the facts. It turns out, to take a big example, the Lovings had only one lawyer, Bernie Cohen, not two: Phil Hirschkop, fully as central as Cohen to the successful outcome of the court case and the Lovings' quest, never existed. Until the very end of the film — with Mildred carrying around new baby Peggy as the Lovings were shown preparing to leave their DC place and return at last to Virginia after their victory at the Supreme Court — they had only two children. Asked what she thought about it, Mrs. Loving hesitated before offering gently: "It is a nice story." At first she had missed Peggy's late arrival, and thought she was missing a child, but only she knew how much more had been distorted about her family's private lives.

A caption at the outset of the movie alerts viewers as to the year the two young people began their romance — 1960. After what seems to have been a lengthy time apart as though he had been away in the military,

Mildred and Richard are at an interracial dance in Caroline County, happy to meet up with each other, in a moment of growing love that would lead to marriage. In truth, by mid-1960, they had been married for two years, were already parents of their three children, and were living in exile in the nation's capital after their conviction for a marriage that, according to the movie's time line, had not yet taken place.

But if the film distorted some key aspects of the story beyond recognition, it generated a palpable awareness of their story in any number of viewers, powerfully affecting many people in highly personal ways. As a nine year old living in North Carolina in 1998—her mother white, her father black—Brittany Houser had seen the movie, had adopted a new hero, and had determined to meet her, and soon found herself with her mom, Leslie Houser, visiting in Caroline County, where, as she wrote the story up for her grade school class, "My mom told her that my daddy's mom had died and I missed her a lot and that I wonder would she be my other grandmother. And that's when she told me I could call her grandma. I was so happy. I feel so special now that I have met Mildred."

A few years after the movie *Mr. and Mrs. Loving* came out, the story of the Lovings gained greater circulation through other media. A book published by historian Peter Wallenstein in 2002 carried as its title the words Richard Loving was said to have spoken to Bernie Cohen shortly before the case was argued before the Supreme Court's nine justices: *Tell the Court I Love My Wife.* But the Lovings' story, though playing a climactic role in the book's sweep across all of American history, took up little more than one chapter out of sixteen and emphasized the legal history of the case. Early the next year another book came out, this one by law professor Randall Kennedy, exploring the years after the decision in *Loving* as well as before it: *Interracial Intimacies: Sex, Marriage, Identity, and Adoption* (2003).

An additional book, published in 2004, developed the Lovings' story at greater length. The author, Phyl Newbeck, introduces her book by explaining that she, a white woman living in the North, and her husband, a black man, watched the movie *Mr. and Mrs. Loving* one night in 1997. Acting on a keen need to know more about the *Loving* case, she tried to find and read a book that would tell her more. Unable, to her surprise, to find such a book, she set out to write one. She visited Caroline County, spoke with people there, developed some of the missing detail, and wrote it up, thus supplying a potential readership the fullest account in print of the Lovings' saga. More than that, between fall 1998 and spring 1999 she identified and tracked down a collection of other interracial couples who had found themselves stymied by state laws like the one the Lovings had encountered, interviewed them, and wrote up their experiences, thus supplying an irreplaceable addition to the historical literature. Playing off Virginia state tourism's official slogan—"Virginia Is for Lovers," which, designed to appeal to prospective vacationers, had originated in 1969, just two years after the Supreme Court decided *Loving*—she used the title *Virginia Hasn't Always Been for Lovers: Interracial Marriage Bans and the Case of Richard and Mildred Loving*. The earlier period of the long history is not well comprehended, however, and Mrs. Loving supplies only a scant couple of lines of the narrative. Still, like the two books published a year or two earlier, one by a historian, the other by a law professor, Newbeck's book contributed to a widening and deepening awareness of the mid-twentieth-century history of antimiscegenation laws in general and of the Lovings' experience at their hands in particular.

Mildred Loving's death in May 2008 led to national, even international, news coverage, a renewed recognition of her story, and a new film. Inspired by the story, songwriter Nanci Griffith wrote and performed "The Loving Kind." Another person struck with Mildred Loving's story was Nancy Buirsky, who set out to make a film on the subject, at least if she could find materials and funding. Together with the film's producer, Elisabeth Haviland James, they had the immense good fortune of tracking down a pile of Grey Villet's still photographs, the proofs of which the family has always had, and an even more astonishing amount of Hope Ryden's film footage, which she had stored away in a closet and forgotten, both collections from the mid-1960s as the Lovings were making their way through America's court system. They obtained seed money from the Virginia Foundation for the Humanities, which they parlayed into a big grant from the National Endowment for the Humanities. So they were able to develop *The Loving Story*, a documentary film that, for the first time, effectively brought viewers face to face with this dramatic historical tale from less than a half-century before. In the 2012 Oscar Award sweepstakes, it was one of the fifteen semifinalists for best documentary film but did not make the list of five finalists.

On February 14, 2012—Valentine's Day—HBO screened that film, which was starkly different from its Showtime predecessor. *The Loving Story* was not a fictional rendition "based upon a true story." Based largely on the still photographs and film footage, it gave direct entry to much of the texture of the Lovings' family life and the emotional turmoil of their legal travails, and it also tried to sketch the tortuous path their case took through the courts. The film begins with and thereafter highlights Judge Bazile's words about how "God created the races," though it leaves some uncertainty as to the context in which he said or wrote those words. Given the timing of both the photographs and the film footage, the images of the Loving family almost all come from the period after Judge Leon Bazile rendered his famous words in January 1965 and before Chief Justice Earl Warren wrote his in June 1967. Donald appears often in the film, Peggy even more, Sidney infrequently.

In addition to Mildred and Richard Loving—the dominant figures, of course, from the images of the 1960s taken mostly in their home—the film highlights three people who appear both in the original footage and again as talking heads reflecting on the long-ago events. The Lovings' lawyers, Phil Hirschkop and Bernie Cohen, each appear both then and, separately, now. Peggy, by the time of the film's completion the sole surviving Loving child, takes viewers back and forth between the five- or six-year-old in the early images and her older self as the reluctant but willing and able spokesman for the family and their lived experience.

The Loving Story made the rounds of film festivals, thus reaching varied audiences and at the same time accompanied by panel discussions and opportunities for viewers to ask questions of the panelists. At the Virginia Film Festival in Charlottesville, panelists included daughter Peggy Loving, attorney Philip Hirschkop, historian Peter Wallenstein, and filmmaker Nancy Buirsky. The film also went home to Bowling Green, in Caroline County, where it was screened in the auditorium of Mildred Loving's old high school, and panelists included Peggy Loving again and, this time, Bernard Cohen—both of whom appeared in the film from back in the day, also in the film long afterward, and in person as well.

What new works of art or scholarship might *The Loving Story* inspire?

Loving Day

In 2001, at about the same time as these books were coming along, a young man in New York City was stunned to learn about the Lovings while trolling through the Web at work one day. Ken Tanabe found particularly jolting the 1965 statement by Judge Bazile about God's having put the different races on separate continents and wanting them to stay separate. Tanabe realized that a law such as the Lovings had encountered in the 1950s would have barred his own parents' marriage, since they, a Japanese man and a white Belgian woman, could not have legally married in Virginia before the Supreme Court's ruling in *Loving*. He had been born in Washington, DC, a decade after *Loving*, but he nonetheless took it personally. He came to understand that a law like Virginia's affected everyone—black, white, Asian American, Native American, everyone.

Two years later, as a graduate student at the Parsons School of Design at the New School, he was working on a master's degree in design and technology, and he remembered the story and found a way to put his discovery to work. Why not a special day, Loving Day, to commemorate the Supreme Court's ruling? He could combine his new mission, his skills as a graphic designer, and perhaps even his music. A Website on the Lovings became his thesis project, completed in May 2004.

Immediately he set about throwing a Loving Day party in New York City. After the inaugural one in 2004, another followed each year, and each year's grew bigger. Moreover, the celebrations spread to other cities. On the occasion of the 2005 Loving Day get-together in New York, he told a reporter: "I was shocked because I didn't know about it even though I am a product of an interracial couple," and it "dawned on me that there's a generation gap; younger people who didn't live with that law don't know anything about it." The goal of the Loving Day project is "for the *Loving* decision to become a part of our civil rights history," as he explained in 2006. "We know about *Brown*," he went on, and about Rosa Parks, Martin Luther King, and the lunch counter sit-ins, yet few people, he said, "know about *Loving*."

As he put it in 2007, on the decision's fortieth anniversary, "It's rare to have an opportunity to identify something that society needs, that it doesn't have, and to fill that need." Loving Day celebrations take place in many communities. At the New York event in 2007, he took a microphone and told the crowd: "I'd like to take this opportunity to say, 'Thank you Mr. and Mrs. Loving.' Can I get everyone to join me? I want you to say the words on the count of three!"

"Interracial Marriage"

When scholars measure the incidence of "interracial" marriage in the twenty-first century against the figures for any time before 1967, two problems can easily creep in. One is that, by the time the Lovings brought their case to the Supreme Court, most Americans lived in states that had no such laws governing the racial identity of the person they might marry. At the end of World War II, thirty states out of forty-eight maintained miscegenation laws. The tipping point, with twenty-four out of forty-eight, had been reached by 1958, the year the Lovings went to DC to marry only to find that Virginia law enforcement authorities rejected their marriage, or rather regarded it as the very basis for their prosecution. In 1961, when Barack Obama's parents married in Hawaii, the number had dropped some more but still stood at twenty-two. Another problem, often ignored, is what we choose to understand as "interracial."

An index of demographic distribution can help us gauge the significance of *Loving* in terms of its implications for a greater rate of black-white intermarriage. In the 1960s, more than half of all African Americans lived in the seventeen states in which miscegenation statutes persisted into 1967. Yet few such marriages had taken place before 1967 in New Jersey or New York, two states that had never enacted restrictive laws, or in Pennsylvania or Massachusetts, two states that had repealed their statutes long before the Civil War. Looking back on these patterns, one might have projected a fairly limited quantitative impact in any additional states in which such laws could no longer be enforced.

But of course the adjective "interracial" covers pairings of kinds other than only black-white, although most Americans in 1967 — regardless of race or region — thought of race, and therefore would have considered "interracial" marriage, in terms of black and white. Then again, when

Barack Obama's mother married a second time, her new husband was Indonesian—in Judge Bazile's terms, "Malay"—and young Barry grew up for a time in Indonesia. A mere two years after the Immigration Act of 1965 became law, little had yet changed on the social landscape in the United States to complicate matters such that, four or five decades later, most interracial marriages would not include an African American. One huge difference, then, between then and now is the significant numbers of "white"-"Asian" marriages as well as other combinations.

The law of race and marriage had always served as a rough proxy for the law of race in other sites, such as voting and education, and that observation might usefully serve as a guide to further research on the pre-*Loving* era as well as the post-*Loving* world. In Mississippi, where segregation in marriage more or less mirrored segregation in the schools, the state supreme court ruled in *Moreau v. Grandich* (1917) that two people both white enough to marry as "white" people (each less than one-eighth black, if black at all) might nonetheless together have a child not white enough to qualify for attending a school for white children. How does "interracial marriage" relate in the twenty-first century to recent or contemporary patterns of housing segregation, school segregation, and so on?

What gave two Los Angeles residents, Andrea Perez and Sylvester Davis, the chance to run into each other, get to know each other, fall in love, and want to marry was the cluster of situations that had both of them working at the same Lockheed Aviation assembly plant, and both attending St. Patrick's Catholic Church, regardless of whether their residences were nearby as well. So they lived in an environment that was structured in ways that contrasted with most other Americans, whatever their race under the law and regardless of whether the law had a say against their getting together across some racial line.

To take another example—one that relates to integrated higher education—until after a federal court ordered the University of Georgia to admit its first two black students, including Atlanta resident Charlayne Hunter, in January 1961, there was no chance that she and Walter Stovall, a white student from faraway rural South Georgia, would find each other there and then set out to marry.

So, despite the lack of a law against any kind of interracial marriage in New York, despite the fallen statutes of California and other states that had abandoned the antimiscegenation regime in the years before 1967, and even regardless of *Loving v. Virginia*, relatively few Americans were going to encounter one another in ways that might lead to marriage. Reflecting those facts, the data for black-white and other forms of interracial marriage showed small—albeit growing—numbers in every census year thereafter.

The term "interracial" continued often to be taken, without even being noticed, as a synonym for black-white, even while most "interracial" married couples were not black and white. In the run-up to the screening of the documentary film *The Loving Story* in February 2012, many stories in newspapers and other publications announced the upcoming broadcast, giving it a vibrant buzz. They all tried to place the story in some kind of context, both historical and present-day, and they all got something wrong. In a particularly impressive error of conflation, one story observed cheerfully that, in a recent reporting year, a full 8 percent of all new marriages involved black-white couples. Such was, of course, far from true. So in announcing the film, they offered all manner of statements that perpetuated—or created—myths about what had occurred a half-century earlier, as well as what had been happening in American life since.

The very same week that the film went on national television, however, a new report came out that showed a substantial increase in all of its categories of interracial and interethnic marriage. The Pew Research Center issued a report, "The Rise of Intermarriage," based on an analysis of recent census and other data, led by Wendy Wang, and it went far to reveal the evolving patterns of interracial marriage in twenty-first-century America. In order to crunch the numbers, the people who worked up the report divided Americans into "white," "black," "Asian," and "Hispanic," with a residual category of people who reported some combination of identities.

According to the analysis of the categories employed, about every seventh marriage taking place recently is either interracial or interethnic. It continued to be true that relatively few African Americans showed up in the overall numbers, but the numbers there, too, had in fact grown. The state with the greatest proportion of new black-white marriages turned out to be Virginia, at 3.3 percent, where 13.8 percent of all new marriages comprised "married out" couples, people who had crossed either one of the racial lines employed or a line between Hispanic and non-Hispanic.

"In the past half century, intermarriage has evolved from being illegal, to being taboo, to being merely unusual," according to the Center's director, Paul Taylor, and "with each passing year, it becomes less unusual." In a crisp summary of the history and the report, he observed: "The face of the country is changing, and behaviors are changing with it." Changing, yes, although one out of seven leaves six out of seven.

Stateways and Folkways — a Global Context for the Lovings

The stories that make up the statistics and that make up the bulk of this book — illuminating as they may be for domestic affairs in American society, law, culture, and politics — may profitably be placed briefly in larger contexts in time and space, situated in other parts of the world in the generation following World War II, and especially during the years when the Lovings were in the courts seeking to overturn their convictions and exile.

In Sicily in 1965, teenager Franca Viola turned down her rich, powerful suitor, Filippo Melodia. He in turn, following what was called a regional tradition dating from the Middle Ages, abducted and raped her. After that, according to the tradition, she had to accept him or be dishonored, for no one else would ever marry her. Instead she brought criminal charges and told him in court, "I do not love you. I will not marry you." He would have gotten off had she consented to marry him. Instead, he was sentenced to eleven years in prison, and other young women in Sicily followed her lead. Although having been described as "destined to live as a spinster," two years after her ordeal she married Giuseppe Ruizi. Not only had he chosen her, but she had chosen him. Italy's president, Giuseppe Saragat, one of her many well-wishers, sent a gift. A new day had dawned in Sicily. A movie came out in 1970, *The Most Beautiful Bride*, dramatizing Franca Viola's story.

In South Asia, Hindus and Muslims long clashed over many matters. So severe were communal tensions in the subcontinent that when Great Britain conceded political independence to India and Pakistan after

World War II, it was to two separate nations, one predominantly Hindu and the other mostly Muslim. Yet people of more than one heritage continued to live in proximity in many communities, albeit in vastly different proportions, and their cultural differences were often compounded by tensions over such matters as access to political power and occupational opportunity. Against that background, violence broke out in summer 1967 in Kashmir—the greatest violence there since the time of independence—after a young Hindu woman, Parmeshwar Handoo, was allegedly abducted by a Muslim man, Gulam Rusool Kanth. Once she was located, she claimed that she had freely converted to Islam and married the young man, a coworker, and she refused to return to her family.

In 1927, the government of South Africa banned sexual relations between whites and "Africans," a measure broadened over the next thirty years to outlaw marriage and to cover all nonwhites. Such stateways did not prevent all such folkways. Susan Schoeman, a white woman, and Harry May, a native of China, though unable to marry, began living together in the mid-1960s. In 1969, after they had had three children together, they were convicted under the Immorality Act, which called for imprisonment for up to seven years. Schoeman took her case to the Interior Department, which granted her a racial reclassification as Chinese. Free to marry Harry May, and to escape further prosecution, she observed happily: "This is all I've ever wanted—to be Harry's legal wife. We will be married as soon as possible."

Another story from the 1960s has its origins in early post–World War II Great Britain and southern Africa. Seretse Khama—whose grandfather and father had each been paramount chief, or king, of the Bangwato people and who himself was named king in 1925 at the age of four—went to England in his twenties to study law, and there he met and in 1948 married a white woman, Ruth Williams. But he found that he could not permanently return home as chief with her to his native Bechuanaland, in part because of opposition from his kinsmen, who nonetheless came around, but far more because the Union of South Africa, which had a ban against black-white marriage and which was unprepared to allow a neighbor area to have a ruler with such a marriage, threatened England with cutting off supplies of uranium, a vital ingredient in a Cold War world. Later, with all these challenges resolved, and after pushing hard for democratic self-government, in 1965 Seretse Khama became the first prime minister of Bechuanaland and in 1966 the first president of a newly independent Botswana. With a national creation myth radically at odds with its neighbors South Africa and Southern Rhodesia, Botswana moved into independence committed to a racially open political society. Reelected time and again, Khama served until his death in 1980 at age fifty-nine from cancer. His successor would later characterize him as "the Mandela of Botswana."

Marriage and Family after *Loving*

So the story of the Lovings played out at a time during which traditional rules of social relations were becoming attenuated, both in private relations and in public law, and not only in America but in places around the world. In Virginia in particular and the United States more generally, attitudes and behavior were becoming less oppositional regarding "interracial" marriage among relatives and neighbors and strangers, too, much as they were becoming less oppositional toward interethnic and interreligious marriages. A new set of questions soon arose regarding "same-sex" marriage.

CHAPTER 9

The Freedom to Marry

From Interracial to Same-Sex

A new social phenomenon—and a new legal one—emerged in the United States in the last three decades of the twentieth century, as more and more same-sex couples sought to secure what Chief Justice Earl Warren in the *Loving* decision called "the freedom to marry." Like black southerners on a wide range of issues during the half-century between the 1910s and the 1960s, same-sex couples saw little prospect of securing change through legislative politics. In view of the ruling in *Loving v. Virginia*, however, they saw some possibility in the courts.

The resulting litigation reflected an important development in American social history, although similar developments in Canada, Denmark, and elsewhere revealed the phenomenon to be global, not local or national. One social group and its supporters tried to redefine marriage, as it had been long recognized in both the law and the dominant culture, so as to bring same-sex couples within the legally recognized institution of the family. On the other side, people went so far as to argue that one of the basic institutions of society was not worth saving if it were redefined in the way that the advocates of change called for. The contest over a social institution, embedded in the dominant culture, was played out in the political system, especially in the state courts. *Loving v. Virginia* rippled through these developments.

Private Behavior and Public Policy

Between about 1964 and 1972, a legal revolution in the United States mirrored in part, and fostered in part, a revolution in social relations and individual behavior. In matters of birth control—first for married couples, in *Griswold v. Connecticut* (1965), then for unmarried couples, too,

{ 176 }

in *Eisenstadt v. Baird* (1972) — the US Supreme Court broadened the concept of personal privacy in a constitutionally protected zone of behavior. The Court followed those decisions up with the abortion case *Roe v. Wade* (1973). On another front, the Civil Rights Act of 1964 emerged as a monument to the Civil Rights Movement's efforts to secure an end to the old order of state laws restricting activities on the basis of race. By 1972, Congress enacted protections against discrimination against women, whatever their race, in employment and education.

In the meantime, the last states outside the South with antimiscegenation laws repealed them, and in 1967 the privacy argument and the Civil Rights Movement merged when the Supreme Court, in *Loving v. Virginia*, overturned all state miscegenation laws. The federal courts had long considered marriage a matter best left to the states to regulate as they saw fit, a position enunciated in 1888 in *Maynard v. Hill.* The Court's new interpretation of the Fourteenth Amendment in *Loving v. Virginia* brought to an end the authority of states to sort prospective marriage partners according to racial identity.

Chief Justice Earl Warren and his colleagues on the Supreme Court in 1967 spoke in *Loving v. Virginia* about equal protection, due process, and the "freedom to marry." In doing so, they had in mind bringing down any racial barriers to the right of two otherwise qualified people who loved each other to enter into a heterosexual marriage. The decision had a great impact, very soon, on countless Americans. So decisive was it that the complex of questions that *Loving v. Virginia* addressed soon vanished as a significant policy issue anywhere in the nation.

Same-sex couples soon began seeking whatever privileges and legitimacy — whatever benefits, substantive or symbolic — that are bestowed by formal marriage. *Loving v. Virginia* was about race, privacy, and the right to marry. But a new set of questions emerged: Should the right to marry be detached from the racial element? Should the right to privacy and the right of marriage be extended to same-sex sexual and marital relations?

Gay Pride, Gay Rights

In June 1969, police raided the Stonewall Inn, a gay bar in New York City, and to their surprise the men and women at the place fought back. Riots and demonstrations took place over several nights, and solidarity emerged in other US cities. To that event, gay and lesbian Americans have often dated the beginnings of a "gay pride" and gay rights movement, a commitment to resist police harassment and seek to overturn legal obstacles to their freedoms. As one manifestation of this new social movement, various gay couples sought licenses to marry.

Some courts in the South were still busy seeing to it that *Loving* was recognized as the law of the land in matters of race and marriage, when people began to call upon *Loving* in support of same-sex marriage. In Hennepin County, Minnesota, law student Richard John Baker and librarian James Michael McConnell decided on New Year's Eve 1969 to get married—married under the law, more than having the religious ceremony that some other gay couples had managed. They applied for a marriage license in May 1970 and were turned down by the clerk, Gerald R. Nelson. They took him to court, where he agreed that the two men were fully qualified for a license, had either of them wished to enter a heterosexual marriage. Not only did the trial judge, Tom Bergin, quash the request for a writ of mandamus to order Nelson to issue a license to Baker and McConnell, he ordered him not to issue a license to them.

The case went to the Minnesota Supreme Court, where their attorney, Michael Wetherbee, drew on *Loving* to argue the case:

> In *Loving v. Commonwealth of Virginia*, . . . the issue was whether Virginia's anti-miscegenation statute prohibiting marriages between persons of the white race and any other race was constitutional. The Court struck down the statute. . . .
>
> The discrimination in this case is one of gender. . . . Just as Virginia was attempting to maintain White Supremacy in *Loving*, Minnesota is attempting to maintain "heterosexual supremacy" here by denying to appellants one of the basic rights of Man. But . . . there is no more rational reason for discriminating against appellants on account of their sex than there was in *Loving*, on account of their race.

The Minnesota Supreme Court, when handing down its decision in *Baker v. Nelson* in October 1971, rejected the idea that *Loving* had any bearing on the case at hand and went on to reject every one of the couple's contentions. Did the absence of a specific statutory prohibition against same-sex marriage mean that they had a right to a license? Common usage of the term, especially in view of such words in the statute as "husband and wife," did not leave that possibility open, the court determined. Did denial of a license on the basis of sexual identity go against the Fourteenth Amendment? True, the right to marry and form a family was a "fundamental right," but that "historic institution" involved the "procreation and rearing of children," and, the court insisted, "[t]he due process clause of the Fourteenth Amendment is not a charter" for transforming the family "by judicial legislation."

As for *Loving v. Virginia*, the Minnesota court ruled, that decision could not support the couple's case, for what had been thrown out was a law that embodied "patent racial discrimination." Rather than say that "all state restrictions upon the right to marry are beyond the reach of the Fourteenth Amendment," *Loving* had left room, the court concluded, for "a clear distinction between a marital restriction based merely upon race and one based upon the fundamental difference in sex." In short, a state's traditional authority over marriage remained in place, with the sole exception of restrictions based on racial identity. So far had the world turned since 1967 — or so far was the Upper Midwest from Virginia — that the Minnesota court could dismiss the importance of "a marital restriction based merely upon race."

The case went to the US Supreme Court, but there the appeal was "dismissed for want of substantial federal question." The Court was not about to move, four years after transforming the constitutional law of race and marriage in *Loving*, to dealing with a same-sex version of the marriage question. The dismissal was more damaging than no response at all, but the couple had been overconfident about the ruling they would get.

Then again, by then they were already married. They had appeared in *Look* magazine in January 1971, featured in a spread on "The American Family." In April, Jack Baker had been elected president of the University of Minnesota Student Association, after his campaign to get students some representation on the governing board of the institution so that they might have a say in how the place was run drew tremendous support. And in September, having navigated the niceties of Minnesota law, which permitted someone to adopt a person and then marry that person, they managed to obtain a license, had their ceremony, and issued a press release asserting: "This is America's first legally-recognized same-sex marriage." They pressed on in their court action, however, recognizing that their own marriage was a fluke, not the result of a change in law or policy, and so could hardly change things for any other couple.

A case similar to the one in Minnesota soon arose in Kentucky, where two women, Tracy Knight and Margery Jones, were denied a marriage license in Louisville. The outcome in *Jones v. Hallahan* (1973) was much the same. The Kentucky Court of Appeals cited dictionary definitions of marriage, such as a "legal union of a man with a woman for life," as well as the recent Minnesota decision in *Baker v. Nelson*, both the state court decision and the Supreme Court's dismissal of the appeal.

In another such case from the 1970s, Paul Barwick and John Singer challenged the validity of a restrictive law under the Washington state constitution, and the *Loving* analogy was more fully considered in the court's opinion. To support their position, the two men called on the 1948 California Supreme Court decision *Perez v. Sharp*, as well as the 1967 US Supreme Court decision in *Loving v. Virginia*. They urged, said the court, "an analogy between the racial classification involved in *Loving* and *Perez* and the alleged sexual classification involved" in their own case. The court distinguished the two earlier decisions by reference to the generally accepted definition of a marriage: "In *Loving* and *Perez*, the parties were barred from entering into a marriage relationship because of an impermissible racial classification. There is no analogous sexual classification involved in the instant case." The couple were "not being denied entry into the marriage relationship because of their sex; rather, they are being denied entry into the marriage relationship because of the recognized definition of that relationship as one which may be entered into only by two persons who are members of the opposite sex." It was as if the court was channeling *Pace v. Alabama* (1883) and its language about the interracial couple in that case having been convicted of an entirely different crime of cohabitation than if they had shared a racial identity, and the law they broke prescribed "a punishment for an offense that can only be committed where the two sexes are of different races."

Here the legal issue related to the two people, no matter what their race, being of the same sex.

The couple had challenged the "recognized definition." They insisted on the analogy in that, when *Perez* and *Loving* were decided, the definition of a valid marriage under state law in California and Virginia had excluded interracial relationships. The courts had—in those decisions, through their interpretations of the Constitution—changed the very definition of marriage. Said the court, "We disagree. The *Loving* and *Perez* courts did not change the basic definition of marriage as the legal union of one man and one woman; rather, they merely held that the race of the man or woman desiring to enter that relationship could not be considered by the state in granting the marriage license." The statute stood.

One subsequent case brought into focus the kinds of benefits that a legal marriage conferred and the kind of responsibilities that it imposed. John DeSanto and William Barnsley had been together for a decade, but then they broke up, and in February 1981 DeSanto filed for divorce. He sought a legal end to their common-law marriage, which dated, he said, from June 14, 1970, until November 15, 1980. He sought a division of their property, and he sought alimony from Barnsley, who denied, however, that they had ever been married. The trial court dismissed the complaint, and on appeal the Pennsylvania Superior Court, in *DeSanto v. Barnsley* (1984), noted that the case "presents the novel issue of whether two persons of the same sex can contract a common law marriage. We hold that they cannot." Maybe there had been an agreement, witnesses, a mutual commitment, but there had been no marriage. Breaking up was hard enough to do, all the more so if the presence of a marriage was itself contested.

In the face of such total defeats, efforts to achieve constitutional victories receded. As for dictionary definitions and legislative intent, moreover, the Minnesota legislature responded to the litigation in *Baker v. Nelson* by adding to the legal definition of marriage the words "between a man and a woman." The controversy would not go away, however. It took various shapes and directions in the 1980s and 1990s.

Same-Sex Sex

In 1986, the Supreme Court confronted a case, *Hardwick v. Bowers*, regarding homosexual behavior—not a case regarding marriage, but rather one regarding sexual relations necessarily outside of marriage. The case resembled, in some respects, the 1883 fornication case *Pace v. Alabama* and the 1964 cohabitation case *McLaughlin v. Florida*, though it tended for good reason to get compared with *Loving v. Virginia*. Michael Hardwick had been arrested in Atlanta, Georgia, in 1982 for the crime of sodomy, and his challenge to the Georgia sodomy law had gone to federal court.

The district court had upheld the Georgia statute, but the appeals court reversed that ruling, whereupon the state appealed the case to the Supreme Court. There the state of Georgia, represented by the senior assistant attorney general, Michael E. Hobbs, urged the Court to uphold the sodomy law, for to invalidate it would open the way to similar overturns of laws prohibiting "polygamy; homosexual, same-sex marriage; consensual incest; prostitution; fornication; adultery." The two sides jousted over "privacy" versus "morality," and distinctions were urged and denied between sexual relations inside and outside marriage and consensual sodomy that was heterosexual and homosexual. Along the way, Hobbs conceded that, in light of *Griswold v. Connecticut*, "it would be unconstitutional" to attempt to apply the statute to a married heterosexual couple, but this case involved an unmarried same-sex couple.

Was "homosexual sodomy" a fundamental right, or was it a crime? Having accepted jurisdiction in the case, the Court had to choose between options that the justices did not necessarily feel comfortable with. The Court was narrowly divided. Early on, Justice Lewis F. Powell leaned toward affirming the appeals court ruling and invalidating the statute, but in the end he voted to reverse and uphold the statute. Either way, the ruling would have been 5–4, but Powell's defection meant that the Court went one way rather than the other.

Thus the effort to overturn state sodomy laws failed. Some of the people who carried the case no doubt saw that they had made a mistake in seeking a ruling at all, since a decision of the sort they obtained hardly served their purposes. They had overreached.

Loving v. Virginia was very much on the justices' minds in *Hardwick v. Bowers*. Speaking for the majority, Justice Byron R. White opened by attacking the notion that the Court's privacy decisions since the 1920s, including *Loving*, predetermined the outcome in this case. To the contrary, he declared, those rulings on privacy were not to be construed as extending to "homosexual sodomy." In angry dissents, Justice Harry R. Blackmun wrote, "The parallel between *Loving* and this case is almost uncanny," and Justice John Paul Stevens observed, "Interestingly, miscegenation was once treated as a crime similar to sodomy."

Justice Stevens detected a contradiction in the majority opinion, which had depended in large part on the historical nature of legal and cultural bans on sodomy. He noted that the state of Georgia and the Court majority had both seemed prepared to declare unconstitutional the enforcement of sodomy laws against heterosexual couples but that in fact heterosexual and homosexual sodomy had both been similarly outlawed "for a very long time."

Some member of the Court might have written, paraphrasing (as follows, changing one noun) what Justice Potter Stewart and Justice William O. Douglas had said a quarter-century earlier in *McLaughlin v. Florida*, overturning *Pace v. Alabama*: "I think it is simply not possible for a state law to be valid under our Constitution which makes the criminality of an act depend upon the gender of the actor. Discrimination of that kind is invidious *per se*." No member of the Court did say that, though.

Transgender People and Marriage

Gender identity in the final years of the twentieth century — and its importance in view of everything from criminal statutes to inheritance and alimony practices, and the unending problems of determining where to draw the line and on which side of it to place various individuals — proved to be remarkably like racial identity. Again, individuals and the law generally demanded an unambiguous dividing line in what was seen as a binary world. Again, many people insist that every individual be clearly placed on one side of the line or the other — and that they stay there. The analogy to racial identity, though by no means perfect, can be remarkably appropriate. If same-sex marriages are not valid, what must the sexual identity of a transgender person's be for the marriage to be heterosexual and valid?

Born in 1952 in San Antonio, Texas, Lee Cavazos Jr. grew up with male physical features, but a female sexual identity, and as an adult adopted the name Christie Lee Cavazos in 1977, underwent surgery, and received female hormones. As a woman, in 1989 she married Jonathon Mark Littleton in Kentucky and became Christie Lee Littleton, and they lived together as husband and wife until his death in Texas in 1996. Christie Littleton filed a wrongful death suit against Dr. Mark Prange, who sought to deflect the suit by asserting that Christie Littleton, born a male, could not be the surviving wife of the dead man. When the trial court granted the doctor's motion for a summary judgment, Christie Littleton appealed to the Texas Court of Appeals in San Antonio. There, in *Littleton v. Prange* (1999), Chief Justice Phil Hardberger began his opinion with the statement, "This case involves the most basic of questions. When is a man a man, and when is a woman a woman?" More particularly, he went on, "Is Christie a man or a woman? There is no dispute that Christie and Jonathon went through a ceremonial marriage ritual. If Christie is a woman, she may bring this action. If Christie is a man, she may not." Was "she" a "man," or was she not? To medical experts, Christie Littleton was "medically a woman." In the words of the appeals court, however, "We hold, as a matter of law, that Christie Littleton is a male. As a male, Christie cannot be married to another male. Her marriage to Jonathon was invalid, and she cannot bring a cause of action as his surviving spouse."

But now we turn back to people about whom there is no legal or medical doubt in anyone's mind — the individual, the partner, or the representative of the state — as to whether he or she is male or female, and yet they find a controversy. Might there come to be a time and place in which one person can lawfully marry another even though both potential partners shared the same sexual identity, which they had at birth and continued to have at the time of the ceremony?

Equal Benefits and State Constitutions

In the 1990s, cases regarding "same-sex marriage" came to state courts based not on the Fourteenth Amendment but rather on provisions in the *state constitution*, looking for interpretations of those provisions in a way that required access to marriage, or at least benefits to same-sex partners equal to those of their heterosexual counterparts. Some state courts had previously ruled against recognition: Minnesota in 1971, Kentucky in 1973, Washington in 1974, and Pennsylvania in 1984. The US Supreme Court had refused an appeal of the first of these, the case from Minnesota, in 1972, and evidently potential litigants saw no point in taking that path again. Seeking favorable rulings on the basis of state constitutional provisions might prove far more fruitful. So it seemed in Hawaii.

In December 1990, three couples, including Ninia Baehr and Genora Dancel, attempted to obtain marriage licenses in Hawaii but were turned down on the basis that the couples were same-sex rather than heterosexual. They all then went to court in 1991, only to see their case dismissed by a local judge. When they appealed to the Hawaii Supreme Court, they won a victory in the sense that the trial judge was directed to try the matter on its merits. The state supreme court did not exactly rule, in *Baehr v. Lewin*, that same-sex marriages were legal in Hawaii, but it was hard to distinguish that conclusion from what was actually said there in May 1993.

The court majority took the approach in *Loving v. Virginia* and applied it to same-sex marriages. Written by Justice Stephen Levinson, the court's opinion worked from the premise that, like racial discrimination, discrimination on the basis of sex had to be strictly scrutinized to see whether there was compelling justification for restrictive state action. As for the right to marry, it remained a "fundamental right." The combination of "strict scrutiny" and "fundamental right" made it difficult for the court to come to any conclusion other than the one it did.

The question was, the court said, "whether we will extend the *present* boundaries of the fundamental right of marriage to include same-sex couples, or, put another way, whether we will hold that same-sex couples possess a fundamental right to marry." The answer lay in the court's reading of the Hawaii state constitution's equal protection clause, which was more elaborate than its counterpart in the US Constitution. No person, said the Hawaii provision, shall "be denied the equal protection of the laws, nor be denied the enjoyment of the person's civil rights or be discriminated against in the exercise thereof because of race, religion, sex, or ancestry."

The case took a long time coming to trial, mostly because the state requested extensions, with the state attorney general hoping that the matter would be settled not by the judiciary but through legislative politics. At last, in December 1996, Judge Michael S. C. Chang ruled that the state had failed to make the case for restricting marriage to heterosexual couples. "In Hawaii and elsewhere," he wrote, "same-sex couples can, and do, have successful, loving, and committed relationships." As for children raised by same-sex couples, they tend, he said, "to adjust and develop in a normal fashion."

The state had, therefore, no compelling need to ban same-sex marriages. Evan Wolfson, one of the lawyers for the three couples, exulted: "This decision marks the beginning of the end of sex discrimination in marriage just as we brought an end to race discrimination in marriage a generation ago." And yet he knew that, even in Hawaii, the fight was far from over, and gay couples from the mainland were advised "against hopping on planes for Waikiki." To begin with, the Hawaii Supreme Court might not uphold Judge Chang's decision, and in any case the outcome there might not be known for another year or more. In fact the story promptly left the courts and headed into legislative politics.

The Hawaii legislature responded with two initiatives. In early 1997, it approved an amendment to the state constitution, for submission to the voters in November 1998, that would authorize the legislature to restrict marriage to heterosexual couples. But it did not mean to turn away empty-handed such couples as Ninia Baehr and Genora Dancel. It also passed the Reciprocal Beneficiaries Act, which conferred on same-sex couples some of the benefits that came with marriage between heterosexuals, among them the right of the surviving partner to inherit in the absence of a will. The next year, the electorate did in fact ratify the amendment, by a margin of more than two to one.

Once the "marriage amendment" was ratified, the Hawaii state constitution contained the language "The legislature shall have the power to reserve marriage to opposite-sex couples." When the Hawaii

Supreme Court ruled again on the matter, in *Baehr v. Miike*, it dismissed the case in December 1999. At the time of Judge Chang's ruling three years earlier, said the court, the statute might have been in violation of the Hawaii constitution's equal protection clause; but, in view of the marriage amendment, the court observed, it "no longer is."

Resisting Same-Sex Marriage

The events in Hawaii could hardly be contained there. Advocates elsewhere of the kind of change that Hawaii had seemed to signal were enthusiastic at the breakthrough, but the constitutional initiative was swiftly attacked. Groups opposed to same-sex marriage mobilized across the country, as did proponents of a Hawaii-type court victory of the sort that had come in 1996 and then had been turned back. By no means did the history of law and marriage come to an end, and further initiatives, on both sides of the debate, emerged in state after state, in the 1990s and beyond.

Meanwhile, under the Supreme Court's ruling in *Hardwick v. Bowers*, even as same-sex couples could not marry anywhere in the United States, their carrying on sexual relations outside marriage left them vulnerable to criminal prosecution. *Pace v. Alabama* went bust in 1964, with respect to racial relations. For same-sex couples, by contrast, *Pace* lived on. No outcome like that in *McLaughlin v. Florida* had yet come to pass, let alone one like that in *Loving v. Virginia*.

Beginning in the second half of the 1990s, efforts to contain, or roll back, the same-sex revolution took place not only in state legislatures and state constitutions but also in Congress. The developments in Hawaii sufficed to mobilize forces both on the islands and on the mainland seeking to maintain a heterosexual definition of marriage. At the same time, supporters of initiatives like those in Hawaii pushed elsewhere to broaden the definition.

Proponents of same-sex marriage had celebrated the news from Hawaii with declarations that comity—states recognizing contracts entered into under each other's laws—would force a nationalization of same-sex marriage; opponents decried what the other side celebrated. In one episode in the TV series *The West Wing*, the writers had President Jed Bartlet voice that position. That is, both sides in the debate on same-sex marriage seemed to assume that, if one state recognized such marriages and then marriages were solemnized there, other states would have to recognize those contracts as valid, even though the long history of the law of interracial marriage scarcely demonstrated any such imperative.

In October 1996, President Bill Clinton signed the Defense of Marriage Act (DOMA), a direct response in Congress to the developments in Hawaii, when it looked like that state would become the first to recognize same-sex marriages. Anticipating the kind of decision that Judge Chang handed down, DOMA defined marriage as a union between a man and a woman. The definition had no criminal sanctions, but it was designed to guarantee that no American could secure federal benefits as a consequence of a same-sex union.

More than that, DOMA offered to insulate every state from what might develop in any other state. The 1996 measure made it clear that no state had to recognize a same-sex union, no matter whether it was valid in the state where it had been solemnized. In marriage at the end of the millennium, as with race during the long reign of the antimiscegenation regime, comity had its limits. Congress was imposing a national definition of marriage in terms of federal benefits, at the same time authorizing states to deny efforts to import same-sex marriages valid elsewhere. Just as most states with miscegenation laws had long refused to recognize many kinds of interracial marriages undertaken in states where such marriages were valid, according to DOMA any state could refuse to recognize same-sex marriages entered into in Hawaii or any other state where they might become valid.

Yet, also in 1996 — earlier in the year, in May — the Supreme Court ruled in a case from Colorado, *Romer v. Evans*. Several Colorado municipalities had enacted ordinances prohibiting certain kinds of discrimination against gays and lesbians, and in 1992 the statewide electorate had sought to overturn all such ordinances and, moreover, prohibit the state legislature from enacting any similar measures. The Colorado courts had rejected these efforts, and the state had appealed. Writing for a 6–3 majority, Justice Anthony Kennedy spoke for the US Supreme Court when it upheld the Colorado Supreme Court in what writers Joyce Murdoch and Deb Price, in their book *Courting Justice: Gay Men and Lesbians v. the Supreme Court* (2001), characterized as the Court's "first landmark gay-rights decision."

Alaska

In 1995, after the early developments in Hawaii but before passage of the Defense of Marriage Act, Jay Brause and Gene Dugan applied for a marriage license in Anchorage, Alaska. In part, they were inspired by developments in Hawaii. In part, they were acting in accordance with a gender-neutral Alaska marriage statute that used the term "person" rather than "man" and "woman," a statute that a local judge in Fairbanks, Meg Greene, had suggested earlier that year might be construed as permitting same-sex marriage.

Turned down by a local official, Brause and Dugan sued the Alaska Bureau of Vital Statistics to obtain a license. Before their suit reached court, the Alaska legislature changed the marriage statute in 1996. Under the new law, marriage could be contracted in Alaska only by "one man and one woman," and also any out-of-state same-sex marriage would be void in Alaska. Judge Greene's interpretation could no longer have any place, nor could events in Hawaii lead to a same-sex couple's importing their marriage to Alaska. Brause and Dugan amended their suit. Instead of challenging the constitutionality of the state's interpretation of the previous statute, they challenged the constitutionality of the new law. It denied them due process, they claimed, and it infringed their right to privacy under the Alaska constitution.

At a hearing in February 1998, Judge Peter Michalski sided with Brause and Dugan. He emphasized the matter of privacy under the Alaska constitution and ordered a trial, at which the state would have to demonstrate a compelling interest in retaining a ban on same-sex marriage. Within days of Judge Michalski's ruling, however, the state legislature began considering an amendment to the Alaska constitution. Both houses approved it, and that November, by 68 percent to 32 percent, the voters ratified the "marriage amendment": "To be valid or recognized in this State, a marriage may exist only between one man and one woman." The Alaska story came to a dead end.

The Defense of Marriage Act left Hawaii free to do whatever Hawaii chose to do, but offered some assurance to other states that they need not recognize Hawaii's handiwork, let alone emulate it in their own states. It guaranteed, too, that the Hawaii law—or any state's—would not govern the national definition of marriage as it related to the receipt of federal benefits from their marriage status.

Moreover, the Hawaii and Alaska decisions—judicial interpretations of the state constitution—were each turned back by an amendment to the state constitution. Voters in both states made it clear that the constitution was theirs. If one or more judges seemed to think that the language voiced in that constitution permitted—or even required—an interpretation that would validate same-sex marriages, the sovereign people would rectify that matter by changing the language to make it clear that such was not the case. DOMA restrained the degree and reach of any change that might be secured at the state level, and then states themselves turned back from consolidating the change.

The *Loving* decision had been consolidated as regarded miscegenation. Yet, despite initiatives, assertive and optimistic, in the three decades after *Loving* was handed down, its reach had not been extended to same-sex marriage. In the meantime, more and more same-sex couples had wedding ceremonies that provided the ritual equivalents of a heterosexual marriage but that did not, however, bring state recognition of the couple's married status and did not necessarily confer any legal benefits, certainly not any federal benefits.

A letter to the editor of the *New York Times* just after the November 1998 elections summed up one perspective on race, gender, and the law of marriage: "Three states held ballot initiatives on marriage" during the 1998 elections, observed Michael Pasnik. "South Carolina voted to end their State Constitution's 103-year-old ban on interracial marriage," yet, at the same time, "residents of Alaska and Hawaii voted to amend their State Constitutions to ban same-sex marriages." Supporters of the modern ban characterized same-sex marriages as immoral and unnatural, he said, "the same arguments used . . . when miscegenation was banned." He concluded, "I hope gay people do not have to wait 103 years to overcome the prejudice that generated the Alaska and Hawaii initiatives and to see those proposed discriminatory amendments erased."

The same-sex question at the end of the twentieth century looked a lot like the opposite-race question had at various points in the past, whether in the 1870s or the 1960s. The matter was controversial. Most people, when asked, disapproved, as a large majority of the voters in Hawaii and Alaska demonstrated. But constitutional rights are designed in part to protect minorities from majorities, and the Vermont Supreme Court took center stage on the matter in 1999.

Vermont

Nina Beck and Stacy Jolles were a couple, and as a couple they wished to marry. Because both of them were female, however, they were denied a license to marry in Vermont. They went to state court, where they argued that the Vermont constitution's common benefits clause required that they be granted the recognition and benefits that they sought. That clause—modeled on Pennsylvania's, itself borrowed from Virginia—declared that "government is, or ought to be, instituted for the common benefit, protection, and security of the people, nation, or community, and not for the particular . . . advantage of any single person, family, or set of persons, who are a part only of that community." The trial court ruled against them. Vermont's marriage statutes were not intended to cover same-sex couples, it ruled, and, because they furthered a legitimate state interest in fostering "the link between procreation and child rearing," they were constitutional in their limited definition.

Together with two other Vermont same-sex couples—Lois Farnham and Holly Puterbaugh as well as Stan Baker and Peter Harrigan—Beck and Jolles appealed the trial court's ruling to the Vermont Supreme Court. In oral argument in November 1999, their attorney, Beth Robinson, pointed toward the pathbreaking *Perez v. Sharp* decision in the California Supreme Court a half-century earlier, in which California's miscegenation law was overturned. That decision "was controversial, it was courageous and it was correct," she told the Vermont court, which should follow its lead and apply the same reasoning to the matters under dispute here. Employing language from *Perez* as well as *Loving v. Virginia*, Justice Denise R. Johnson asked Eve Jacobs-Carnahan, the attorney for the state, if marriage was "a fundamental right." Jacobs-Carnahan, relying on a narrow approach more like that taken by the US

Supreme Court back in *Pace v. Alabama*, replied, "Yes, but it's a fundamental right between a man and a woman."

The Vermont Supreme Court, in ruling that December, began its opinion with a question: "May the State of Vermont exclude same-sex couples from the benefits and protections that its laws provide to opposite-sex married couples?" Given the justices' understanding of the common benefits clause, the answer had to be no: "We hold that the State is constitutionally required to extend to same-sex couples the common benefits and protections that flow from marriage under Vermont law." The court's decision quoted the statement in *Loving v. Virginia* that "the freedom to marry has long been recognized as one of the vital personal rights." How that recognition related to the Vermont state constitution governed the court's decision.

The Vermont legislature would have to implement this ruling, but it had discretion: "Whether this ultimately takes the form of inclusion within the marriage laws themselves or a parallel 'domestic partnership' system . . . rests with the Legislature." All Vermonters, said the court, must receive the same "benefit, protection, and security" from their state government. The 1857 *Dred Scott* decision had long since been overruled in matters of race and slavery. Perhaps, the court suggested, a similar sea change was overdue in matters of gender and marriage.

Early in the year 2000, the Vermont legislature passed, and the governor signed, a bill to establish a category called "civil union" that would give all the benefits of marriage to same-sex couples under state law that heterosexual married couples enjoyed.

From the perspective of either side in the continuing controversy, much had changed. Much, however, had not. Each couple was celebrating a "civil union," not a marriage, and the newly validated relationship carried no benefits under federal law. As for the question of comity, DOMA had already declared that no state had to recognize such relationships, and any number of states had declared their intent to confer no recognition of same-sex marriages, no matter what they were called.

Perhaps Vermont would rescind its pioneering legislation. Two opponents of civil unions, David Orgon Coolidge and William C. Duncan, soon published a law review article calling for Vermont to adopt its own marriage amendment. Initiatives in Hawaii and Vermont, straws in the wind that showed a movement building power and acceptance, were no more conclusive than they were universal. Hawaii voters had deflected the initiative that a handful of judges had taken. Vermont voters might do the same, although under Vermont's constitution an amendment of the sort that Hawaii and Alaska voters approved would be several years away, so the Vermont law would have time to grow roots. Either way, traditional barriers to same-sex marriage had come under assault. Public barriers to private choices had become a matter of public debate.

As with interracial marriages in some places and at some times, same-sex marriages had long been unthinkable. Evan Wolfson, a lawyer with the Lambda Legal Defense and Education Fund, spoke for the proponents of change. "Through this law," he said, "Vermont becomes a pioneer for families and equality." The very name of Wolfson's group reflected one way in which same-sex advocates had emulated the strategy of the Civil Rights Movement and its longtime leading organization in pushing for legal change, the NAACP with its Legal Defense Fund. Wolfson said about the events of July 1, "American will see that when lesbians and gay men are given access to most of the rights and obligations of civil marriage, the sky will not fall and the institution of marriage will be even stronger."

Separate, Unequal

Decades after *Loving v. Virginia*, most Americans had made their peace with the *Loving* decision as to the law of race and marriage. By that time, many were prepared to consider the merits of applying the decision to same-sex relationships. More were not. Debates continued over the definition of marriage, and over the meaning of the Constitution, the jurisdiction of federal and state authority, and the roles of the courts on the law of marriage. Much of that debate—what was the meaning of *Loving* for same-sex marriages?—took place in law journals and in courtrooms. Much took place in political campaigns, on the floor of Congress, in newspapers, and in state legislatures.

On election day in the year 2000, one chapter ended, and another took fuller shape regarding state restrictions on who could marry whom. On November 7, Alabama voters removed from their state constitution the ancient—and by that point long-since unenforceable—prohibition against interracial marriage. Alabama was the last state to do so. On the same day, voters in Nebraska put into their state constitution a ban against recognizing same-sex marriage, and voters in Nevada did the same.

Nebraska and Nevada weren't the first to take the action they did. They followed Hawaii and Alaska; but people in those two states, when they acted two years earlier, had been intent on reining in their state judiciary, responding to developments in their own state, not elsewhere. Moreover, when Nebraska and Nevada changed their constitutions, they preempted successful litigation as well as legislation there. According to Nebraska's marriage amendment, "Only marriage between a man and a woman shall be valid or recognized" there. Going further, it continued: "The uniting of two persons of the same sex in a civil union, domestic partnership, or other similar same-sex relationship shall not be valid or recognized in Nebraska." This constitutional amendment was itself, in part, declared unconstitutional, in *Citizens for Equal Protection v. Bruning* (2005), by US District Judge Joseph F. Bataillon. The US Court of Appeals for the Eighth Circuit, however, drawing in part on the US Supreme Court's dismissal of the Minnesota case *Baker v. Nelson* back in 1972, reversed Judge Bataillon the next year and upheld the Nebraska initiative.

In the *Loving* litigation, the Virginia Supreme Court held to precedent and upheld the restrictive law, but then the US Supreme Court insisted on privileging race as a special category under the Fourteenth Amendment. Viewed another way, the Supreme Court insisted that race be dethroned as a category according to which people's choices were sorted out under the law. Similarly — and necessarily first, before *Loving* — the Court had, in *Brown v. Board of Education*, overruled *Plessy v. Ferguson* and its "separate-but-equal" formula. Only if gender achieved a comparable level of significance — only when matters relating to sexual identity and sexual orientation were subject to similar strict scrutiny — might a federal court rule favorably on same-sex marriages.

In the world of *Pace*, whites could not marry blacks, nor could blacks marry whites, so both were similarly restricted, and violations — getting married anyway, or acting in ways that looked much the same — brought identical penalties to each party. Under that analogy, a century later, men could not marry men any more than women might marry women. The disabilities persisted in that, if a same-sex couple achieved legal recognition in one state, whether the legal relationship could be transported into another state was open to doubt, and in fact—as often had been true for interracial couples as late as the Lovings—expressly denied.

The concept of separate but equal failed in any case. Black-black as well as white-white marriages were fully recognized in every state after the end of slavery in 1865, and each group could develop its own communities. Under the prevailing law same-sex communities, by contrast, could not fully develop alongside heterosexual communities. William N. Eskridge Jr., in his book *The Case for Same-Sex Marriage: From Sexual Liberty to Civilized Commitment*, wrote in 1996: "The prohibition against same-sex marriage is even more discriminatory than the prohibition against different-race marriage. Even under *Pace* the states could not enact a law saying African Americans could not marry one another. Yet this is how current state law affects the class of so-called homosexuals: we cannot marry one another." The observation might have gone on to point toward the preemancipation denial of slaves' rights to marry at all.

In the end, only a change in federal understanding could amend the law across the land. As in *Loving*, such a change would more or less track changing attitudes about what rights individuals ought to have that no state could fail to respect. The right to privacy would have to include sexual orientation, as well as racial identity, in family formation. It would have to go beyond the formula in *Loving* about race and marriage to incorporate homosexual relations as well as heterosexual.

To achieve the objective being sought by many couples in the early twenty-first century, marriages within one biological sex—in fact, regardless of sexual identity—would have to become as constitutionally protected as were marriages across some line that had once been drawn to distinguish racial identities. Two-thirds of the way through the twentieth century, in *Loving v. Virginia*, the US Supreme Court revolutionized the constitutional relationship of race and marriage. At the end of the century, it had done no such thing with regard to the law of gender identity or sexual orientation and marriage. Across the country, however, same-sex couples pressed their case, seeking to achieve legal change that would reflect the social change. They drew upon *Loving v. Virginia* to accomplish that.

The parallels between race and sexual orientation were by no means fully evident. For one thing, *Pace v. Alabama*, like *Loving v. Virginia*, was a matter of criminal law, and the litigation on same-sex relations was typically brought by couples who claimed civil rights they wanted recognized; they were not responses to state prosecutions for acting out those rights.

Yet *Hardwick v. Bowers* (1986) had revealed a criminal prosecution, and in 2003 the Supreme Court heard argument in another such case, *Lawrence v. Texas*. The Georgia statute in the 1986 case criminalized sodomy whether by heterosexuals or homosexuals; the Texas law in the 2003 case did so only with same-sex couples in mind. Most states, like Texas, had by this time repealed their sodomy statues in general, but some, like Texas, targeted same-sex relationships. The Court majority overruled *Hardwick* and threw out all such laws, regardless of people's gender. No longer, anywhere, were same-sex couples by definition in violation of state law.

Massachusetts

Back in August 1970, not long after Richard John Baker and James Michael McConnell had applied for a marriage license in Minnesota, President Richard M. Nixon had mused at the prospect of same-sex marriage: "I can't go that far—That's the year 2000. Negroes [and whites]—OK; but that's too far." The year 2000 eventually came, and Thomas Lang and Alexander Westerhoff, dealers in antiques, had visited Vermont from an adjacent state, Massachusetts, as soon as civil unions became available there. They recognized the limits on the civil union that they nonetheless celebrated in Brattleboro that first possible day. Going public and lobbying for further change, they celebrated their ceremony in front of television cameras as well as friends. Lang observed: "We have a long fight ahead of us" in Massachusetts "to see these rights and these freedoms."

Perhaps Massachusetts would come to emulate Vermont? In 2003 that question arose in the case of *Goodridge v. Department of Public Health*, which was argued in March, the same month as *Lawrence v. Texas*, but was decided several months after *Lawrence*. The Massachusetts court's

4–3 majority opinion, issued in November, determined that marriage licenses for same-sex couples in the Bay State could not constitutionally be denied, and that even civil unions did not go far enough. Starting from the premise that "absolute equality before the law is a fundamental principle" of the Massachusetts constitution, the court determined even the Vermont arrangement to be too limited, and in May 2004 Massachusetts began granting marriage licenses to same-sex couples.

Three passages from the court's majority opinion, written by Chief Justice Margaret H. Marshall, demonstrate both its reasoning and its reliance on such cases as *Perez v. Sharp, Loving v. Virginia,* and, from earlier that same year, *Lawrence v. Texas.* One of these comes from the text of the decision, the other two from footnotes to that text:

> For decades, indeed centuries, in much of this country (including Massachusetts) no lawful marriage was possible between white and black Americans. That long history availed not when the Supreme Court of California held in 1948 that a legislative prohibition against interracial marriage violated the due process and equality guarantees of the Fourteenth Amendment, *Perez v. Sharp,* . . . or when, nineteen years later, the United States Supreme Court also held that a statutory bar to interracial marriage violated the Fourteenth Amendment, *Loving v. Virginia.* . . . In this case, as in *Perez* and *Loving,* a statute deprives individuals of access to an institution of fundamental legal, personal, and social significance — the institution of marriage — because of a single trait: skin color in *Perez* and *Loving,* sexual orientation here. As it did in *Perez* and *Loving,* history must yield to a more fully developed understanding of the invidious quality of the discrimination.

> When the Supreme Court of California decided *Perez v. Sharp,* . . . a precursor to *Loving,* racial inequality was rampant and normative, segregation in public and private institutions was commonplace, the civil rights movement had not yet been launched, and the "separate but equal" doctrine of *Plessy v. Ferguson* . . . was still good law. The lack of popular consensus favoring integration (including interracial marriage) did not deter the Supreme Court of California from holding

that that State's antimiscegenation statute violated the plaintiffs' constitutional rights. Neither the *Perez* court nor the *Loving* Court was content to permit an unconstitutional situation to fester because the remedy might not reflect a broad social consensus.

Recently, the United States Supreme Court has reaffirmed that the Constitution prohibits a State from wielding its formidable power to regulate conduct in a manner that demeans basic human dignity, even though that statutory discrimination may enjoy broad public support.

Yet a resolution of the larger controversy might very well go in a very different direction than proponents of same-sex legal equality and sexual opportunity wished, as had *Hardwick v. Bowers*. It was one thing for the nation's highest court to decriminalize same-sex sex as it did in *Lawrence v. Texas*. It was far worse, it seemed to many, for the highest state court in Massachusetts, that same year, to mandate the availability of same-sex marriage as it did in *Goodridge v. Department of Public Health*.

So in 2003 and on through the presidential campaign of 2004, support built for amending the US Constitution to deflect any likelihood that judges might interpret a law to require recognition of same-sex marriage. Nor, under the proposal, could any state be required to recognize a same-sex marriage contracted elsewhere: "Marriage in the United States shall consist only of the union of a man and a woman. Neither this Constitution or the constitution of any state, nor state or federal law, shall be construed to require that marital status or the legal incidents thereof be conferred on unmarried couples or groups." The language seemed to bar even something short of marriage — including the legal alternative of civil unions, Vermont's choice — from being enacted by any state legislature. Left unchallenged, perhaps, were domestic partnership statutes, ordinances, and company policies that conferred benefits on same-sex partners.

The pioneering developments in Massachusetts brought same-sex marriage to one state, but it also galvanized opponents of same-sex marriage in other states to go to the polls in the 2004 presidential election, as legal scholar Michael Klarman has recounted. They likely made the difference in Ohio, in which case they put President George W. Bush over the top in the electoral college and gave him a second term. As a candidate for reelection, Bush had supported a federal amendment to ban same-sex marriage, and in Ohio he benefited from the ballot's inclusion of a state amendment to ban such marriages. Given the opportunity, he nominated John Roberts and Samuel Alito to the US Supreme Court, where they were expected to turn back any attempt that might reach the Court to legitimate same-sex marriage.

After Massachusetts

Under federal law, at the dawn of the new millennium, there had been no evidence of movement, and certainly no wholesale change. If there was change, DOMA—together with the rise of marriage amendments to state constitutions—represented the sort that the NAACP had feared about school segregation as well as the marital color line in the 1940s, a premature effort that might obtain a retrograde outcome. In the meantime, however, a favorable end could perhaps be achieved at retail through decisions of state courts interpreting state constitutions. Hawaii had pointed the way.

As early as 1970, just three years after *Loving*, two men in Minnesota had sought to recruit the law and logic of *Loving* to their cause, but state judges were not buying those arguments. Subsequent efforts in other states came to a similar end, and the effort was abandoned. The litigation mine had played out, it seemed, before yielding anything of value. Yet later, the rulings in Hawaii and Alaska—and in Vermont and Massachusetts—showed that state courts could go the other way.

When same-sex couples returned to court in the 1990s, they took a very different approach than in the 1970s, calling instead on provisions in their state constitutions, to be interpreted in state courts, to obtain marital benefits. At first, in jurisdictions that had not yet even become states when the Lovings were arrested in 1958, their efforts proved successful, both in Hawaii and in a lesser-known case in Alaska. In each of those states, however, voters soon reversed the judicial ruling by amending the language in the state constitution that had been construed to grant marriage licenses to same-sex couples. A similar effort in Vermont also led to a court victory, but in that instance "civil unions" were established in 2000. In 2003 the highest state court in Massachusetts interpreted "absolute equality before the law" as requiring the legalization of gay marriage. The decisions in neither Vermont nor Massachusetts had been undone.

Each year Loving Day, established at first to celebrate the right of interracial marriage, welcomes couples of all kinds of interethnic combinations. It also welcomes gay and lesbian couples, not just straight folks. *Loving v. Virginia*, as history unfolded, pointed in divergent ways in 1967, and Loving Day reflects both of those directions. The Court had spoken in very clear terms about "the freedom to marry," but it had also spoken directly only to heterosexual couples. Same-sex couples had very soon gone to court seeking to reconcile the two directions, to bring them into harmony by extending "the right to marry" beyond its interracial and heterosexual orientation.

At the time of Loving Day 2007, on the fortieth anniversary of the 1967 decision, two lawyers got together to join the two causes. Bernie Cohen had been cocounsel in the *Loving* case in Virginia back in the 1960s. Evan Wolfson had been cocounsel in the Hawaii case, *Baehr v. Lewin*, a quarter-century later. Cohen and Wolfson saw the direct connections between the court rulings in *Loving* and *Baehr*, on the one hand, and the victory in Massachusetts in 2003, for example, on the other. Wolfson took the lead, phoned Cohen, and asked him to add his name to a column he was writing. This was at a time when many straight Americans remained uncomfortable with the subject, even if sympathetic, and Cohen remembers that Wolfson was able to clarify matters every time he raised a concern and, moreover, that his son and daughter had no such ambivalence as their dad and helped him step resolutely into the issue. Regardless, Cohen had sponsored a measure a quarter-century earlier that, though it passed only one house of the Virginia legislature, would have, as the language went, decriminalized intimate sexual acts between consenting adults in private venues, regardless of the gender of the participants. Receptive, he agreed, and "Loving Equality," arguing against "exclusion from marriage," came out in the *Huffington Post*.

Cohen and Wolfson called for an extension of the law and logic of *Loving* and marriage to same-sex couples. "Today," they wrote, "we rightly celebrate *Loving v. Virginia* as a milestone in racial equality, an important vindication of marriage as a cherished civil right, and a testament to the importance of fighting for equality." Four decades after the US Supreme Court had ruled against restrictions in interracial marriage—put an end to them, not only in Virginia but throughout the country—they looked for a similar acceptance of same-sex marriage: "Hopefully, legislators and judges will find their courage, and our nation won't need too many lawyers working too much longer on behalf of too many couples and their kids before we end ongoing marriage discrimination—the best way to celebrate the anniversary of what *Loving* is really all about."

At the same time, it is said, Mrs. Loving herself came out with a statement in support of same-sex marriage. The statement was evidently written by others, given the ways some facts are rendered, such as the timing of Judge Bazile's assertion about the separate races. But it is designed to address connections between her battle in the 1960s and that of so many others four decades later, and it concludes:

> My generation was bitterly divided over something that should have been so clear and right. The majority believed that what the judge said, that it was God's plan to keep people apart, and that government should discriminate against people in love. But I have lived long enough now to see big changes. The older generation's fears and prejudices have given way, and today's young people realize that if someone loves someone they have a right to marry.
>
> Surrounded as I am now by wonderful children and grandchildren, not a day goes by that I don't think of Richard and our love, our right to marry, and how much it meant to me to have that freedom to marry the person precious to me, even if others thought he was the "wrong kind of person" for me to marry. I believe all Americans, no matter their race, no matter their sex, no matter their sexual orientation, should have that same freedom to marry. Government has no business imposing some people's religious beliefs over others. Especially if it denies people's civil rights.
>
> I am still not a political person, but I am proud that Richard's and my name is on a court case that can help reinforce the love, the commitment, the fairness, and the family that so many people, black or white, young or old, gay or straight seek in life. I support the freedom to marry for all. That's what *Loving*, and loving, are all about.

An account in the *New York Times* in December 2008, some months after Mildred had died, described in some detail the thoughtful response she gave in a spring 2007 meeting in her Central Point home to an invitation by people from the gay rights group Faith in America to link the two causes. It told how she spoke of it with friends and family and then, some days later, decided to go ahead. The account sounds plausible. It seems that Mildred agreed to the statement for the group to take with them, but for use at an upcoming gathering of that group and not beyond. She and they had established a personal connection, but she retained her wish to remain a private person.

2012

In February 2012, movement along multiple fronts pointed up how much had changed, and how much had not, in the years since a few same-sex couples in Hawaii first went to court in the early 1990s for the right to obtain a marriage license. A federal appeals court handed down its ruling in a long-running case from California, one that began in 2008 with a decision inaugurating same-sex marriage in that state by the California Supreme Court—a divided court, split 4–3, just as in the 1948 *Perez* case, on which the court majority drew for its ruling sixty years later. Approval by 52 percent of the voters that fall, however, of Proposition 8, providing a marriage amendment for California, brought an end to any new same-sex marriages and a beginning of litigation that stretched on for years. The ruling in February 2012 rejected Proposition 8. Observing that legal changes in California had offered just about all the material benefits that marriage could, the 2–1 court majority asked what—aside from invidious discrimination, a denial of full human dignity—was keeping the state from recognizing same-sex marriage. Opponents of same-sex marriage pondered their approach, including a possible appeal to the US Supreme Court, where, however, if the Court agreed to take the case, neither side could be confident of victory and the stakes were potentially huge.

Within days of the appeals court ruling, while parties were still mulling their next steps, a federal district judge in California declared the 1996 federal Defense of Marriage Act itself unconstitutional, as it applied to the case before him. Health benefits had been denied to the female spouse of a federal worker who happened to be lesbian, and this denial, Judge Jeffrey White ruled, denied her right to equal protection of the laws. Other such rulings followed.

That same month, legislatures in Washington State, New Jersey, and Maryland—on the Pacific Coast and the Atlantic—passed same-sex marriage measures; but in none of these instances could a permanent change in the legal environment be anticipated right away. In Washington, Democratic Governor Chris Gregoire gave her approval to a bill legalizing same-sex marriage; but the law was due to go into effect only on June 7, and meanwhile opponents, looking to collect enough signatures to put the matter on the ballot in the fall elections, hoped to put the effective date on hold. In Maryland, the legislature passed a similar measure, and Democratic Governor Martin O'Malley had promised he would sign it into law, as he did on March 1, but opponents were already gearing up to gather enough signatures to get the question on the ballot for that fall there as well.

And in New Jersey, both houses of the legislature passed a bill to legalize same-sex marriage, but Republican Governor Chris Christie, as he had promised he would, vetoed it, calling instead for maintenance of the state's civil unions approach and sending the matter to the voters in the fall elections. Democrats in the legislature held the position that gay marriage was a constitutional right and not subject to referendum; the governor held that only a state constitutional amendment changing the definition of marriage could properly validate such a shift in public policy.

Vermont's adoption of civil unions in 2000 supplied, within a few years, a new norm in public opinion and public policy. Americans appeared increasingly ready to accept the notion of more or less equal benefits for same-sex couples. But the word "marriage" seemed much more of a reach. The Supreme Court's 1967 language in *Loving v. Virginia* regarding "the freedom to marry" for interracial couples that were also heterosexual was not yet widely accepted as applying to same-sex couples. Vermont's breakthrough court decision in 1999, followed by the legislature's passage of a law consistent with it, proved, however, insufficient when similar questions came before the Massachusetts high court just a few years later. So Massachusetts adopted same-sex marriage, revealing another big shift, from "civil unions" to "the freedom to marry."

By 2012, even before the legislative action in Washington, Maryland, and New Jersey, six states as well as the District of Columbia had approved same-sex marriage. Vermont moved from civil unions to marriage itself beginning in 2009, and Connecticut and New Hampshire made similar transitions. As of early 2012, the post-*Loving* legal, political, and constitutional history of same-sex marriage continued to play out across America. Perhaps, as one person put it on February 7 in response to the appeals court ruling in California on Proposition 8, "Twenty years from now, the idea that two gay people can't be married will seem as ludicrous as the idea that an interracial couple can't marry is today."

In November 2012, when voters went to the polls in Washington, Maryland, and New Jersey, they approved the handiwork of their state legislatures the preceding February. The change was stark from the 1990s, when voters in Hawaii and Alaska had both rejected, by two-to-one margins, rulings by state courts that seemed about to bring same-sex marriage. The central tendency in American law and culture had already moved to supporting civil unions, and increasingly that central tendency was moving toward supporting marriage itself. In most states, however, same-sex couples were not yet free to marry.

DOMA Gets One Wing Clipped

Meanwhile, two cases made their way toward eventual rulings by the nation's highest court. One had to do with Proposition 8, a referendum that had rejected an act of the California legislature permitting same-sex marriage and thus had put an end to a period during which thousands of same-sex couples had obtained marriage licenses in that state. The other came from New York, a state that recognized same-sex marriages, something the federal government did not, as Edith Windsor discovered when the Internal Revenue Service hit her with a huge tax bill upon the death of her wife (under New York law, but not federal law), Thea Spyer, in 2009. Windsor and Spyer had been together for thirty years when, in 1993, they registered as domestic partners. They married in Canada in 2007, then returned to the home they shared in New York City, where New York state law recognized their marriage.

On June 26, 2013, during the Court's very last week of the 2012–2013 session, a 5–4 decision in *Hollingsworth v. Perry* left in place a lower court ruling that favored restoration of the California statute authorizing gay marriage in that state. Four justices held that the Court should have decided the case on its own rather than conclude that the plaintiffs lacked standing to bring the case to the Court. How each justice in the Court minority, or for that matter the Court majority, would have ruled on the merits, however, was far less certain. When California's law went into effect, the proportion of Americans living in states that authorized same-sex marriage jumped from 18 percent to 30, and the number of states in which gay couples could marry climbed to twelve, plus the District of Columbia.

The other decision that day, *United States v. Windsor*, although limited in scope and reasoning, was a more universal victory for gay rights advocates. It threw out the provision in DOMA defining marriage as between a man and a woman and thus denying federal benefits to same-sex partners even when their marital status was fully recognized under their own state's laws. DOMA lived on, however, in its other provision, which permitted any state to refuse to recognize same-sex marriages initiated under another state's laws. Neither decision, of course, went so far as to declare constitutionally impermissible any state's refusal to countenance same-sex marriage. As for Justice Alito and Justice Roberts, they carried out their projected roles, deeming DOMA constitutional, but by the scantest of margins they had too few allies on the Court to carry the day and sustain the law.

In Virginia, within two weeks of the Court's rulings, the ACLU declared its intent to file suit against the Virginia constitution's prohibition of same-sex marriage, a ban that had been incorporated in 2006 into the state Bill of Rights. The Virginia ACLU executive director, Claire Gastañaga, spoke of how same-sex couples and their children "deserve the legal protections that come with state-recognized marriage." Virginia Cobb, president of the leading organization in Virginia opposed to same-sex marriage, guessed that "the debate over marriage will continue in the legislative and political process, where it belongs," where she hoped, of course, denial of such recognition would continue to prevail. As to the substance of the proposed change, her language sounded ambiguous: "The Family Foundation of Virginia will continue to educate on the reason for marriage as the bedrock of society and the structure through which children are best protected and can most likely mature into productive members of society."

A public opinion poll in Virginia released a few months later, in October 2013, showed a widening reversal from seven years earlier, with 56 percent of those surveyed opposing the restriction and in favor of permitting same-sex marriage, and 36 percent wishing to retain the ban. Some legislators introduced a bill in January 2014 to undo the Virginia constitutional amendment, though the measure failed, and in any event the process of removing the restriction from the state constitution would have taken at least through 2016. Meanwhile, two suits in federal district court were under way in Virginia, one from Norfolk, the other from Harrisonburg.

In early 2014, Virginia's newly elected attorney general, Mark Herring, a Democrat who had narrowly defeated his Republican opponent, announced that he could not see his way to defending the Virginia constitutional provision banning any form of same-sex marriage. Doing so, he took a very different approach than had his predecessor back at the time of the *Loving* litigation, at the same time modeling the position US Attorney General Eric Holder had taken with regard to DOMA.

Despite the breakthrough victories at the Supreme Court in June 2013, the future remained uncertain. On the one hand, the Court's ruling in the DOMA case played significant roles in other litigation. New Mexico's statutes did not expressly bar same-sex marriage, and certainly its state constitution did not, but that did not mean that same-sex couples could obtain marriage licenses. In several New Mexico counties, however, shortly after the DOMA decision, clerks began issuing marriage licenses to same-sex couples, but their validity was uncertain, and the matter went to the New Mexico Supreme Court for resolution. That court, in December 2013, ruled in *Griego v. Oliver* that restricting marriage to heterosexual couples violated the state constitution's equal protection clause. In the weeks that followed, a federal judge in Utah ruled against that state's ban on same-sex marriage, and in January 2014 another federal judge, in Oklahoma, did the same, though both rulings were appealed, so the outcome remained uncertain.

On the other hand, neither of the Court's rulings in June 2013 promised an outcome like that in *Loving v. Virginia* that would take down bans against same-sex marriage everywhere. Rather, the 5–4 majority in *United States v. Windsor* took an approach more akin to the *McLaughlin* case from Florida in 1964, in which the Court expressly declared that it was not addressing the right of marriage in the face of race-based restrictions. *Windsor* took a states' rights approach. Noting, for one thing, that the matter was not before the Court, it did not address the section in DOMA that authorized states to refuse to recognize out-of-state same-sex marriage. As for the section it ruled unconstitutional, on Congress's denial of federal benefits to same-sex couples whose marriages had been recognized under their states' laws, the Court majority insisted that DOMA departed from the "history and tradition of reliance on state law to define marriage." So, wrote Justice Kennedy, "This opinion and its holding are confined to those lawful marriages." Americans had a right to same-sex marriage only insofar as their state recognized such a marriage.

Even after *Windsor,* Americans had no right under the US Constitution to same-sex marriage. While very much an expansion of the recognized rights of a very large and rapidly growing number of same-sex couples, the rationale and rhetoric of *Windsor* seemed to make it more difficult, not less, to assert a right that would override the laws of states that refused to recognize a right to marriage regardless of gender. Such a ruling might take the form, first, that all states, and not only the federal government, had to recognize same-sex marriages that were valid in the state where they had originated, though such would indeed be an innovation. More of a reach would be a ruling that, to constitutionalize a right to marriage by same-sex partners, used the language about discrimination, clearly employed by the Court majority in *Windsor*, to undo that Court's reliance, just as clear, on the rights of states to determine their own marriage laws. The Court might soon rule in support of a right to same-sex marriage, but it might well rule the other way.

Regardless, the constitutional question, important as it was, comprised only a part of the equation. In the meantime, legislatures continued to work their own way through the question. Individuals who opposed judicial intervention, arguing that the "people" should decide the matter, whether by referendum or legislation, often objected less to the process than to the substance of policymaking.

The 1996 Defense of Marriage Act had been a congressional response on the mainland to efforts in Hawaii to obtain a judicial ruling in support of same-sex marriage based on the state constitution, an effort turned back at home when voters in Hawaii amended their constitution to prevent such a ruling in state court. As a mark of how much had changed since the 1990s, in November 2013 the Hawaii legislature passed, and the governor signed, a law recognizing same-sex marriage in that state. After the twin rulings in June 2013, more particularly the ruling in *Windsor* throwing out a key part of DOMA, Democratic Governor Neil Abercrombie had called a special session to consider the matter. New Mexico and Hawaii brought the total number of jurisdictions permitting same-sex marriage at the end of 2013 to sixteen states plus the District of Columbia.

The Supreme Court's ruling in *Windsor* meant, meanwhile, that the same-sex marriages that took place in Hawaii beginning in December would immediately bring the many federal benefits of marriage that had been at issue when the Supreme Court ruled in support of same-sex marriages wherever a state gave them recognition. Then again, the couples celebrating their new marital status in Hawaii, though the federal benefits would stick wherever they might go, could not export that relationship to a prohibitionist state like Virginia and have it recognized there under that state's law.

So two main questions remained. New state laws might recognize marriages entered into in other states, but little in the historical record concerning interracial marriage suggested that such would happen until the same state recognized marriages conducted within its own jurisdiction. Federal courts might weigh in there and, clipping DOMA's other wing, decide that out-of-state marriages must be accepted anyway, perhaps under the full faith and credit clause—though as long as marriage remains largely a state matter, that clause seems less likely to work, getting things backward—or under the equal protection clause. The kind of litigation that might lead to such a ruling could well relate to property, as in the 1917 home-ownership case *Buchanan v. Warley*, but in this instance where a family member of the deceased will have stepped forward to contest a claim to inheritance, in the absence of a will, by a same-sex spouse living in another state. Harry, we'll say, had property as well as family in Mississippi but was living in Massachusetts where he had married Fred, and when Harry died Fred claimed the Mississippi property but was challenged by Harry's relatives.

The larger question has to do with nationalizing the freedom to marry regardless of gender identity. The case that leads to such a broad ruling might well come (1) after a number of additional states have adopted same-sex marriage, whether as a result of legislation or a judicial ruling; and (2) with the passage of additional time more Americans have become amenable to seeing such a standard apply across the nation; not to mention (3) with the appointment—or the change of mind—of an additional Supreme Court justice or two who support such a ruling.

It might develop, for example, out of a question of one spouse's ability to make medical decisions for another, when the ill spouse happened to be in a resistant state and authority was denied on the grounds that the marriage was same-sex and therefore not recognized where the decision had to be made. In this case, we'll say, Rachel was visiting her elderly parents in Mississippi but fell gravely ill, and her wife Susan flew there from their home in Massachusetts to look after her but was denied visiting rights or authority over medical decisions. The case might go into federal court and, on appeal, make its way to the nation's highest court. At that point a single standard will more likely appear to be just, necessary, and timely, and the Supreme Court will move from its limited *McLaughlin*-type stand in 2013 to an actual *Loving*-type ruling on the freedom to marry. Then again, such a case might give rise to a ruling restricted to addressing, and establishing, the transferability of a same-sex marriage, though a ruling that a state must recognize an out-of-state marriage would come close to nationalizing the freedom to marry.

Contests over the legal status of same-sex marriage continued up to and beyond the decision in *Windsor* with or without *Loving*, but the *Loving* case had, for decades by the twenty-first century, shaped and often propelled the development of the central issue of law and marriage that emerged after the end of America's antimiscegenation regime in 1967.

To get from *McLaughlin* to *Loving* took the Supreme Court three and one-half years. What would, what should, follow *Windsor*? The Court, likely divided, might provide an answer. Meanwhile, as in the days of the antimiscegenation regime, a patchwork of laws on gender and marriage prevailed.

Mr. and Mrs. Loving learned on a June day in 1967 that they, together with their three young children, were free to live in Virginia, unchallenged by any law of race and marriage. For them, their wedding in 1958 in Washington, DC, put them at risk, as they soon learned, of prosecution and imprisonment. The Virginia law treated their going out of state to marry, with the intent of evading the law that barred their marrying within Virginia, as indistinguishable from violating the law by marrying within Virginia.

Virginia had outlawed interracial marriage ever since 1691. The specifics had certainly changed over time—how the races were defined, which ones came under the ban of marrying people classified as white, what the penalties were. But the persistence of such laws, and their continued enforcement, even if in more or less random fashion—all this said that something important remained at stake in the eyes of those who promulgated or maintained those laws.

An equal-opportunity penalty directed against both parties, as well as the express ban on going out of state to marry in evasion of Virginia's laws—these two central components of the Lovings' experiences dated from 1878. The Racial Integrity Act itself dated mostly from 1924, secondarily from 1930—legislation that made it of no legal significance what racial mix or nonwhite identity Mildred might have. And the Lovings' penalty of one year's confinement, albeit in their case suspended on condition of their exile, was reduced from a minimum of two years to a single year in 1932.

Between the 1920s and the 1960s, the Lovings' home state went further than had most states with laws against certain kinds of interracial marriage, in very narrowly defining who was a "white" for purposes of marriage, in refusing to recognize out-of-state marriages for in-state residents, and in making a marriage between a "white" person and a "colored" person a crime, in fact a felony that carried a prison sentence.

Had the Lovings settled for the relationship they had before deciding to marry, Virginia's criminal law would not likely ever have come down on them for living together. Entering formally into an interracial marriage—more specifically, one in which only one of them was "white"—led to their arrest, conviction, and exile from the state, until they returned to court and carried an appeal, eventually successful. Their marriage had made them more vulnerable, not less, yet in the long history of the antimiscegenation regime any number of couples had been prosecuted regardless of a formal marriage.

For countless couples in states that still maintained miscegenation laws the evening before the Court's ruling, a new day suddenly dawned. Resolution of a case in Delaware regarding denial of a marriage license probably and of a case from Oklahoma over an inheritance dispute certainly came swiftly in a manner different from how each would have had *Loving* not been ruled upon when and how it was. For countless additional couples, living as they did in states that had never had such restrictions, or had rescinded them, the change did nothing to remove obstacles to their marrying, but it did free them up to move to any state in the nation, and that was no small thing.

For people in a great many "interracial marriages," 1967 held no legal significance in their home states. Taro Kishi, a native of Japan and mainstay on the Texas A&M football team in the 1920s, was a "white" resident of Texas because he was nonblack. His first wife was a Japanese violinist, Mary Oni, with whom he lived in New Jersey, which had no miscegenation law anyway. His second wife was a white woman, Elizabeth Carter, whom he married in Texas in 1957, ten years before the US Supreme Court struck down the miscegenation laws that would have barred his legally marrying a white woman in Virginia or a black woman in Texas. So the antimiscegenation regime could not reach him and his second wife unless they wanted to move to a state, like Virginia or Georgia, that classified their marriage as interracial, and void, and illegal. After 1967, they could marry anyone and live anywhere, no matter what their spouse's racial identity.

The three great religious communities in American life in the 1960s came together as a force for social change. Leaders and followers alike spoke out in support of the Civil Rights Movement, and they participated in the March on Washington for Jobs and Justice and then, later, the Selma march. They reflected, even as they pushed along, the emergence of a broad-based public opinion in support of changes of the sort that the Lovings were seeking for their own family. Already by 1964, the Court overturned *Pace v. Alabama* in the *McLaughlin v. Florida* decision. Three years later, there was reason for confidence, but not for certainty, that the Court was ready to do what in fact it did in *Loving* and overturn all miscegenation laws.

By June 1967, when the Supreme Court handed down its ruling in the case of *Loving v. Virginia*, thirty-four of the fifty states had no miscegenation laws. As far as the law was concerned in those states, people could marry without regard to their racial identity. Had the political process continued on that had led such northern laggards as Wyoming and Indiana to finally repeal their miscegenation laws in 1965, and the southern vanguard Maryland to do so in 1967, there is no basis for projecting that the process would in fact have gone anywhere, or at least very far, in many of the remaining states for a great many years. Missouri might have joined Maryland, and then perhaps West Virginia or Kentucky or Delaware, and maybe Oklahoma or Texas, but no others seemed at all likely. One measure of how long full dismantling of America's antimiscegenation regime might have taken had the Court not ruled the way it did is this: the last two states to repeal their constitution's bans on black-white marriage, even though these had been unenforceable for more than three decades, were South Carolina in 1998 and Alabama in 2000.

Absent the Supreme Court's ruling in *Loving v. Virginia*, had Congress sometime after 1967 sought to enact legislation declaring it the public policy of the nation to permit marriage regardless of racial identity, it could conceivably have done so. But surely there would have been constitutional challenges in some of those sixteen remaining states that, in June 1967, continued to enforce miscegenation statutes. The political ability to enact a federal law would hardly have settled the constitutional status of miscegenation laws in those states that continued to enforce them. The matter would no doubt have gone into the courts after all. Officials in any number of states would no doubt have argued that *Maynard v. Hill* remained good law, continuing to grant states authority over marriage law, and that nothing in the Constitution prohibited states from using race as one of the indicators of who could marry whom.

Short of an amendment to the US Constitution (like the one in 1964 that put an end to the poll tax as a barrier to voting in federal elections)—by no means a sure thing, in fact quite improbable—only the Supreme Court could do that. The poll tax amendment served the material interests of electorates far from the poll tax states, and it did not touch the poll tax as a barrier to participation in state elections. The poll tax analogy does not work. Some dozen states, more or less, would continue to maintain and enforce miscegenation laws, or the Supreme Court would outlaw them. As of the mid-1960s, no other solution appeared viable for many years.

And the nation's highest court could rule the way it did when it did, but it could not have done so on any earlier case, at least before the *McLaughlin* decision in 1964. The *Loving* decision embodied a sea change in American constitutional law of historic proportions. The case the Lovings brought to the US Supreme Court ended a law and policy that, in Virginia, had stood in one form or another since 1691.

Loving v. Virginia ended the antimiscegenation regime in which a large majority of American states had participated into the 1950s, one that directly affected not only the millions of people living in those states but also the many other Americans who might not have been able to move freely to those states. And of course it freed the Lovings to go home to Caroline County, Virginia, not just to visit, but to live out their lives.

The Racial Integrity Act lost its power in Virginia's public policy of marriage in 1967. Yet does the world of Walter Plecker live on, despite his death in 1946 and the ruling in *Loving v. Virginia* two decades later? Citizens and scholars and journalists, "white" and "black" alike, display the rhetoric of race that Plecker's words and actions embodied. Everyone for Plecker was either "white" or "colored," and "colored" for Plecker meant indisputably "negro," later "Negro," or "black," or "African American." Mildred Loving is sometimes "part Indian and part black," but almost always "black," and virtually never "Indian." The 1924 conflation of her identity preceded her birth, and it outlives both her and the case she brought and won. Her freedom to marry, like her staying out of jail, would no longer depend on how she is defined, but Mildred Loving is still not in charge of declaring her own racial identity. The one-drop rule, in a binary world, persists. In the rhetoric of race in American culture, Plecker lives.

——————

The Supreme Court wrote in expansive terms in *Loving* about "the freedom to marry." And yet it also ruled in a narrow way, expressly though unobtrusively leaving intact a precedent, *Maynard v. Hill* (1888), in which the Court had declared the law of marriage to be entirely in the hands of state legislatures. There it remained even after *Loving*, with the crucial exception that states had henceforth to be bound by the Supreme Court's new interpretation of the Fourteenth Amendment when it came to the law of race and marriage. The Court needed to go, and in fact did go, only so far in attaching a right of privacy to the selection of a partner.

Unbundling all the categories or characteristics that state legislatures had traditionally employed in determining the suitability of two people to marry—among them age of consent, first cousins, and racial identity—the Court pulled race out of the bundle but otherwise left the bundle, and the authority, intact. Attorneys for the Lovings never raised, and the Court did not address, the matter of whether a state, such as Virginia, had, under the Constitution's full faith and credit clause or perhaps the privileges and immunities clause, to recognize a marriage entered into elsewhere. And with the invalidation of all miscegenation laws, there was no further occasion for the question to come up as regarded the law of race and marriage.

The relatively narrow definition of "the freedom to marry" came into view when, as early as 1970, gay and lesbian plaintiffs began seeking to apply the law and logic of *Loving* to same-sex marriage. The next year, the Supreme Court of Minnesota, a state that had no law against interracial marriage to be thrown out in 1967, dismissed the *Loving* case as irrelevant, related to "a marital restriction based merely on race." Other attempts in the 1970s were similarly unsuccessful, so the effort trailed away. These plaintiffs did not face prosecution for their marriage; they were trying to secure a marriage license for themselves, much as "interracial" couples had long been denied a license to marry in many states.

Beginning in the 1990s, however, other such couples changed legal strategies and sought victory by claiming benefits under their state constitutions. When state supreme courts subsequently reached the conclusion that Vermont, for example, could no longer deny the equal benefits of marriage (even if the statute that followed used the term "civil unions") and that Massachusetts could not even deny marriage itself, they did so in part on the basis of *Loving*.

Many same-sex couples simultaneously cross racial boundaries, thus capturing both the change associated with *Loving* and the further change of which, to many minds, it holds a promise. Just as not all heterosexual couples contemplate the birth and raising of children, not all "biracial" and "multicultural" children are born to parents who are married to each other. Regarding same-sex marriage, a court could hold that, much as the Supreme Court spoke in *Brown v. Board of Education* of the transformed place of public schools since the framing of the Fourteenth Amendment, the place of marriage in the modern world is a study in contrast to earlier times.

One challenge is to reconfigure the bundle of characteristics and the locus of authority in such a way as to extend the right to freely choose an adult partner, regardless of gender and whether for life or for a season, and then also to have all the rights associated with marriage, including hospital visitation and power over medical decisions. Much of that, at least, has already been happening. By the early 2010s, the center of gravity in American political culture had come to approve "civil unions" for same-sex couples—legal relationships with many of the privileges of marriage, but with no federal benefits—even while continuing to reject their "freedom to marry." But there continued to be regional differences, as there were in 1967, and something of a state-by-state patchwork pattern like that during the long history of the antimiscegenation regime. Beyond that, restrictions on same-sex marriage at the national level went beyond those in place on race into the 1960s.

———

In January 1965, shortly before Judge Bazile declared how "God Almighty created the races," Mrs. Loving countered with her gospel: "The law should allow a person to marry anyone he wants." Just as the Fourteenth Amendment gained an interpretation by the 1960s that worked in a very different way than it had—most of the time, not always—since the 1860s, her own words might come to mean something even more robust than when she voiced them.

Mrs. Loving's Home Going Ceremony, 2008

Mildred Loving died on May 2, 2008. It was one month to the day before her fiftieth wedding anniversary. For nine years after that wedding, the state of Virginia refused to recognize her marriage as anything but an evasion of the law and a felony. During those nine years, the state of Virginia denied her the name "Mrs. Loving."

Early Responses to Mildred Loving's Death

By 2008, much had changed. Not everything had. Nor was everything understood in terms she would have recognized. Newspaper stories, though sympathetic in tone, routinely misstated the facts and misconfigured the larger contexts of the couple and their case. Outsiders, whether from haste and carelessness or a simple lack of comprehension of the particularities of Mrs. Loving's life and community, often got it wrong.

An AP story, which went everywhere, spoke airily about there having been "at least seventeen states" with miscegenation laws on the books when the *Loving* decision was handed down. Yet in the *New York Times* one could read that, at the time of the couple's arrest in 1958, sixteen states had such laws, as though the number had never changed during those nine years or had actually gone up. A number of books on the law of race and marriage, as well as their authors, could have clarified the actual number of states with miscegenation laws in 1958 (twenty-four of forty-eight) or in June 1967 (sixteen of fifty, eight having since repealed their laws, including, weeks earlier, one southern state, Maryland).

The early stories lined the Lovings' three children up as "Donald, Peggy and Sidney," instead of placing Sidney first. And when they gave details from 1958, they typically said, as the *New York Times* did, that "when Mildred became pregnant at 18, they decided" to get married. That statement mixed up the actual story, though those facts were far less readily available for news writers to obtain, since the earlier books had not told anything approaching the full story, nor had they reliably sorted the facts out.

All the press accounts spoke of Mildred as a "black woman." In the parlance of the twenty-first century, she was African American. That is, she had some African ancestry, so under the culture's adoption of the one-drop rule of black racial identity, she was black. But the one-drop rule had come to Virginia law in 1924, not before, and its relevance to marriage had vanished in 1967. Using such a word, using that short-hand way to describe her, violated her self-definition by denying her Native American descent. The use of such easy outsiders' terminology, one could say, privileged the racist legislation of the 1920s by erasing her Indian background and consigning her to a catchall "colored" category, recalibrated to "black" or "African American," an updated rhetoric that retained the categories established in the Racial Integrity Act, as though the world that produced that particular law persisted down to the present.

Press accounts typically attributed the couple's 1958 arrest to Virginia's 1924 Racial Integrity Act and spoke of the 1967 court ruling as having finally legitimated "interracial marriage." Such shorthand distorts the story in multiple ways. By 1967, far more states than not already recognized "interracial marriages," whatever their stance had been at earlier times. Virginia's ban against marriages between whites and other people, whether black, Indian, or mixed, dated from 1691. So did the penalty of exile, at least for the white person in the marriage. Over the years, the specifics, all of them, underwent modification, but the underlying ban against black-white marriages persisted without a ripple. The law that deemed it a felony for both parties dated from 1878, whether the marriage took place within Virginia or was imported from another jurisdiction by a couple who evidently sought to evade the Virginia law by making a day trip to DC, as the Lovings had in 1958. So did the two-to five-year penalty that was long attached to the crime. The one-year term in prison (actually, jail) handed down at the couple's trial in January 1959, then suspended on condition that they leave the state, came a few years after the 1924 Racial Integrity Act.

What did the 1924 Racial Integrity Act have to do with any of it? Two things, and two only, though they were very important to many couples, perhaps including the Lovings. Fewer people than before could reliably make their way past the "one-drop" rule and maintain a white racial identity. And various groups were, for the first time, expressly assigned to the "colored" side of the great racial divide, a category that included people who were "Negro, Mongolian, American Indian, Malay, or any mixture thereof." The 1924 law banned marriages between "white" people and "colored" individuals, but it in no way challenged the right of someone who was ethnic Chinese to marry someone African American. The only racial identity to be safeguarded in its "integrity" was "Caucasian." That is, "interracial" marriage had for centuries remained entirely legal in Virginia, so long as no "white" person was party to it.

As for the one-drop rule of black racial identity, that hardly came into play, when no one, including Mr. Loving, ever suggested that he was anything other than white, and everyone assumed that Mrs. Loving was not. Was she at least one-fourth black, as the nineteenth-century rule had specified would make a person "colored" or "negro" in Virginia? Was she at least one-sixteenth black, as the 1910 law had set for the boundary between white and black? She had described herself in 1963 as "part negro, + part indian," though her 1958 application for a marriage license in Washington, DC, identified her simply as "Indian."

Conversation by E-Mail

Discussions of Mrs. Loving took place in other venues. One was a listserve operated by the state library, the Library of Virginia. One participant cut rudely across the grain of most of the postings on her death. A lawyer by trade, and operating under the pseudonym "J South," this person wanted to know: "Weren't John Smith and Pocahontas a mixed race marriage in Virginia some time before the Loving's decided to make a Federal case out of the whole thing." One doubter retorted: "Do you mean John Rolfe?"

To which J South replied, still seeking to provoke his readers: "John whomever. He was still a white guy who married this Indian chick way back in the day in Virginia. The Loving case was a test case to get rid of a law that was essentially un enforced in Virginia much as the 55 mile an hour speed limit is largely un enforced. It apparently had no chilling effect on anyone, including the Lovings, who wanted to get married in the state. It was a vestige of Jim Crow that had long died and just needed to be taken off the books. The NAACP funded and backed the whole thing, and since the Lovings were living in DC at the time, there was no risk of any sort of enforcement by the Commonwealth." He concluded: "What else did she ever do for the public good?"

Replies of amazement greeted this outburst. One writer expressed himself in a single word, and then his electronic voice trailed away: "Wow . . . "

Law professor Paul Finkelman, never at a loss for words, pounded out a paragraph or two: "The police went into the Loving's bedroom in the middle of the night and arrested them; the judge sentenced them to long prison sentences if they did not leave the state; and furthermore, the NAACP refused to take the case; it was not their case. In other words everything you say below is utterly incorrect. I would suggest you read 'Tell the Court I Love My Wife' by Va. Tech's Peter Wallenstein before you babble on about things you do not know and mislead members of this list by your lack of knowledge."

Another writer observed: "Your cynicism is astounding. They wanted to move back to Caroline County, from which they had been kicked out. Aren't we supposed to be able to live wherever we want? They lived in DC because they'd have been thrown in jail if they went back home. There were a lot of white/native marriages at the beginnings of Virginia, but that has nothing to do with later miscegenation laws."

Richard E. Dixon, of the Thomas Jefferson Heritage Society, made a different contribution. "With respect to the issues on the Loving case," he told the list, "I queried the appellate attorney. My post to him: Phil, There is a history discussion group (VA-HIST) on the Internet operated by the Library of Virginia. At present, there is a dispute about the Loving case in two respects: One, whether the case was funded by the NAACP, and two, whether the arrest was legitimate or was staged to create a test case. If you would like to comment on this I will post your comments (without alteration) to the list. Hope all is well with you. Dick Dixon."

Hirschkop got right back to Dixon: "Dick — The NAACP in no way funded or assisted in the Loving case, other than Bob Carter did file an amicus brief in the US Supreme Court on behalf of the NAACP. The case was funded solely by the ACLU, which paid out of pocket costs. Bernie Cohen and I volunteered all of our time without payment. As far as some allegation that the case was staged to create a test case, that is totally incorrect. The Lovings were arrested, prosecuted and convicted of felonies years before we got involved in any legal challenge. Phil Hirschkop."

Electronic Guest Books

The funeral home had an electronic "memorial guestbook" for well-wishers from distances great or small to convey their condolences and reminiscences. At other sites, too, people put their remarks on the Web. Quite a few reported having seen the movie *Mr. and Mrs. Loving* in the previous dozen years, and while it fudged some important facts, it captured the emotional tenor and the broad outlines of the Lovings' experience as a family and in the courts. A considerable number, from all around the country but most notably in the South, expressed their gratitude to Mr. and Mrs. Loving for blazing a path that had permitted them to live their own interracial lives. Some expressed a wish that they could have known her; others had known her at some point over the years, either in Caroline County or, as they recounted, from long-distance conversations or correspondence that took her voice as far away as Florida or Texas. Whatever their situation, women proved particularly responsive to the death of another woman.

From a writer in Woodbridge, Virginia, came the statement that she "did not personally know Mr. and Mrs. Loving but I feel I owe them both a deep gratitude. My husband and I are an interracial couple as well, and are growing stronger and stronger each day, going on 19 yrs of marriage.... As my Mother once told me, my husband is the best thing that ever happened to me. This came from a woman who came from a time that Mrs. Loving lived in, where mixed marriage was not accepted." From Glen Allen, Virginia, came a similar note that "it was their strength and courage that allows me to have the wonderful life I have today with my husband." A woman from Colonial Beach, Virginia, echoed the thought: "Your parents struggle paved the freedom for other couples like myself." From Roanoke, Virginia, came another such message: "I guess i owe my whole life to your mother, i too live in Virginia, and i did not know until i read your mother's obit, that it was against the law to marry outside of your race here, well i have been with the same wonderful man for 30 years and i guess i owe it all to her, wish i had known of her before she passed, but i just wanted you to know you are in my prayers."

Yet another, recounting a story of race, love, and early loss, said of the Lovings: "Because of their courage, my parents were able to marry in Virginia in 1968, my mother black, my father white. My parents truly had a love story of a life and my father was tragically taken at a young age but my mother never remarried, pledging her love only to my father."

Other voices of thanks, too, sought to be heard, from people in Georgia ("your mother made it possible for me to love and marry who I choose"), Louisiana ("your fight has made my marriage possible"), and elsewhere. Two women from Florida wrote, one saying that "the love she had for her husband made it legal for me to marry my husband" and the other observing that "my husband and I would probably not be together had it not been for Mildred's effort to make interracial marriage legal." A woman in Greensboro, North Carolina, wrote of the Lovings: "because of them, my husband and I can also be married here in the south."

Some wrote with recognition that, though it did not take the *Loving* decision to open the door to their being married in their own state, nonetheless the ruling greatly enhanced their freedom. A woman in New York wrote: "I cannot imagine living in a country where my husband and I could not freely move as a married couple, and yet that could have been the case had not Mildred Loving and her husband protested an unjust law."

Again and again, people voiced the thought that the couple was at last together again. From Bedford, Virginia, came the message, "What a beautiful love story, Mildred and Richard together again," and from Richmond, "can't no court system separate them." From Wisconsin: "Mildred is now with her true love and no one can keep them apart." From Maryland: "Now no man or court can ever break that union. Richard and Mildred WILL love forever more." And from North Carolina: "Rest Well, peaceful warrior. You are now reunited forever with the love of your life."

Civil Rights Heroine

A number of writers pointed out how Mrs. Loving deserved to be included in the pantheon of figures who made up the Civil Rights Movement. Valerie Peyton, from King George, a few miles north of the Rappahannock, wrote: "Even though not recognized they were a part of the civil rights movement." A law professor in Maryland, M. T. Hall, termed *Loving v. Virginia* "the inspiring story of a fight to obtain a fundamental civil right. The courage displayed by Mrs. and Mr. Loving shows my students that just one couple can right a wrong and can turn a ripple into a mighty tide." From the Estelle family in Florida, whose members had spoken with Mrs. Loving on "numerous" occasions, came the message: "Her strength and fortitude to persevere and stay true to her heart despite huge obstacles shows that she is truly an American icon for civil rights in America. Mildred's name will be synonymous in the history books for generations to come as a true pioneer towards creating a colorblind society."

Going Home

Caroline County was, aside from her years in exile, the only home Mrs. Loving ever had. Her going home took place at venues scattered throughout that big though sparsely populated county in eastern Virginia.

One week after her death, a viewing took place in Port Royal, a tiny village on the Caroline side of the bridge that takes US 301 traffic across the wide Rappahannock River. Throughout the afternoon and early evening that Friday, various members of her extended family and other admirers stopped by the Cedell Brooks Funeral Home to pay their respects. Some stayed a few minutes, some longer, some in silence, some murmuring their greetings to one another or saying soft goodbyes to Mrs. Loving. Mr. Brooks found himself constantly bringing in new bouquets of flowers, until he wondered where to put the latest ones.

The next morning, for what her pastor called Mrs. Loving's "home going celebration," three hundred or more people crowded into the auditorium of the Caroline Community Center, which also housed the main branch of the Caroline County Library. Formerly the Union High School, which had served until 1969 as the high school for "colored" teenagers from the entire county (whatever their mix might be among the three racial identities to be found in Caroline), it was the same building where Mildred had attended high school in the 1950s. The building's foyer displayed photos on a wall as well as trophies from glory days in the parallel world of "colored" high school athletics in the county from the 1940s through the 1960s.

A great many of the people in attendance were members of the extended family. These included her two surviving children, Sidney Jeter and Peggy Fortune; Donald's widow, Kathi Loving; and Mildred's grandchildren and great-grandchildren, as well as a large number of siblings, in-laws, cousins, and other family members. Also seated as part of the family were Richard's aging sister, Margaret Cropper, and Mildred's old friend and attorney from the 1960s, Bernie Cohen, and his wife, Rae. Still others were Phyllis Jeter, a white woman who had for a time been married to Sidney, and her sister, Leslie Houser, Mildred's great confidante and solace her last few years. Leslie Houser's daughter, Brittany Houser, was there with her own young daughter, paying tribute to the woman she recognized as having made possible her parents' North Carolina marriage in the 1970s, paying tribute also to the gentle lady who had agreed to serve as Brittany's "other grandmother."

Attorney Cohen was uncertain that he belonged as part of the family. He felt out of place there entirely. "I'm Jewish, you know," he observed. Maybe so, he was assured, but today "you are a Baptist." Today he was clearly very much a Loving. He had been instrumental in the Lovings' being allowed to return permanently to Caroline County and raise their children there, and now, together with the other family members, he was there to bid her a fond farewell. Mildred, just hours before she died, had asked Peggy to request that he drive over to see her, and he and Rae had rushed to make that final visit.

Ken Tanabe and Madeleine Kanai also arrived for the funeral. Representing Loving Day (as the organization's president and vice president), they had taken a train to DC from New York, then rented a car to find their way to Fredericksburg and on to Bowling Green. Peter Wallenstein, who had written a book on interracial marriage throughout

American history first inspired by the story of the Lovings, was there with his wife, Sookhan Ho. They remembered with gratitude and fondness an afternoon many years before spent with Mildred at the home of her son Donald and his wife and son, and they were paying tribute to the brave woman who made their own marriage in Virginia possible.

Rev. Dr. Charles F. Baugham Sr., of St. James Baptist Church, also located on Sparta Road but closer to Bowling Green, offered up a prayer. He spoke of "joy, peace, and power." He spoke of "history books" and "our lives." And he lauded "a courageous spirit, committed to justice."

Floyd Thomas, another of the three black men speaking at the service, was next. In his capacity as chair of the county board of supervisors, and thus embodying the tremendous change that had come to Caroline County in the fifty years since the arrest of Mildred and Richard, he could speak on behalf of all the residents of Caroline. He attended the same church, he said, as Mrs. Loving and her daughter Peggy. And he described the lamented "Mrs. Loving" as "an icon of America" and "a heroine of Caroline County." She "never wanted this attention," he went on, "never wanted to be in the national spotlight." Rather, he repeated the words she had often used to explain her motivation: "I just wanted to get married."

Rev. William Gibson, the pastor of Mildred's church, brought to the audience's attention multiple dimensions of the significance of the life being celebrated that morning. He began his remarks by noting that he had first encountered Mr. and Mrs. Loving in Massachusetts. Knowing that most people in attendance would be surprised to hear that the couple had ever ventured so far from home, he clarified his meaning, going on to explain how he had been in law school there back in the late 1960s and had found their case to be of great interest. He had no idea then, he explained, that, some three decades and more later, he would find himself a pastor in Virginia, at Mildred's church, where she had joined at an early age, a great many years before he met her. He spoke of her early years as the wife of Richard Loving, no matter that her home state denied her that legal role: "She stood her ground on the rock of love."

Knowing what most of his audience would already know, and what everyone at the service could readily see, he spoke of Mrs. Loving's "flower project," "the diversity among us," not just one kind or color of flower, but a beautiful diversity of flowers. The people in the audience ranged in hue across much of the human rainbow, and he celebrated that as a consequence of Mrs. Loving's dedication to her family and to her commitment to the idea that love knew no color. One might have reversed the chronology in his analysis, of course, and observed that the community in which she and Richard grew to adulthood, already a garden of diverse flowers, fostered her and his lack of recognition that the garden should have only one kind of flower in it—or only two varieties, carefully kept separate.

Moreover, knowing what many in the audience would already know, but that some might not know and that regardless ought to be highlighted, he pointed up the presence of the outsider who had done so much to make her married life in Virginia finally possible. "Brother Cohen," he asked her longtime friend and lawyer, "please rise" and be acknowledged. Bernie rose reluctantly from his place in the middle of the left side of the room, where the family had mostly been seated, and the crowd gave him a warm expression of inclusion and gratitude.

Most of the people at the funeral knew one another, but not all had previously met. Whether during the hour before the service, or the short time afterward, they had a chance to make one another's acquaintance or renew their acquaintances. So after the service, people milled about, outside the old Union High School, before they began climbing into cars to make their way south on 301, then east on 721—just as Mr. and Mrs. Loving and her sister had done back in 1975, the night he died—toward far eastern Caroline County, the location of Mildred's church, St. Stephen's Baptist. In the most striking occurrence along the route to the church, the procession passed the home of the Sparta Volunteer Fire Department. Out in front, a fire truck was parked, with its lights blazing, and three men, who appeared white, stood in salute to Mrs. Loving. It turned out that Peggy's son Mark, Mildred's grandson, was a fellow volunteer fireman there in Sparta. The trio were paying tribute to what Floyd Thomas had called "a heroine of Caroline County" and, at the same time, to the beloved grandmother of their friend and colleague.

At the church, with a soft rain falling, people made their way to the site of Mildred's burial. To the left of her gravesite stood a bold granite stone with the name Richard Perry Loving and the dates 1933–1975. Nearby were the names of Mildred's parents, Theoliver Jeter (1884–1968) and Musiel Parker (March 6, 1911–May 6, 1997). And then one saw another premature stone, this one for Donald Lendberg Loving (October 8, 1958–August 31, 2000) and his wife, who found herself attending yet another wrenching farewell, albeit this burial was not entirely unexpected nor was it of someone still in his early forties.

The birth year for Donald struck at least one viewer as improbable. Peter Wallenstein asked Bernie Cohen about it, and Bernie asked Sidney Jeter, whose last name had also struck us as out of order. Sidney gave his own birth date as January 27, 1957, then repeated it, and suddenly Bernie and I each had a new understanding of the story of a teenager in rural Caroline County in the late 1950s. When Mildred was thrown into the Bowling Green jail for several days and nights in July 1958, she had been about six months pregnant. But it was not Sidney, the eldest, that Mildred was pregnant with when she and Richard rode north to DC to get married. It was Donald—it was her second pregnancy that evidently drove her, or her and Richard, to figure they really ought to get married. So her eldest child came along not at about the time of their being sentenced to exile in DC. Rather, when the couple had to leave Virginia, they took two children with them, the oldest about to turn two years old, his baby brother three months old. Mildred had not returned to Virginia, as later statements had it, for the birth of each of her children, but only for Peggy.

Other uncertainties and controversies swirled through the cool damp air. In one conversation that day, Bernie Cohen heard that Mildred had indicated "Indian" on her marriage license. He paused. Did she consider herself as—did I think of her as—Native American only or African American as well? Assured that she described herself as both, he returned to his longtime sense of her identity. Another thought troubled him. The formal statement attributed to her the previous summer, that she had publicly come out in favor of gay marriage? That had disturbed her, he observed. However she herself might have felt about the application of her case to a related but very different question, one thing seemed clear there: she was not happy about having her name appropriated, without her consent, for other people's agendas. She wanted people each to be free to be with the love of his or her life, but she had never wanted any publicity and, over the years, had gone public ever less often, and in fact had left the public sphere just about entirely the last several years of her life.

The crowd waited in the cemetery, visiting and moving among the stones, in soft voices, making out the names of various family members whose names each signified an earlier departure. Delaying the proceedings was the fact, rumored and soon confirmed, that Mr. Brooks had seen to it that Mildred in her coffin take a circuitous route to the church, so she could once more go past the home that Richard had built soon after the court victory and that the family had shared for nearly four decades.

Then five people began drumming and singing, as a Rappahannock ritual accompanied Mildred's passing into the spirit world. The three men sat drumming and singing. The two women stood behind and also sang. When they had concluded, one of the women, the chief, came over to the tent, the crowd, and the burial site to declare that, though some people might wish to deny Mrs. Loving her heritage, she had always been and would forever remain a member of the Rappahannock nation.

The crowd made their way across the road and into the church, downstairs to the fellowship hall, where the eating commenced and the visiting continued. Eventually, people singly and in groups made their way back out of their church and then back home. Many family members waited for the time to make their way over to Mildred's home, getting together at the home of the family matriarch each to celebrate her life and continue with their own. In one conversation with Lourdes and Don Parker, about Richard Loving as a child riding a tractor on an Indian farmer's land during World War II, Mr. Cohen's name came up again. Though Bernie had left by this time, the musings revisited his having that day become a Baptist, a member of the Loving family, and, in addition, an Indian.

Three cars eventually left to return to Bowling Green, this time together for a visit to the courthouse complex where the Lovings had many years earlier been jailed and then tried. Ken Tanabe and Maddy Kanai wanted to see the courthouse and, especially, the monument to diversity and inclusion out in front of it, at the other end from the jail. Phyllis Jeter and Leslie Houser revisited the site, reminiscing, for example, about what a challenge it had been to have the language included on one face of the monument: "Mildred Loving, who along with her husband Richard, helped strike down laws prohibiting interracial marriage in the United States." Leslie pointed out the small old jailhouse, where a pregnant teenager had been housed on one floor, while, for the first of her several anxious nights there, Richard had been jailed on the other. Joining the four of them in front of the courthouse were two other people, who thus had an opportunity to build on their brief visits with Ken, Maddy, Phyllis, and Leslie from earlier in the day, as one of them took more notes toward recounting the history of a community, a couple, and a case.

Hundreds of people had converged that day at the old "colored" high school, and many of them had made their way to a church and cemetery. Most of those people were part of the community, either for time generations deep or by marriage into the family and its embracing inclusiveness. All had been brought together, even made possible, by the couple and the case the couple brought. Mr. and Mrs. Loving, both having moved off into the spirit world, were together at last, again, forever.

It was a day of immense sadness—and glorious celebration. The public significance of the day's proceedings would not have escaped Mrs. Loving. Terri Givens wrote Mildred's children from Nashville, Tennessee, of her sorrow at "the loss of your dear mother": "Her heroic efforts have surely touched the lives of many." Greg Jacobson wrote from Salt Lake City, Utah, upon her death: "Your legacy lives on in the world you leave behind." Lydia Glover wrote from Atlanta, Georgia, about how people can leave "legacies that impact our everyday lives and we are totally unaware." Or as someone wrote from Washington, DC, where the Lovings had gone to get married and then had been exiled for several years: "Our lives are impacted by the Loving family more than most of us realize." William Joseph Simmons wrote from Atlanta: "A nation is grateful for a couple who simply said 'This is not right' and stood up for their beliefs. The world needs more Lovings in it."

But the absolute centrality of family would have been, for her, the key. The greater family she did so much to build and nurture was the monument she wished, if she had to, to leave behind. Meanwhile, of course, a host of other families had a chance to grow because of the case she and Richard had brought many years before. As a lawyer from the Pacific Northwest, Donna Hamilton, wrote of Mr. and Mrs. Loving a few days after Mildred's death: "Their simple act of loving one another changed the legal landscape for the many loving families who came after them."

1614	Marriage between the Native American Pocahontas and the Englishman John Rolfe brings a peaceful respite to the awful warfare that had been going on between the two peoples.
1691	The Virginia General Assembly enacts a bill "for prevention of that abominable mixture" (marriages between whites and non-whites, whether blacks, Indians, or mixed) and "spurious issue" (mixed-race free children of white women).
1780 and 1843	Pennsylvania and Massachusetts are the first states to repeal their laws against black-white marriage, but many other states inaugurate such laws.
1857	The Supreme Court decides the *Dred Scott* case, in which Chief Justice Roger B. Taney uses the many state laws against interracial marriage at the time of the Revolution and the Philadelphia Convention of 1787 to bolster his stance about African Americans' disqualification for citizenship or equal inclusion in American society.
1863–1864	David Goodman Croly and George Wakeman, two Democratic newspapermen hoping for President Abraham Lincoln's defeat in his anticipated bid for reelection, write a hoax pamphlet—its title a word they invent, "miscegenation" (a substitute for "amalgamation")—depicting (in fact celebrating) sex and marriage between black men and white women as one outcome of the Republicans' struggle against slavery.
1865	End of the Civil War; universal emancipation from enslavement; the Freedmen's Bureau is established and oversees formalization of marriages between former slaves, schools for freedpeople, and labor contracts between whites and former slaves.
1866	Congress passes the Civil Rights Act of 1866, which declares all native-born Americans to be citizens (thus deliberately including African Americans, overturning the *Dred Scott* ruling), with such rights as making contracts and purchasing land; Congress proposes the Fourteenth Amendment, which (for one thing) incorporates the 1866 Civil Rights Act into the Constitution, lest there be doubt about its constitutionality and permanence.
1868	The Fourteenth Amendment is ratified, with its equal protection and due process clauses.

1871	The Indiana Supreme Court, in *State v. Gibson*, insists that the Fourteenth Amendment in no way overrode the state's law making interracial marriage a crime.
1872	In *Bonds v. Foster*, the Texas Supreme Court, validating a marriage between a white man and his former slave, says the Texas miscegenation statute was "abrogated by the 14th Amendment."
	In *Burns v. State*, the Alabama Supreme Court's three white Republican justices strike down that state's law against interracial marriage under the Civil Rights Act of 1866.
1873	The Mississippi Supreme Court rules in *Dickerson v. Brown* that "with the adoption" of the 1868 state constitution, "former impediments to marriage between whites and blacks ceased."
1874	In *Hart v. Hoss and Elder*, the Louisiana Supreme Court rules that, in view of the 1866 Civil Rights Act, an 1867 interracial marriage was valid despite a contrary state law.
1878	In *Green v. State*, the Alabama Supreme Court overrules *Burns v. State* and fully recommits the state to the antimiscegenation regime.
	Virginia updates its miscegenation law to provide two-to-five-year prison sentences, applicable to both parties, regardless of whether a black Virginian and a white Virginian marry each other within Virginia or go outside to marry and then return.
1883	In *Pace v. Alabama*, a unanimous US Supreme Court, noting that both partners had received the same prison terms as an equal penalty for violating the same statute, upholds an Alabama statute that imposes greater sentences on cohabiting unmarried couples who are of different races than if they are both white or both black.
1888	In *Maynard v. Hill*, the US Supreme Court speaks of marriage as having "more to do with the morals and civilization of a people than any other institution"; and as having "always been subject to the control of the Legislature"; *Maynard* also observes that marriage is "not a contract within the meaning" of the US Constitution's full faith and credit clause, which in general requires that a contract made in one state be recognized as valid in other states.
1894–1895	Louisiana restores its law against interracial marriage in 1894; and the Arkansas Supreme Court, in *Dodson v. State* (1895), asserts that the Arkansas statute had continued in force, whatever blip there might have been in the 1870s; so the former

Confederate South is solid once again in this respect, for the first time since 1868.

1896   *Plessy v. Ferguson* endorses "equal, but separate" public transportation facilities, noting that public education and marriage have long been widely segregated.

1910   Virginia changes the definition of a "colored person" from someone of at least one-quarter African ancestry (with one black grandparent) to someone at least one-sixteenth (with one black *great-great*-grandparent).

1912   Congressman Seaborn Roddenbery of Georgia (unsuccessfully) proposes an amendment to the US Constitution to ban black-white marriages everywhere in the nation.

1917   In the housing case *Buchanan v. Warley*, both sides assume that miscegenation statutes are constitutional.

1924   The Racial Integrity Act of 1924 becomes law in Virginia: anyone having any black ancestry is black; and other nonwhites are defined as colored, too, for purposes of marriage and therefore cannot marry people still defined as white.

1932   Virginia reduces to one year the minimum prison sentence for interracial marriage (it had been two years since 1878), not trying to reduce the penalty so much as increase the likelihood of conviction.

1931–1939   Arizona, California, Maryland, and Utah, each with men from the Philippines in mind, enhance their laws against interracial marriage to target members of "the Malay race" and include them among the groups barred from marrying whites.

1948   Thirty of the forty-eight states have laws against interracial marriage, a figure unchanged since 1913; but in *Perez v. Sharp*, the California Supreme Court overturns that state's miscegenation law; the Fourteenth Amendment's equal protection clause is the primary basis for this breakthrough 4–3 decision; but, with a case concerning two Catholics, the First Amendment's freedom of religion proves critical as well.

Having already established commissions to explore and advocate on civil rights matters, President Harry S. Truman orders the military desegregated and directs his Justice Department to support black plaintiffs in higher education cases.

The US Supreme Court, in *Shelley v. Kraemer*, rules that courts can no longer enforce restrictive covenants designed to maintain residential segregation.

The United Nations adopts the Universal Declaration of

Human Rights, declaring everyone "equal in dignity and rights" (article 1), with a right to "privacy" (article 12), and stating too: "Men and women of full age, without any limitation due to race, nationality or religion, have the right to marry and to found a family" (article 16).

1953   Former California governor Earl Warren becomes chief justice of the US Supreme Court.

1954–1955   The US Supreme Court bans state-mandated public school segregation in *Brown v. Board of Education* (1954), overturning *Plessy v. Ferguson*'s application to the field of education, and in *Brown II* (1955) urges implementation "with all deliberate speed."

1954–1956   The US Supreme Court refuses to hear two cases, from Alabama and Virginia, regarding miscegenation statutes, leaving the statutes there and elsewhere intact.

1956   Both senators and every congressman from Virginia, together with most of their colleagues from the other former Confederate states, sign the *Southern Manifesto*, supporting the principle of "separate but equal," decrying the decision in *Brown v. Board of Education*, and calling for resistance by "all lawful means" to its implementation.

To ensure that no white child need ever attend school with a black child, the Virginia General Assembly enacts a policy of Massive Resistance; one of the many provisions directs the governor to close any public K–12 school that a federal court orders to become desegregated.

The board of supervisors of Caroline County determines that it will withhold all county funds from any public school where "the mingling of white & Negro pupils took place."

1958   South Dakota and Colorado having repealed their interracial marriage laws in 1957, the nation is divided evenly between twenty-four states with miscegenation laws and twenty-four without.

Mildred Delores Jeter and Richard Perry Loving go to Washington, DC, to marry, then return to Caroline County, and are subsequently arrested for "interracial cohabitation."

1959   Convicted and (in lieu of one year each in jail) exiled from Virginia, the couple move with their children Sidney and Donald to Washington, DC.

Decisions by a federal court and the Virginia Supreme Court overturn Virginia's Massive Resistance, the one on the basis that it violated the Fourteenth Amendment, the other that it violated the Virginia constitution.

1963   Mrs. Loving writes a letter to Attorney General Robert F. Kennedy, who directs her to the American Civil Liberties Union, and attorney Bernard S. Cohen takes the case.

The National Catholic Conference on Interracial Justice approves a resolution calling for action to obtain legislative repeal or judicial invalidation of all miscegenation statutes.

1964   Congress enacts the Civil Rights Act of 1964, which has nothing to say, however, about interracial marriage.

Philip J. Hirschkop joins Cohen on the *Loving* case; the two lawyers go to federal district court, which stipulates that the case first run its course in Virginia's state courts.

The NAACP enters the fray as an active proponent of bringing such laws down.

The US Supreme Court, in *McLaughlin v. Florida*, overturns *Pace v. Alabama* as regards higher penalties for interracial cohabitation than for same-race cohabitation, but expressly declines to go so far as to overturn the Florida law against interracial marriage.

1965   Judge Leon M. Bazile, in turning down the Lovings' plea to have their conviction and banishment rescinded, speaks of God's intention that the (five different) races stay separate and not intermarry.

Wyoming and Indiana repeal their laws against interracial marriage, leaving just the seventeen southern states with such laws, the identical states that had required statewide segregated schooling at the time of *Brown v. Board of Education*.

Congress enacts the Voting Rights Act of 1965.

Caroline County begins to desegregate its public schools.

1966   The Virginia Supreme Court upholds the Virginia laws against interracial marriage, and the Lovings' convictions under them, but takes exception to their banishment.

1967   Maryland, with a newly reapportioned legislature as well as enhanced black enfranchisement and new black legislators, repeals its laws against interracial marriage.

In *Loving v. Virginia*, the US Supreme Court unanimously overturns the Lovings' convictions, and in fact overturns all remaining state laws against interracial marriage.

1969   In April, it is announced that the private Caroline Academy has been chartered and will begin classes that fall; the Caroline

County public schools open that fall on a "fully integrated" basis.

1971   In *Baker v. Nelson*, the Minnesota Supreme Court becomes the first of several state appellate courts to reject the argument that the US Supreme Court's interpretation of the Fourteenth Amendment on race in *Loving v. Virginia* should be applied to same-sex marriage, so that a gay couple could obtain a marriage license.

1975   Richard Loving dies, and Mildred is injured, when a drunk driver crashes into their car.

1984   In *Palmore v. Sidoti*, about a divorced white woman who had lost custody of her white children after she married a black man, the Supreme Court rules against race as a criterion for reassigning child custody when a parent remarries across a racial line.

1986   In *Hardwick v. Bowers*, the Supreme Court upholds a Georgia sodomy statute being applied to a same-sex couple.

1996   In *Romer v. Evans*, the Supreme Court invalidates a Colorado initiative that had terminated local ordinances protecting same-sex couples and had forbidden subsequent passage of such laws.

Congress passes the Defense of Marriage Act, authorizing states to ban same-sex marriage, in the face of new efforts in state courts in the early 1990s, most notably in Hawaii, to secure, under the provisions of state constitutions, what early efforts failed to obtain under the Fourteenth Amendment, beginning with Minnesota in 1971.

1998   Hawaii and Alaska each adopt a marriage amendment to their constitution, thus barring a legislative effort to permit same-sex marriage or, more immediately, a judicial ruling that might end traditional impediments.

1999–2000   In *Baker v. State of Vermont*, which directs the state legislature to "extend to same-sex couples the common benefits and protections that flow from marriage under Vermont law," the Vermont Supreme Court quotes *Loving v. Virginia* about the "freedom to marry"; to comply, the Vermont legislature adopts "civil unions."

2000   In a referendum in that fall's elections, Alabama is the last state to remove from its constitution a clause banning interracial marriage.

Nebraska and Nevada each constitutionalize a ban on same-sex marriage.

2003   In *Lawrence v. Texas*, the Supreme Court overrules *Hardwick v. Bowers* and throws out all sodomy laws, including one that specifically targeted same-sex couples.

In *Goodridge v. Department of Public Health*, the highest court of Massachusetts, partly on the basis of *Loving v. Virginia* and partly on the basis of its state constitution, says that even civil unions are not enough and calls for full marriage rights for same-sex couples.

2004   Ken Tanabe establishes Loving Day to celebrate the *Loving* decision on June 12 each year.

2008   Mildred Loving dies, of cancer and pneumonia.

2012   In stark contrast to developments beginning in Alaska and Hawaii in the 1990s, voters in Maryland, Washington State, and elsewhere approve legislative action to inaugurate same-sex marriage.

2013   The US Supreme Court rules in two cases on same-sex marriage, one from New York challenging the constitutionality of DOMA's denial of federal benefits, the other from California regarding the status of same-sex marriage in that state, and each 5–4 ruling supports gay rights. Implications of the DOMA ruling quickly ripple out.

Hawaii enacts same-sex marriage.

The New Mexico Supreme Court rules that restricting marriage to heterosexual couples violates the state constitution.

Social Security benefits become available to same-sex married couples living in states that recognize their marriages.

Same-sex married couples can file joint federal tax returns, no matter where they live.

By the end of 2013, fifteen states (plus DC) recognize same-sex marriages, up from seven a year earlier; and an Illinois law passed in November took effect in June 2014.

Baehr v. Lewin, 74 Haw. 530 (1993).
Baehr v. Miike, 92 Haw. 634 (1996).
Baker v. Nelson, 291 Minn. 310 (1971).
Baker v. Nelson, 409 U.S. 810 (1972).
Baker v. State of Vermont, 170 Vt. 194 (1999).
Bonds v. Foster, 36 Tex. 68 (1872).
Browder v. Gayle, 352 U.S. 903 (1956).
Brown v. Board of Education, 347 U.S. 483 (1954).
Brown v. Board of Education, 349 U.S. 294 (1955).
Buchanan v. Warley, 245 U.S. 60 (1917).
Burns v. State, 48 Ala. 195 (1872).
Calma v. Calma, 203 Va. 880 (1962).
Citizens for Equal Protection v. Bruning, 368 F. Supp. 2d 980 (2005).
Citizens for Equal Protection v. Bruning, 455 F.3d 859 (2006).
City of Richmond v. Deans, 37 F.2d 712 (1930).
City of Richmond v. Deans, 281 U.S. 704 (1930).
Cleveland Board of Education v. LaFleur, 414 U.S. 632 (1974).
Cohen v. Chesterfield County School Board, 326 F. Supp. 1159 (1971).
Cohen v. Chesterfield County School Board, 468 F.2d 262 (1972).
Coleman v. Dick and Pat, 2 Va. (1 Washington) 233 (1793).
Davis v. Gately, 269 F. Supp. 996 (1967).
DeSanto v. Barnsley, 328 Pa.Superior Ct. 181 (1984).
Dickerson v. Brown, 49 Miss. 357 (1873).
Dick v. Reaves, 434 P.2d 295 (1967).
Dodson v. State, 61 Ark. 57 (1895).
Dred Scott v. Sandford, 60 U.S. 393 (1857).
Eggers v. Olson, 104 Okla. 297 (1924).
Eisenstadt v. Baird, 405 U.S. 438 (1972).
Ex Parte Francois, 9 F.Cas. 699 (1879).
Ex Parte Kinney, 14 Fed. Cas. 602 (1879).
Frasher v. State, 3 Tex. App. 263 (1877).
Fuller v. Commonwealth, 189 Va. 327 (1949).
Gong Lum v. Rice, 275 U.S. 76 (1927).
Goodridge v. Department of Public Health, 440 Mass. 309 (2003).
Grant v. Butt, 198 S.C. 298 (1941).
Green v. State, 58 Ala. 190 (1878).
Greenhow v. James Executor, 80 Va. 636 (1885).
Griffin v. County School Board of Prince Edward County, 377 U.S. 218 (1964).

Griswold v. Connecticut, 381 U.S. 479 (1965).
Hardwick v. Bowers, 478 U.S. 186 (1986).
Harmon v. Tyler, 273 U.S. 668 (1927).
Harrison v. Day, 200 Va. 439 (1959).
Hart v. Hoss and Elder, 26 La. Ann. 90 (1874).
Hollingsworth v. Perry, 133 S.Ct. 2652 (2013).
Honey v. Clark, 37 Tex. 686 (1873).
Hoover v. State, 59 Ala. 57 (1878).
Hudgins v. Wrights, 11 Va. (1 Hening and Munford) 134 (1806).
Jackson v. State, 37 Ala. App. 519 (1954).
Jackson v. State, 260 Ala. 698 (1954).
Jackson v. Alabama, 348 U.S. 888 (1954).
James v. Almond, 170 F. Supp. 331 (1959).
Johnson v. Branch, 364 F.2d 177 (1966).
Johnson v. Virginia, 373 U.S. 61 (1963).
Jones v. Alfred H. Mayer Co., 392 U.S. 409 (1968).
Jones v. Hallahan, 501 S.W.2d 588 (Ky., 1973).
Kinney v. Commonwealth, 71 Va. (30 Gratt) 858 (1878).
Kirstein v. Rector and Visitors of the University of Virginia, 309 F. Supp. 184 (1970).
Lawrence v. Texas, 539 U.S. 558 (2003).
Littleton v. Prange, 9 S.W.3d 223 (Tex. App. 1999).
Loving v. Commonwealth, 206 Va. 924 (1966).
Loving v. Virginia, 388 U.S. 1 (1967).
Maynard v. Hill, 125 U.S. 190 (1888).
McLaughlin v. Florida, 379 U.S. 184 (1964).
McPherson v. Commonwealth, 69 Va. (28 Gratt.) 939 (1877).
Meyer v. Nebraska, 262 U.S. 390 (1923).
Monks v. Lee, 326 U.S. 696 (1946).
Moon v. Children's Home Society of Virginia, 112 Va. 737 (1911).
Moreau et al. School Trustees v. Grandich et ux., 114 Miss. 560 (1917).
Mullins v. Belcher, 142 Ky. 673 (1911).
Naim v. Naim, 197 Va. 80 (1955).
Pace v. Alabama, 106 U.S. 583 (1883).
Palmore v. Sidoti, 466 U.S. 429 (1984).
Perez v. Sharp, 32 Cal.2d 711 (1948).
Plessy v. Ferguson, 163 U.S. 537 (1896).
Randolph v. Virginia, 374 U.S. 97 (1963).
Red Lion Broadcasting Co. v. FCC, 395 U.S. 367 (1969).
Reynolds v. United States, 98 U.S. 145 (1879).
Rice v. Gong Lum, 139 Miss. 760 (1925).
Roe v. Wade, 410 U.S. 113 (1973).

Romer v. Evans, 517 U.S. 620 (1996).

Scott v. State, 39 Ga. 321 (1869).

Shelley v. Kraemer, 334 U.S. 1 (1948).

Singer v. Hara, 11 Wn. App. 230 (1974).

Sipuel v. Board of Regents of the University of Oklahoma, 332 U.S. 631 (1948).

State v. Gibson, 36 Ind. 389 (1871).

State ex rel. Farmer v. Board of School Commissioners of Mobile County, 226 Ala. 62 (1933).

Stevens v. United States, 146 F.2d 120 (1944).

Tucker v. Blease, 97 S.C. 303 (1914).

United States v. Brittain, 319 F. Supp. 1058 (1970).

United States v. Dougherty, 473 F.2d 1113 (1972).

United States v. Windsor, 133 S.Ct. 2675 (2013).

Van Camp v. Board of Education, 9 Ohio 406 (1859).

Williams v. School District, 1 Wright (Ohio) 578 (1834).

BIBLIOGRAPHICAL ESSAY

Note from the Series Editors: The following bibliographical essay contains the major primary and secondary sources the author consulted for this volume. We have asked all authors in the series to omit formal citations in order to make our volumes more readable, inexpensive, and appealing for students and general readers. In adopting this format, Landmark Law Cases and American Society follows the precedent of a number of highly regarded and widely consulted series.

Particularly in the past dozen years or so, a good many people have written on Mr. and Mrs. Loving and their travails and eventual triumph in the courts. The results have included news items and feature stories, various essays in law reviews or historical journals, and a small collection of books. Though errors abound in many of these accounts, whether on the story of the Lovings or on the long history that preceded them, each of these clusters is of importance in any attempt to reconstruct the story of the community, the couple, or the case. Most of the books in the literature cited in this review of sources focus on the interracial marriage dimension, while some comment on questions of identity, adoption, and custody, especially as these have emerged in the years since the Supreme Court spoke in the Lovings' case, and another literature, mostly even more recent, addresses marriage between people of the same sex.

A far fuller account of Virginia history than in the present book can be found in Peter Wallenstein, *Cradle of America: Four Centuries of Virginia History* (Lawrence: University Press of Kansas, 2007), with a revised edition titled *Cradle of America: A History of Virginia* published in 2014. Far more detailed explorations of the sweeping historical context of the Lovings' story can be found in Peter Wallenstein, *Tell the Court I Love My Wife: Race, Marriage, and Law—an American History* (New York: Palgrave Macmillan, 2002), which established the research field (and then appeared with a few corrections in paperback in 2004), and in Peggy Pascoe, *What Comes Naturally: Miscegenation Law and the Making of Race in America* (New York: Oxford University Press, 2009). *What Comes Naturally*, while matching *Tell the Court* in sweep across both space and time, as well as in surefootedness of fact and analysis, deepens the analysis and broadens the terrain—it enlarges upon the treatment of several key cases and expands the treatment of developments in the American West. The cover photo of the labor leader Harry Bridges and his fiancée, Noriko Sawada, taken at the time of their successful effort to get married in Nevada despite that state's miscegenation law, captures the shift in emphasis toward the West as well as toward interracial couples that included no African American.

The sociologist William J. Goode's book *World Revolution and Family Patterns* (New York: Free Press, 1963) caught the cusp of great change in family patterns around the world; in the United States, the minuscule number of black-white marriages was creeping up, and in terms of religion the incidence of out-marriage was much greater than a generation earlier. Much more recently, four excellent general histories of marriage and family in the United States are Stephanie Coontz, *The Way We Never Were: American Families and the Nostalgia Trap* (New York: Basic Books, 1992); Hendrik Hartog, *Man and Wife in America: A History* (Cambridge, Mass.: Harvard University Press, 2000); Nancy F. Cott, *Public Vows: A History of Marriage and the Nation* (Cambridge, Mass.: Harvard University Press, 2000); and Stephanie Coontz, *Marriage, a History: From Obedience to Intimacy, or How Love Conquered Marriage* (New York: Viking, 2005). Other approaches are Carole Shammas, *A History of Household Government in America* (Charlottesville: University of Virginia Press, 2002), as to composition, and Mark E. Brandon, *States of Union: Family and Change in the American Constitutional Order* (Lawrence: University Press of Kansas, 2013), as to historical variations. Declaring the continuing central importance of nuclear families in a post-*Loving* world is Kay S. Hymowitz, *Marriage and Caste in America: Separate and Unequal Families in a Post-Marital Age* (Chicago: Ivan R. Dee, 2006).

Among the scholars who pioneered significant parts of the long history of racial identity and the law of marriage in the United States is David H. Fowler, *Northern Attitudes towards Interracial Marriage: Legislation and Public Opinion in the Middle Atlantic and the States of the Old Northwest, 1780–1930* (New York: Garland, 1987), a published edition of a dissertation from 1963 that reaches well beyond the eight states that are its focus. Other such works are Byron Curti Martyn's encyclopedic "Racism in the United States: A History of Anti-Miscegenation Legislation and Litigation" (Ph.D. diss., University of Southern California, 1979), on three centuries of statutes and court cases, and Chang Moon Sohn, "Principle and Expediency in Judicial Review: Miscegenation Cases in the Supreme Court" (Ph.D. diss., Columbia University, 1970). Retaining some utility is an early effort by Robert J. Sickels, *Race, Marriage, and the Law* (Albuquerque: University of New Mexico Press, 1972).

Exemplary explorations of their respective topics are Peter W. Bardaglio, *Reconstructing the Household: Families, Sex, and the Law in the Nineteenth-Century South* (Chapel Hill: University of North Carolina Press, 1995), and Joshua D. Rothman, *Notorious in the Neighborhood: Sex and Families across the Color Line in Virginia, 1787–1861* (Chapel Hill: University of North Carolina Press, 2003). Charles F. Robinson II, *Dangerous Liaisons: Sex and Love in the Segregated South* (Fayetteville: University of Arkansas Press, 2003), emphasizes evasion as well as enforcement of miscegenation laws. Elise Lemire, *"Miscegenation": Making Race in America* (Philadelphia: University of Pennsylvania Press, 2002), introduces nineteenth-century background to larger issues. A particularly insightful scholar of the history of racial identity is Joel Williamson, most notably in *New People: Miscegenation and Mulattoes in the United States* (New York: Free Press, 1980). An important essay on the 1948 *Perez* case is Dara Orenstein, "Void for Vagueness: Mexicans and the Collapse of Miscegenation Law in California," *Pacific Historical Review* 74 (August 2005): 367–407. Important new work by Jane Dailey, on race, sex, religion, and the white southern side of the mid-twentieth-century conflict over civil rights, includes "Sex, Segregation, and the Sacred after *Brown*," *Journal of American History* 91 (June 2004): 119–144.

Among the many excellent writings that have shaped my thinking in the broad areas of African American history, race relations, and racial identity is Frank Tannenbaum's essay in comparative history *Slave and Citizen: The Negro in the Americas* (New York: Knopf, 1946). Tannenbaum has been rightly faulted for his overemphasis on the roles of religion and law in ameliorating slavery in Catholic parts of the New World, but his primary interest was in tracking the transition of former slaves into freedom. He did not emphasize intermarriage as one marker of that transition, but his overall approach remains a pregnant force for transformation in historians' understanding of these matters, even if often they do not recognize or acknowledge his work's importance to their own. Fay Botham, *Almighty God Created the Races: Christianity, Interracial*

Marriage, and American Law (Chapel Hill: University of North Caroline Press, 2009), in tilling new ground by emphasizing the role of religion in shaping attitudes toward regulating interracial marriage, can be seen as taking Tannenbaum in a new direction in her comparison of Protestant and Catholic theologies of race and marriage in US history.

Pauli Murray, comp. and ed., *States' Laws on Race and Color* (1951; Athens: University of Georgia Press, 1997), supplies a marvelous compilation as of mid-century, including miscegenation laws outside as well as inside the South. Rachel F. Moran, *Interracial Intimacy: The Regulation of Race and Romance* (Chicago: University of Chicago Press, 2001), includes an exemplary exploration of the post-*Loving* world, of policy changes in adoption and custody, as well as of the limited incidence of black-white marriage even as the numbers of other kinds of interracial marriages increased. Randall Kennedy, *Interracial Intimacies: Sex, Marriage, Identity, and Adoption* (New York: Pantheon Books, 2003), supplies a rich tapestry both on the era of miscegenation laws and on such central questions in the post-*Loving* era as identity, custody, and adoption. Julie Novkov, *Racial Union: Law, Intimacy, and the White State in Alabama, 1865–1954* (Ann Arbor: University of Michigan Press, 2008), is an extraordinary state study, all the more significant in view of Alabama's importance from the *Burns* case in the 1870s through the last repeal of a state constitution's ban on interracial marriage in 2000.

Renee C. Romano, *Race Mixing: Black-White Marriage in Postwar America* (Cambridge, Mass.: Harvard University Press, 2003), provides a strong cultural study of interracial marriage in the American imagination since World War II. Suzanne W. Jones, *Race Mixing: Southern Fiction since the Sixties* (Baltimore: Johns Hopkins University Press, 2004), supplies an insightful analysis of modern literary themes related to interracial marriage. Rickie Solinger, *Wake Up Little Susie: Single Pregnancy and Race before Roe v. Wade* (New York: Routledge, 1992), offers a national context for Mildred Jeter and Richard Loving in the late 1950s. Susan Courtney, *Hollywood Fantasies of Miscegenation: Spectacular Narratives of Gender and Race, 1903–1967* (Princeton: Princeton University Press, 2005), closes with a chapter on *Guess Who's Coming to Dinner*. Political scientist Priscilla Yamin's *American Marriage: A Political Institution* (Philadelphia: University of Pennsylvania Press, 2012) is clever but historically misinformed. Elizabeth H. Pleck, in *Not Just Roommates: Cohabitation after the Sexual*

Revolution (Chicago: University of Chicago Press, 2012), writes of the freedom *not* to marry. Contributing to the international context of the Loving story is Susan Williams, *Colour Bar: The Triumph of Seretse Khama and His Nation* (London: Allen Lane, 2006).

Anthropologist Helen C. Rountree has developed an extremely important body of work on Native Americans in eastern Virginia, most notably for the purposes of this book her *Pocahontas's People: The Powhatan Indians of Virginia through Four Centuries* (Norman: University of Oklahoma Press, 1990). Two other important sources are Paul T. Murray's terse but helpful sketch "Who Is an Indian? Who Is a Negro? Virginia Indians in the World War II Draft," *Virginia Magazine of History and Biography* 95 (April 1987): 215–231 (although Murray emphasizes Indians in Amherst County, not Caroline), and Sandra F. Waugaman and Danielle Moretti-Langholtz, *We're Still Here: Contemporary Virginia Indians Tell Their Stories* (Richmond: Palari, 2000). Also valuable in approaching this dimension of the story is Brewton Berry, *Almost White* (New York: Macmillan, 1963).

Arica L. Coleman has brought the Native American dimension of the Loving story to the fore in " 'Tell the Court I Love My [Indian] Wife': Interrogating Race and Self-Identity in *Loving v. Virginia*," *Souls* 8 (Winter 2006): 67–80; *That the Blood Stay Pure: African Americans, Native Americans, and the Predicament of Race and Identity in Virginia* (Bloomington: Indiana University Press, 2013); and "Mildred Loving: The Extraordinary Life of an Ordinary Woman," in *Virginia Women: Their Lives and Times*, ed. Cynthia A. Kierner and Sandra G. Treadway (Athens: University of Georgia Press, forthcoming). Arica Coleman first tracked down the Lovings' DC marriage license, in which Mildred Jeter identified herself as "Indian," and also Sidney Jeter's application for a Social Security number, in which he identified Richard Loving as his "stepfather."

Several studies develop the story of the Oklahoma alternative, in which Mrs. Loving, if she had no traceable African ancestry, would have been classified as white and thus an entirely suitable marital partner for Richard Loving. A major scholar of issues of black and Indian identity is the late Jack D. Forbes, whose work includes *Africans and Native Americans: The Language of Race and the Evolution of Red-Black People*, 2nd ed. (Urbana: University of Illinois Press, 1993). A fine collection of essays along these lines is James F. Brooks, ed., *Confounding the Color Line:*

The Indian-Black Experience in North America (Lincoln: University of Nebraska Press, 2002). Claudio Saunt, *Black, White, and Indian: Race and the Unmaking of an American Family* (New York: Oxford University Press, 2005), supplies one significant exploration of these matters; Fay A. Yarbrough, *Race and the Cherokee Nation: Sovereignty in the Nineteenth Century* (Philadelphia: University of Pennsylvania Press, 2007), provides another, as does David A. Chang, *The Color of the Land: Race, Nation, and the Politics of Landownership in Oklahoma, 1832–1929* (Chapel Hill: University of North Carolina Press, 2010). The twentieth-century consequences of those nineteenth-century beginnings are traced through appellate court cases in Peter Wallenstein, "Native Americans Are White, African Americans Are Not: Racial Identity, Marriage, Inheritance, and the Law in Oklahoma, 1907–1967," *Journal of the West* 39 (January 2000): 55–63.

Four remarkable recent books examining interracial families and racial identity elsewhere are Annette Gordon-Reed, *The Hemingses of Monticello: An American Family* (New York: Norton, 2008); Julie Winch, *The Clamorgans: One Family's History of Race in America* (New York: Hill and Wang, 2011); Daniel J. Sharfstein, *The Invisible Line: Three American Families and the Secret Journey from Black to White* (New York: Penguin, 2011); and Rachel L. Swarms, *American Tapestry: The Story of the Black, White, and Multiracial Ancestors of Michelle Obama* (New York: HarperCollins, 2012).

First-person accounts of interracial relationships and the families that have resulted have followed two trajectories. Those tracing long-ago couples and bringing the story down to the recent past are Shirlee Taylor Haizlip, *The Sweeter the Juice* (New York: Simon & Schuster, 1994); Neil Henry, *Pearl's Secret: A Black Man's Search for His White Family* (Berkeley: University of California Press, 2001); and Thulani Davis, *My Confederate Kinfolk: A Twenty-First Century Freedwoman Discovers Her Roots* (New York: Basic Books, 2006). Autobiographical accounts by people whose parents brought differing racial or ethnic identities to their own marriages include Brent Staples, *Parallel Time: Growing up in Black and White* (New York: Pantheon Books, 1994); Patricia Penn Hilden, *When Nickels Were Indians: An Urban Mixed-Blood Story* (Washington, DC: Smithsonian Institution Press, 1995); Scott Minerbrook, *Divided to the Vein: A Journey into Race and Family* (New York: Harcourt Brace, 1996); James McBride, *The Color of Water: A Black Man's Tribute to His White Mother* (New York: Riverhead Books, 1996); and Kevin R. Johnson, *How Did You Get to Be*

Mexican? A White/Brown Man's Search for Identity (Philadelphia: Temple University Press, 1999).

The fullest previous account of the Loving couple and the case they brought is Phyl Newbeck, *Virginia Hasn't Always Been for Lovers: Interracial Marriage Bans and the Case of Richard and Mildred Loving* (Carbondale: Southern Illinois University Press, 2004). Newbeck makes a tremendous contribution in bringing in many voices of other parties to court cases on interracial marriage in the 1950s and 1960s. Various other books, some tracing national patterns, others emphasizing Virginia, relate to one facet or another—cultural, scientific, political, legal—of the story of *Loving v. Virginia.* J. David Smith, *The Eugenics Assault on America: Scenes in Red, White, and Black* (Fairfax, Va.: George Mason University Press, 1993), opened up an investigation that Paul A. Lombardo, in *Three Generations, No Imbeciles: Eugenics, the Supreme Court, and* Buck v. Bell (Baltimore: Johns Hopkins University Press, 2008), substantially extended, as did Gregory Michael Dorr, *Segregation's Science: Eugenics and Society in Virginia* (Charlottesville: University of Virginia Press, 2008), though Dorr is unreliable in his brief account of *Loving.*

Coming in from related angles are Samuel N. Pincus, *The Virginia Supreme Court, Blacks, and the Law, 1870–1902* (New York: Garland, 1990), and Pippa Holloway, *Sexuality, Politics, and Social Control in Virginia, 1920–1945* (Chapel Hill: University of North Carolina Press, 2006). Tracking the workings of Jim Crow in Virginia, and black resistance to Jim Crow, are J. Douglas Smith, *Managing White Supremacy: Race, Politics, and Citizenship in Jim Crow Virginia* (Chapel Hill: University of North Carolina Press, 2002), and Peter Wallenstein, *Blue Laws and Black Codes: Conflict, Courts, and Change in Twentieth-Century Virginia* (Charlottesville: University of Virginia Press, 2004), especially chapters 4 and 5.

Among recent discussions of how race worked in southern history, an emerging chorus insists that, on the ground, all manner of patterns could thrive, an endless array of relationships could arise—that no one template actually works in the sense that we can deduce what life was like just because we have some overarching sense of what the law dictated or what southern white or black mores were. Three works making this case are Mark Schultz, *The Rural Face of White Supremacy: Beyond Jim Crow* (Urbana: University of Illinois Press, 2005), on a twentieth-century Georgia community; Melvin Patrick Ely, *Israel on the Appomattox:*

A Southern Experiment in Black Freedom from the 1790s through the Civil War (New York: Knopf, 2004), on Prince Edward County, Virginia; and Kirt von Daacke, *Freedom Has a Face: Race, Identity, and Community in Jefferson's Virginia* (Charlottesville: University of Virginia Press, 2012), on Albemarle County. Why this theme connects to the saga of the Lovings is the prevailing sense that somehow Caroline County was a highly unusual place, such that Richard Loving in particular could be seemingly oblivious that he should not pursue marriage with Mildred Jeter. Perhaps Caroline was not so unusual after all.

Tracking the Supreme Court's evolving interpretation of the Fourteenth Amendment are Linda Przybyszewski, *The Republic according to John Marshall Harlan* (Chapel Hill: University of North Carolina Press, 1999), and Michael J. Klarman, *From Jim Crow to Civil Rights: The Supreme Court and the Struggle for Racial Equality* (New York: Oxford University Press, 2004). The law of privacy is treated in William G. Ross, *Forging New Freedoms: Nativism, Education, and the Constitution, 1917–1927* (Lincoln: University of Nebraska Press, 1994), which details the early cases, and David J. Garrow, *Liberty and Sexuality: The Right to Privacy and the Making of* Roe v. Wade (New York: Macmillan, 1994), which brings the story down to the 1960s. Victoria F. Nourse, *In Reckless Hands:* Skinner v. Oklahoma *and the Near Triumph of American Eugenics* (New York: Norton, 2008), explores another of the key cases drawn upon in *Loving*. Gregory Michael Dorr, "Principled Expediency: Eugenics, *Naim v. Naim*, and the Supreme Court," *American Journal of Legal History* 42 (April 1998): 119–159, addresses a 1950s case from Virginia on the bumpy road to *Loving*. Bruce Ackerman, *We the People*, vol. 3, *The Civil Rights Revolution* (Cambridge, Mass.: Harvard University Press, 2014), offers an astute analysis of the Supreme Court's road to *McLaughlin* and then *Loving*. Biographical studies that recount the *Loving* case—many do not—include Ed Cray, *Chief Justice: A Biography of Earl Warren* (New York: Simon and Schuster, 1997).

Patricia Sullivan's fine centennial book *Lift Every Voice: The NAACP and the Making of the Civil Rights Movement* (New York: New Press, 2009) recounts the organization's first half-century, or through *Brown v. Board of Education*, but it says nothing about *Loving*, which of course came later, or indeed about miscegenation laws as one of the areas that the NAACP engaged almost from its beginnings, as the organization worked to prevent the spread of new laws in the 1910s. Aside from a mention of the *Perez* case, the law of race and marriage is absent from Samuel Walker, *In Defense of American Liberties: A History of the ACLU* (New York: Oxford University Press, 1990). Another study of the ACLU, Leigh Ann Wheeler's *How Sex Became a Civil Liberty* (New York: Oxford University Press, 2013), passes entirely by the organization's crusade against miscegenation laws (though it does mention Philip Hirschkop's involvement in constitutional challenges to sodomy laws in the mid-1970s). Regarding the Japanese American Citizens League, Bill Hosokawa, in *JACL in Quest of Justice* (New York: William Morrow, 1982), when turning to marriage, emphasizes problems of immigration and citizenship, not state laws restricting interracial marriage, and barely mentions the Lovings and the role of William L. Marutani. But he gives the JACL credit for pushing successfully for an amendment to the Soldier Brides Act in 1947, which permitted entry by the Japanese wives and biracial children of American servicemen stationed in Japan, and obtaining repeal of Idaho's miscegenation law in 1959.

John T. McGreevy's *Catholicism and American Freedom: A History* (New York: Norton, 2003) does not index the National Catholic Conference for Interracial Justice, though the same author tells important bits of the story in *Parish Boundaries: The Catholic Encounter with Race in the Twentieth-Century North* (Chicago: University of Chicago Press, 1996). Gerald P. Fogarty, *Commonwealth Catholicism: A History of the Catholic Church in Virginia* (Notre Dame: University of Notre Dame Press, 2001), recounts some important aspects of the story of the Richmond diocese and racial desegregation, but makes no mention of the *Loving* case. A brief account of the bishop and his involvement in *Loving* appears in Virginius Dabney, "The Bishop Russell Story," *Virginia Record* 89 (September 1967): 7–13, 60–61. Fay Botham's marvelous explication of the theologies of race and family at work in the struggle over the antimiscegenation regime appears to me, however, to give too much credit to Bishop Russell's initiative, and too little to the activist leadership role of the National Catholic Conference on Interracial Justice.

Awaiting a stellar author is the opportunity to write a compelling book on the Loving couple and their case for young readers. Karen Alonso, Loving v. Virginia: *Interracial Marriage* (Berkeley Heights, N.J.: Enslow, 2000), a pioneering effort, is riddled with errors large and small.

Susan Dudley Gold, Loving v. Virginia: *Lifting the Ban against Interracial Marriage* (New York: Benchmark Books, 2007), is a substantial improvement but has its own inexplicable errors and contains a menu of factoids. Sorting out the facts and the ideas, and then converting these into concepts and language accessible to young readers, remains a challenge not yet met.

Over the past decade and more, most of the law review literature that mentions *Loving* has focused on the question of whether the line of legal thought that shaped the outcome of that case might apply as well to same-sex marriage, and a series of books develops a wide range of particulars on the topic. A leading proponent makes his case in William N. Eskridge Jr., *The Case for Same-Sex Marriage: From Sexual Liberty to Civilized Commitment* (New York: Free Press, 1996). A later work is George Chauncey, *Why Marriage? The History Shaping Today's Debate over Gay Equality* (New York: Basic Books, 2004). Opponents include David Orgon Coolidge and Lynn D. Wardle, law professors at Catholic University of America and authors of such articles as "The Alaska Marriage Amendment: The People's Choice on the Last Frontier," *Alaska Law Review* 16 (December 1999): 213–268, and "Beyond *Baker*: The Case for a Vermont Marriage Amendment," *Vermont Law Review* 25 (Fall 2000): 61–92.

The Vermont story is admirably recounted by journalist David Moats in *Civil Wars: A Battle for Gay Marriage* (Orlando: Harcourt, 2004). Daniel R. Pinello, *America's Struggle for Same-Sex Marriage* (Cambridge: Cambridge University Press, 2006), tells the human story in Massachusetts, Oregon, and elsewhere in the early years of the twenty-first century. Andrew Koppelman, *Same Sex, Different States: When Same-Sex Marriages Cross State Lines* (New Haven: Yale University Press, 2006), explores key constitutional questions, especially the relevance of the Constitution's full faith and credit clause. An account of Jack Baker, Michael McConnell, and their pioneering case in Minnesota appears in Kay Tobin and Randy Wicker, *The Gay Crusaders* (New York: Arno Press, 1975). My treatment in *Race, Sex, and the Freedom to Marry* builds on and extends the material near the end of my *Tell the Court I Love My Wife*. Permitting me to cut my material on the topic in *Race, Sex, and the Freedom to Marry* down from two chapters to one is the coverage in Michael J. Klarman, *From the Closet to the Altar: Courts, Backlash, and the Struggle for*

Same-Sex Marriage (New York: Oxford University Press, 2013), as well as in Jason Pierceson, *Same-Sex Marriage in the United States: The Road to the Supreme Court and Beyond*, updated ed. (Lanham, Md.: Rowman and Littlefield, 2014). Published just in time to be included here is a close examination of the years 2008–2013 by Jo Becker, *Forcing the Spring: Inside the Fight for Marriage Equality* (New York: Penguin, 2014).

Pioneering the study of gender, past and present, as it relates to sexuality and marriage was John D'Emilio and Estelle Freedman, *Intimate Matters: A History of Sexuality in America* (New York: Harper & Row, 1988). Studies of the sodomy laws and the campaign against them are Joyce Murdoch and Deb Price, *Courting Justice: Gay Men and Lesbians v. the Supreme Court* (New York: Basic Books, 2001); William N. Eskridge Jr., *Dishonorable Passions: Sodomy Laws in America, 1861–2003* (New York: Viking, 2008); and Dale Carpenter, *Flagrant Conduct: The Story of* Lawrence v. Texas*, How a Bedroom Arrest Decriminalized Gay Americans* (New York: Norton, 2012). Another dimension is explored in Joanne Meyerowitz, *How Sex Changed: A History of Transsexuality in the United States* (Cambridge, Mass.: Harvard University Press, 2002).

Useful collections of essays and other materials are Werner Sollors, ed., *Interracialism: Black-White Intermarriage in American History, Literature, and Law* (New York: Oxford University Press, 2000), and Martha Hodes, ed., *Sex, Love, Race: Crossing Boundaries in North American History* (New York: New York University Press, 1999). The sole item that appears in both collections is a fine essay by Peggy Pascoe. The Sollors volume includes several important documents; one shortcoming, however, is the 1924 Racial Integrity Act, taken not from the Virginia statutes but rather from Arthur H. Estabrook and Ivan E. McDougle, *Mongrel Virginians: The Win Tribe* (Baltimore: Williams and Wilkins, 1926), a racist tract from the 1920s, and not identical to the original. Fresh materials and insights appear in a collection of new essays: Kevin Noble Maillard and Rose Cuison Villazor, eds., Loving v. Virginia *in a Post-Racial World: Rethinking Race, Sex, and Marriage* (New York: Cambridge University Press, 2012).

Historical accounts of Caroline County, each by untrained but indefatigable adventurers, include local historian Marshall Wingfield's *A History of Caroline County, Virginia* (1924; Baltimore: Regional Publishing, 1975); county court clerk T. E. Campbell's *Colonial Caroline: A History of Caroline County, Virginia* (Richmond: Dietz Press, 1954); and Episcopalian minister Ralph Emmett Fall's *People, Postoffices, and Communities in Caroline County, Virginia, 1727–1969* (Roswell, Ga.: W. H. Wolfe, 1989). In *Memories of Union High: An Oasis in Caroline County, Virginia, 1903–1969* (Burtonsville, Md.: Woodfork Genealogy, 2011), Marion Woodfork Simmons supplies wonderful material on the history of the high school Mildred Loving attended. Florence C. Bryant, *Memoirs of a Country Girl* (New York: Vantage Press, 1988), recounts the story of someone who graduated from Union High School in 1940, as well as her family and community. Information on Caroline County teachers is available on microfilm at the Library of Virginia in "Lists of Teachers of the Department of Education, 1892–1984." Information on some early black schools in Caroline comes from the online Fisk University Rosenwald Fund Card File Database, http://rosenwald.fisk.edu.

Sources of materials on people and events that appear in the first chapter include Charles L. Perdue Jr., Thomas E. Barden, and Robert K. Phillips, eds., *Weevils in the Wheat: Interviews with Virginia Ex-Slaves* (Charlottesville: University of Virginia Press, 1976); William Cheek and Aimee Lee Cheek, *John Mercer Langston and the Fight for Black Freedom, 1829–65* (Urbana: University of Illinois Press, 1989); David W. Blight, *A Slave No More: Two Men Who Escaped to Freedom, including Their Own Narratives of Emancipation* (Orlando: Harcourt, 2007), for John M. Washington; Lawrence M. Hauptman, *Between Two Fires: American Indians in the Civil War* (New York: Free Press, 1995); and David John Mays, *Edmund Pendleton, 1721–1803: A Biography*, 2 vols. (Cambridge, Mass.: Harvard University Press, 1952). The key source of broad-based information on nonwhite southern officeholders in the decade 1867–1877 is Eric Foner, *Freedom's Lawmakers: A Directory of Black Officeholders during Reconstruction*, rev. ed. (Baton Rouge: Louisiana State University Press, 1996), but Foner includes only Virginia's early legislators. Luther Porter Jackson's *Negro Office-Holders in Virginia, 1865–1895* (Norfolk: *Guide* Quality Press, 1945) remains indispensable, although the Library of Virginia has recently updated Jackson's information. For a provocative history of elite governance in Virginia, see Brent Tarter, *The Grandees of Government: The Origins and Persistence of Undemocratic Politics in Virginia* (Charlottesville: University of Virginia Press, 2013).

Back in the early 1990s, when I was beginning work on this big project, I spoke with Mrs. Loving and her two attorneys about the case. In

January 1994, while I was sitting in the law office of Bernie Cohen in Alexandria, he asked if I might like to speak with Mrs. Loving. I would, I replied, and she consented, and a few days later we had what for me at least was a magical conversation over the telephone. I was smitten with her voice, as well as enthralled by what she told me; and things she told me, in that conversation and later, subsequently appeared—often in her own clear and heartfelt words—in one account or another I wrote. So, scattered conversations with Mrs. Loving in the 1990s contributed immensely to my understanding of her story, as reflected in my earlier writings about her, beginning with my very long law review article "Race, Marriage, and the Law of Freedom: Alabama and Virginia, 1860s–1960s," *Chicago-Kent Law Review* 70, no. 2 (1994): 371–437, which led eventually to my 2002 book *Tell the Court I Love My Wife*, as well as *Race, Sex, and the Freedom to Marry*.

Tell the Court corrected errors of fact in my earlier account in the *Chicago-Kent Law Review*—one on the *Pace* litigation, where I had not yet seen the case file and assumed erroneously that Pace's attorneys had contested Alabama's ban on interracial marriage, and a second about the Reconstruction South, where I had understood incorrectly that Alabama was the only example of a southern state appellate court throwing out a miscegenation law during that time. The paperback edition of *Tell the Court*, which appeared in 2004, permitted me to correct another error, one that had survived from the law review essay, regarding people of Asian ancestry and the Racial Integrity Act of 1924. Some of my writings since then have explored new dimensions and have thereby strengthened *Race, Sex, and the Freedom to Marry*. Among these are "Reconstruction, Segregation, and Miscegenation: Interracial Marriage and the Law in the Lower South, 1865–1900," *American Nineteenth-Century History* 6 (March 2005): 57–76, and "Identity, Marriage, and Schools: Life along the Color Line/s in the Era of *Plessy v. Ferguson*," in *The Folly of Jim Crow: Rethinking the Segregated South*, ed. Stephanie Cole and Natalie J. Ring (College Station: Texas A&M University Press, 2012), 17–53. *Tell the Court* contains material on developments in Virginia in the aftermath of *Loving* that does not appear in *Race, Sex, and the Freedom to Marry*, in particular early interracial weddings that took place there and the Lovings' lawyers gaining assurance that all such marriages could go forward without official hindrance.

On the Lovings themselves, some foundational sources supply the core material through the nine years between their late-night arrest and their Supreme Court victory. Published accounts from the time include "The Crime of Being Married," *Life*, March 18, 1966: 88ff., and Simeon Booker, "The Couple That Rocked Courts," *Ebony* 22 (March 1967): 78–84 (a title that almost always gets cited as "The Couple That Rocked the Courts"). A scholar provides a personal account in Robert A. Pratt, "Crossing the Color Line: A Historical Assessment and Personal Narrative of *Loving v. Virginia*," *Howard Law Journal* 41 (Winter 1998): 229–244. Charles B. Lawing's "*Loving v. Virginia* and the Hegemony of 'Race'" is available at www.charlielawing.com/modhist_lovingv.virginia.pdf, as is a conference paper, "The Family Tree: A Personal Tribute to Richard and Mildred Loving."

The record of the Lovings' legal journey is traced through several sets of material. The case file for *Loving v. Virginia*, originally housed at the Caroline County Circuit Court, is now available in hard copy at the Central Rappahannock Heritage Center in Fredericksburg and on microfilm at the Library of Virginia. The case file before the Virginia Supreme Court, which I obtained at the law library of the University of Virginia, is also in the library of the Virginia Supreme Court, in Richmond. The briefs and the oral arguments from the US Supreme Court case are published in Philip B. Kurland and Gerhard Casper, eds., *Landmark Briefs and Arguments of the Supreme Court of the United States: Constitutional Law* (Arlington, Va.: University Publications of America, 1975), 64:685–1007. A greatly abbreviated version of the oral argument appears in Peter Irons and Stephanie Guitton, eds., *May It Please the Court: The Most Significant Oral Arguments Made before the Supreme Court since 1955* (New York: New Press, 1993), 277–289; the editors include various errors of fact in their own account, but the accompanying cassette recording permits listeners to hear for themselves the exchanges on the Supreme Court floor, and one can access the entire oral argument at www.oyez .org/cases/1960-1969/1966/1966_395.

Manuscript collections relevant to this study include the papers of Leon M. Bazile, in the Virginia Historical Society. Aside from Fay Botham's book from 2009, *Almighty God Created the Races*, Judge Bazile has previously appeared in journalistic or historical accounts as a cartoon, an unfortunate bit player in the larger story, but it is important to know him better, to gauge his background, understanding, and motivation. Supplying a brief account of his life and career is John Edward Lane III, "Leon Maurice Bazile," in *Legal Education in Virginia, 1779–1979: A Biographical Approach*, ed. W. Hamilton Bryson (Charlottesville: University Press of Virginia, 1982), 82–86.

The Earl Warren Papers, at the Library of Congress, reveal the concerns that Justices Hugo Black and Byron White, in particular, expressed about how to frame the Court's decision in *Loving*. Those of John Marshall Harlan, the Justice Harlan of the 1950s and 1960s, are in the Mudd Library at Princeton University. Also at Princeton's Mudd Library are the papers of the American Civil Liberties Union, a key player in the campaign against laws curtailing interracial marriage. The papers of the National Association for the Advancement of Colored People (NAACP) are at the Library of Congress; much of the collection is available on microfilm. Briefs for the same-sex marriage case *Baker v. Nelson* (1971), from the Minnesota Supreme Court, are in the case file at the Minnesota State Law Library, in St. Paul. An interview with David Carliner done in 1997–1998 is available at http://dcchs.org/David Carliner/davidcarliner_complete.pdf.

The papers of Bishop John J. Russell, in the Archives of the Catholic Diocese of Richmond, in Richmond, Virginia, include materials on miscegenation, and I am grateful to Bishop Francis X. DiLorenzo for his permission to use them here, and to archivist Vincent J. Sansone for his assistance. Books previous to Fay Botham's *Almighty God Created the Races* do not develop Bishop Russell's involvement. The papers of the National Catholic Conference for Interracial Justice are in Special Collections at Marquette University, in Milwaukee, Wisconsin; I thank university archivist Phillip Runkel for providing me relevant materials from those papers.

Newspaper stories made up a very important category of materials for this project. Some of these appeared in the *New York Times*, the *Washington Post*, and other state or national papers. Others appeared in local papers: the *Fredericksburg Free Lance-Star* is available on microfilm at the Central Rappahannock Regional Library, in Fredericksburg; and with the great assistance of the staff, I had access to a hard copy of the *Caroline Progress* at the Bowling Green Branch of the Caroline Library, which is housed in the county's former black high school, Union High.

Available at the circuit court of Caroline County, in Bowling Green, are two collections of materials vital to portions of this book: the order books of the county's board of supervisors since 1909 and the marriage licenses, together with the applications for them, of couples married in the county since 1933. Earlier marriage licenses are available on microfilm at the Library of Virginia. Robert W. Vernon, when I asked him in April 2008 if he had a case from Caroline County in his remarkable inventory of acquisitions, introduced me to Annie Gray and her 1808 petition from the Library of Virginia's Free Negro and Slave Records.

Out at about the time of the thirtieth anniversary of the Supreme Court decision was the Showtime movie *Mr. and Mrs. Loving*. Based on the true story, it appears adept at catching some of the emotional dimension of the Lovings' experiences between their arrest in 1958 and their court victory in 1967, yet it takes serious liberties with core facts. First aired on national television on Valentine's Day 2012 was the HBO documentary *The Loving Story*, based heavily on photographs by Grey Villet and film footage by Hope Ryden, both from the mid-1960s while the case was in the courts. With much left unused from both sets of visuals, surely rich material remains for further detailing the Lovings' experiences, both from what might be seen and from what the couple recounted on camera.

Readers of the manuscript for the University Press of Kansas made some very useful observations and suggestions. Especially in the late going, conversations with Philip Hirschkop, Paul Finkelman, Debra Jeter-Thomas, Arica Coleman, David Osher, and Bernard Cohen proved particularly helpful. To all who have propelled me toward writing a better book, thank you.

INDEX

Freeman, Isabel, 15
French, Harold S., 115–116
Friedenberg, Richard, 165
Fugitive Slave Act (1850), 9
Fuller v. Commonwealth, 101–102, 117
full faith and credit clause, 47, 208, 214.
    See also comity

Gabriel, 7
Garnett, Helot, 15
Garrett, Richard H., 3
Gastanaga, Claire, 205
Georgetown University, 98, 103
George Washington University, 112, 144
Georgia, 31, 36–37, 182–183, 196, 222, 229
Gibson, Thomas, 31. See also *State v. Gibson*
Gibson, William, 156, 225–226
Givens, Terri, 229
Glass, Carter, 18
Glen Allen, 221
Glover, Lydia, 229
Goldman, Floyd, 153
Gong Lum v. Rice, 44
Goodridge v. Department of Public Health, 196–197
Gordon, Albert I., 128
Gordon, Annie E., 12
Graham, Fred, 130
Grandich, Antonio, 43
Grasty, I. B., 57
Gray, Annie, ix–x, xiii, xiv–xv, 4
Gray, Jenny, x, xi–xiv
Great Britain, 3, 173–174
Great Migration, 19
Greek Orthodox Diocese of North
    and South America, 91–92
Green, Aaron, 34
Green Berets, 103
Greene, Meg, 189
Greenhow v. James Executor, 108

Green v. State, 34, 45, 108
Gregoire, Chris, 203
Griffith, Nanci, 167
Griswold v. Connecticut, 176, 182
Groner, D. Lawrence, 40
Grymes Memorial School, 146
Guess Who (movie), 165
Guess Who's Coming to Dinner (movie),
    163–164
Guinea Station, 13
Gwathmey, Robert R., III, 89

Hall, M. T., 223
Hall, Mary, 58
Hall, Mary S., 33
Hamilton, Donna, 229
Hampden-Sydney College, 112–113
Hampton Normal and Agricultural
    Institute, 16, 18
Hancock, Winfield S., 14
Handoo, Parmeshwar, 174
Hanover Academy, 143, 146
Hanover County, 14, 77–78, 89, 116
Hardberger, Phil, 184
Hardwick, Michael, 182
Hardwick v. Bowers, 182–183, 187, 196, 198
Hargrove Military Academy, 68
Harlan, John Marshall (19th-century
    justice), 38
Harlan, John Marshall (20th-century
    justice), clerk of, 118–119
Harmon v. Tyler, 41
Harrigan, Peter, 191
Harris, Caroline Johnson, 10
Harris, John C., 72–73
Harrisonburg, 206
Harrison v. Day, 86
Hart, E. C., 30
Hart v. Hoss and Elder, 30
Hawaii, 85, 158, 185–187, 190, 208
Hayashida, George Shigeto, 85